Somewhere Special

★ Premier Hotels ◆ B&B Guest Accommodation ★ Self-Catering Holiday Homes

England

To Begin

All you need to know about the guide and how to use it

Contents

Plus... Useful Information

'Somewhere Special' 2004

Published by: **VisitBritain**, Thames Tower, Black's Road, London W6 9EL *in association with* **Celsius**, 32 Staple Gardens, Winchester SO23 8SR.

Managing Editor, VisitBritain: Michael Dewing
Design, compilation and production: Celsius
Editorial contributors: Tessa Lecomber, Hugh Chevallier
Cartography (regional base maps): Colin Earl
Printing: W&G Baird Ltd

© VisitBritain (except where stated), 2003

ISBN 0 7095 7757 5

Important:

VisitBritain
VisitBritain is a new organisation created on 1 April 2003 to market Britain to
the rest of the world and England to the British. Formed by the merger of
the British Tourist Authority and the English Tourism Council, its mission is to
build the value of tourism by creating world class destination brands and
marketing campaigns. It will also build partnerships with – and provide
insights to – other organisations which have a stake in British and English
Tourism.

Front cover: Linthwaite House Hotel (page 27)
Title page: The Grand Hotel (page 176)
Back cover: Seaham Hall Hotel and Serenity Spa (page 32)

Somewhere Special is the guide for the discerning traveller, featuring hundreds of hotels, B&Bs, inns, farmhouses, guest accommodation and self-catering all offering their guests that little bit extra. The format is easy to use, with attractive, detailed entries cross-referenced to full-colour maps, plus articles and features as well as helpful hints. Whatever your budget, and whether you want a short get-away or a longer break, **Somewhere Special** offers a choice of accommodation that promises a warm welcome and a stay that's special.

Welcome...

Your sure signs of where to stay

As in other VisitBritain guides, all accommodation included in this invaluable title has been assessed and awarded a rating for quality by VisitBritain (see page 9). In **Somewhere Special**, however, you are promised something extra, for every single entry has achieved a top quality Star or Diamond rating or a Gold or Silver Award (see page 9). This means that the full range of facilities on offer will be presented with exceptional care, individuality and quality of service.

Quality first

Whether you're looking for no-holds-barred luxury on a grand scale, a short break in a cosy cottage with character or an intimate bed and breakfast that gives personal attention to perhaps only three or four guests, you're looking in the right guide. The criterion for inclusion in **Somewhere Special** is excellence rather than the range of facilities available – though of course you'll be able to see at a glance exactly what's on offer.

How to use the guide

Somewhere Special will enable you to find that special place to stay – whichever part of the country you are planning to visit. Even if you only have a rough idea of where you wish to go, you can easily use this guide to locate a quality place to stay.

The guide is divided into four distinct sections: England's North Country, England's Heartland, England's West Country, and South & South East England.

Overleaf you will find a break-down of which county is in which region, together with an accompanying 'England-at-a-glance' map.

Regional listings

Entries are listed by their geographical position, so you'll find that the places you are interested in are usually close to each other in the guide. Serviced establishments (hotels and B&B guest accommodation) are listed separatley from self-catering properties and appear first within each regional section. Each of these sub-sections is preceded by a full-colour regional map which clearly plots by number the location of all the **Somewhere Special** entries, as well as the positions of major roads, towns, stations and airports. If you know the area you want to visit, first locate the possible establishments on the regional map and then turn to the appropriate pages in the regional section.

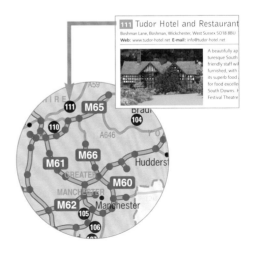

The entries in more detail

The entries are designed to convey as much information as possible in a clear, attractive and easy-to-read format. A fictional sample entry is shown below, together with an explanation of the layout of information.

Each entry shows the establishment's Star or Diamond rating. In **Somewhere Special**, of course, every entry will have a rating of either Four or Five Stars or Diamonds, or a Gold or Silver Award.

1 Entries cross-referenced by number to full-colour maps at the beginning of each regional sub-section

2 Establishment name plus Star or Diamond rating

3 Address and full contact details

4 Full description of establishment

5 Detailed information on prices and facilities, including months open (note: only shown if establishment is **not** open all year) and any credit or charge cards accepted

6 Symbols showing the full range of facilities and services available (see the back cover flap for a key)

111 Tudor Hotel and Restaurant ★★★ Silver Award

Boshman Lane, Boshman, Wickchester, West Sussex SO18 8BU **Tel:** (01842) 173234 **Fax:** (01842) 173459
Web: www.tudor-hotel.net **E-mail:** info@tudor-hotel.net

A beautifully appointed country manor house dating from 1501, set in a picturesque South Downs village, only four miles west of Wickchester. The friendly staff will make you feel very welcome. Bedrooms are all individually furnished, with every modern facility. The Tudor Restaurant is renowned for its superb food and extensive wine list and has been awarded an AA Rosette for food excellence. Enjoy walking on the beautiful riverside or the rolling South Downs. Hambourne Roman Villa, Brickwood House and Wickchester Festival Theatre are all within easy reach.

Bed & Breakfast per night: single room from £59.00–£62.00; double room from £92.00–£115.00
Dinner, Bed & Breakfast per person, per night: £60.00–£75.00
Lunch available: 1230–1400
Evening meal: 1900 (last orders 2130)

Bedrooms: 5 single, 16 double, 10 twin, 2 family
Bathrooms: 33 en-suite
Parking: 44 spaces
Open: All year except Christmas
Cards accepted: Mastercard, Visa, Switch/Delta, Amex, Diners, Eurocard

Other features of the guide

As well as the entries – 327 in all – you'll find many interesting and informative features on a wide variety of subjects scattered throughout the book. The four comprehensive introductions to the regions start on pages 13, 57, 103 and 153. At the back of the book (starting on page 191) you will find more detailed information about booking accommodation. You are strongly recommended to read this before committing yourself to any firm arrangements, bearing in mind the fact that all details have been supplied by proprietors themselves. Finally, you will find a complete alphabetical index to all the establishments featured in the guide, cross-referenced to the page number on which they appear.

England at a glance

This guide is divided into four main regional sections. A map of the area, showing each entry and its nearest town or city, as well as nearby major roads or motorways, can be found after the regional introduction.

England's North Country
Cheshire, Cumbria, County Durham, East Riding of Yorkshire, Greater Manchester, Lancashire, Merseyside, North & North East Lincolnshire, North, South & West Yorkshire, Northumberland, Tees Valley, Tyne & Wear, York.

England's Heartland
Bedfordshire, Cambridgeshire, Derbyshire, Essex, Gloucestershire, Herefordshire, Hertfordshire, Leicestershire, Lincolnshire, Norfolk, Northamptonshire, Nottinghamshire, Rutland, Shropshire, Staffordshire, Suffolk, Warwickshire, West Midlands, Worcestershire.

England's North Country

England's Heartland

South & South East England

England's West Country

England's West Country
Bath & North East Somerset, Bristol, Cornwall, Devon, Isles of Scilly, North Somerset, Somerset, South Gloucestershire, Western Dorset, Wiltshire.

South & South East England
Berkshire, Buckinghamshire, East & West Sussex, Eastern Dorset, Hampshire, Isle of Wight, Kent, London, Oxfordshire, Surrey.

Sea Tree House (page 148)

The National Rating Standard

When you're looking for a place to stay, you need a rating system you can trust. VisitBritain's ratings give you a clear guide to what to expect, in an easy-to-understand form. Properties are visited annually by trained, impartial assessors who award ratings based on the overall experience of their visit. There are strict guidelines to ensure every property is assessed to the same criteria, so you can have the confidence that your accommodation has been thoroughly checked and rated for quality before you make your booking. After all, meeting customer expectations is what makes happy guests.

Gold and Silver Awards

Look out for the Gold and Silver Awards which are exclusive to VisitBritain.

They are awarded to **hotels** achieving the highest levels of quality within their Star rating. While the overall rating is based on a combination of facilities and quality, the Gold and Silver Awards are based solely on quality, with an emphasis on service and hospitality.

They are awarded to **guest accommodation** establishments which not only achieve the overall quality within their Diamond rating, but also reach the highest level of quality in those specific areas which guests identify as being really important for them. They will reflect the quality of comfort and cleanliness you will find in the bedrooms and bathrooms and the quality of service you'll enjoy throughout your stay.

Felbrigg Lodge (page 85)

A note about 'Hotels'

There is no restriction on any property that provides serviced accommodation using the word Hotel in the title. Hotels with a Star rating meet all the requirements for the 1 Star hotel standard and will usually have a drinks licence and offer meals in addition to breakfast. 'Hotel' establishments with a Diamond rating meet the minimum entry requirements for the Guest Accommodation standard but do not automatically meet the Hotel 1 Star requirements.

An assessor calls

Before a quality rating is awarded, one of our qualified assessors visits the establishment to make an independent assessment. For serviced accommodation, the assessor books in advance as a 'normal' guest and does not reveal his or her identity until after settling the bill following an overnight stay. Self-catering properties are generally assessed on a day visit arranged in advance with the owner.

Each assessment will involve a thorough tour of the property together with the proprietor. At the end of the tour, they discuss the conclusions, with the assessor making suggestions where helpful.

Only after the visit does the assessor arrive at a conclusion for the quality rating – so the assessment is 100% independent and reliable.

Chewton Glen Hotel, Health & Country Club (page 165)

Stars for Hotels

Star ratings are your sign of quality assurance, giving you the confidence to book the accommodation that meets your expectations. Based on the internationally recognised rating of One to Five Stars, the system puts great emphasis on quality and is based on research which shows exactly what consumers are looking for when choosing a hotel. Ratings are awarded from One to Five Stars – the more Stars, the higher the quality and the greater the range of facilities and level of services provided.

> Remember that only Star rated hotels with a Gold or Silver Award qualify for entry in Somewhere Special.

Hotel Star ratings explained

At a ★ hotel you will find:
Practical accommodation with a limited range of facilities and services, and a high standard of cleanliness throughout (75% of rooms will have en-suite or private facilities). Friendly and courteous staff. Dining room/eating area offering breakfast to you and your guests. Alcoholic drinks served in a bar or lounge.

At a ★★ hotel you will find:
In addition to what is provided at ★
Good accommodation offering a personal style of service with additional facilities. More comfortable bedrooms (all with en-suite or private facilities and colour television). Food and drink is of a higher standard.

At a ★★★ hotel you will find:
In addition to what is provided at ★ and ★★
Very good accommodation with more spacious public areas and bedrooms, all offering a significantly greater quality and higher standard of facilities and services. A more formal style of service with a receptionist. A wide selection of drinks, light lunch and snacks served in a bar or lounge with greater attention to quality. Room service for continental breakfast and laundry service.

At a ★★★★ hotel you will find:
In addition to what is provided at ★, ★★ and ★★★
Accommodation offering excellent comfort and quality. All rooms with en-suite facilities. Strong emphasis on food and drink. Experienced staff responding to your needs and requests. Room service for all meals; light refreshments and snacks available 24 hours.

At a ★★★★★ hotel you will find:
In addition to what is provided at ★, ★★, ★★★ and ★★★★
A spacious and luxurious establishment offering accommodation, extensive facilities, services and cuisine of the highest international quality. Professional attentive staff, exceptional comfort and a sophisticated ambience.

Farthings Hotel and Restaurant (page 129)

Old Vicarage Hotel (page 70)

Diamonds for Guest Accommodation

The Diamond ratings for Guest Accommodation reflect visitor expectations of this sector – a wide variety of serviced accommodation, embracing B&Bs, inns, farmhouses and guest accommodation, for which England is renowned.

The quality of what is provided is more important to visitors than a wide range of facilities and services. Therefore, the same minimum requirement for facilities and services applies to all Guest Accommodation from One to Five Diamonds, while progressively higher levels of quality and customer care must be provided for each rating.

In Somewhere Special, only those establishments with a Four or Five Diamond rating, or a Diamond rated property with a Gold or Silver Award, qualify for entry in the guide.

Amberley House (page 169)

Guest accommodation Diamond ratings explained

At ◆◆◆ guest accommodation you will find:
A very good overall level of quality in areas such as comfortable bedrooms, well maintained, practical décor, a good choice of quality items at breakfast, customer care and all-round comfort. Where other meals are provided these will be freshly cooked from good quality ingredients.

At ◆◆◆◆ guest accommodation you will find:
In addition to what is provided at ◆◆◆
An excellent level of quality in all areas. Customer care showing very good attention to your needs.

At ◆◆◆◆◆ guest accommodation you will find:
In addition to what is provided at ◆◆◆ and ◆◆◆◆
An exceptional overall level of quality – for example, ample space with a degree of luxury, a high quality bed and furniture, excellent interior design and customer care which anticipates your needs. Breakfast offering a wide choice of high quality fresh ingredients. Where other meals are provided, these will feature fresh, seasonal, and often local ingredients.

The Royal Oak Inn (page 168)

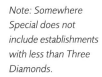

Holmwood House Hotel (page 39)

Note: Somewhere Special does not include establishments with less than Three Diamonds.

Christopher's Farmhouse (page 147)

Stars for Self-Catering

The Star ratings for self-catering reflect the quality that you're looking for when booking accommodation. All properties have to meet an extensive list of minimum requirements to take part in the scheme. Ratings are awarded from One to Five Stars – the more Stars, the higher the quality. Establishments at higher rating levels also have to meet additional requirements for facilities. Some self-catering establishments have a range of accommodation units in the building or on the site and the individual units may have different Star ratings. In such cases the entry shows the range available.

Remember that only Four and Five Star properties qualify for entry in Somewhere Special.

Self-catering Star ratings explained

At a ★★★★ property you will find:
An excellent overall level of quality with very good care and attention to detail throughout. Access to a washing machine and drier if it is not provided in the unit, or a 24-hour laundry service.

At a ★★★★★ property you will find:
In addition to what is provided at ★★★★
An exceptional overall level of quality with high levels of décor, fixtures and fittings, with personal touches. Excellent standards of management efficiency and guest services.

Tourist
INFORMATION
Centres

When it comes to your next England break, the first stage of your journey could be closer than you think. You've probably got a tourist information centre nearby which is there to serve the local community - as well as visitors. Knowledgeable staff will be happy to help you, wherever you're heading.

Many tourist information centres can provide you with maps and guides, and often it's possible to book accommodation and travel tickets too.

Across the country, there are more than 550 TICs. You'll find the address of your nearest centre in your local phone book.

England's North Country

Grace Darling

Few women have attracted such uninvited public adulation as Grace Darling. Daughter of a lighthouse keeper, Grace lived a lonely life on the Farne Islands, off the Northumberland coast. On 7 September 1838 she and her father risked their lives to rescue nine survivors from the wrecked steamer *Forfarshire*, putting out in heavy seas in a tiny rowing-boat. The newspapers made her a national

heroine overnight. At Bamburgh are the Grace Darling Museum and the cottage where she was born. Weather permitting, a boat trip around the Farne Islands is an unforgettable experience (www. farne-islands.com/boat-trips).

Humber Bridge

Parliament approved construction of a Humber bridge in 1959, but it took 22 years to open, and cost £98 million, almost four times the original estimate. The result, however, is impressive. With a central span of almost a mile (4,626ft - 1,410m), the Humber Bridge

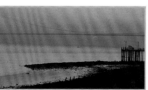

was until very recently the longest unsupported section of bridge in the world. Visitor facilities include viewing areas at both ends; the northern side also has a tourist information centre and country park; views of and from the bridge are magnificent. www.humberbridge.co.uk

Peak after peak

The soul of England's North Country lies in the Pennines, England's mountainous backbone stretching from the borders of Scotland to the borders of the Midlands. The North boasts the Lake District, two glorious coastlines, countless imposing castles and, in York, one of the most perfect cities one could ever wish for, but somehow the sheer scale of the Pennine ridge dominates. The mountains run for around 200 miles (320km), the peaks rising above 2,000ft (610m), too many to count.

Exploring on foot

The most famous way to savour the Pennine experience, fitness and time permitting, is to walk Britain's oldest long-distance path. About 10,000 people each year complete the 268 miles (431km) of the Pennine Way, though many more – perhaps 300,000 – join it for a mile or two from one of 535 separate access points. Two of these are intersections with other long-distance waymarked paths. The Coast-to-Coast Walk, as its name suggests, links the Irish Sea with the North Sea, traversing the Lake District, Yorkshire Dales and North York Moors national parks on its 190 mile (306km) route, while the Dales Way (81 miles, 130km) is a low-level path along the banks of the Wharfe, Dee, Lune and Kent rivers. The Cumbria Way (Ulverston to Carlisle) guides you through Lakeland grandeur. The Cleveland Way falls almost entirely within the North York Moors national park, but still extends over 100 miles (160km). Roughly following the river from its source high in the Dales to the sea near Preston, the wise walker tackles the Ribble Way in a downhill direction. Altogether quieter and less dramatic is the Wolds Way, wending from near Hull to Filey, where it joins the Cleveland Way. Needless to say, all these – as well as Hadrian's Wall, which can be walked for its entire length – explore scenery of the utmost beauty. All make an ideal starting point for shorter strolls, too.

Mills to museums

Towards the southern end of the Pennines the valleys become more populated. The fast-flowing rivers that long ago powered the mills are lined with the characterful small houses built for the workers. Once reviled but now revered, towns such as Holmforth and Hebden Bridge have justly become visitor attractions in their own right. And the factories have in many instances been turned into imaginative museums and galleries. The Armley Mills Industrial Museum, Leeds, occupies what was once the largest woollen mill in the world; Saddleworth Museum and Art Gallery houses working woollen textile machinery; much of Salts Mill, near Bradford is devoted to the works of the artist, David Hockney; and, at Macclesfield, Paradise Mill produced silk until the 1980s. At Sheffield, those with an interest in industrial archaeology can indulge themselves at either the Abbeydale Industrial Hamlet or

Kelham Island Industrial Museum. If you prefer more modern scientific endeavour, then try the Jodrell Bank Science Centre & Arboretum, south of Manchester, home of a massive steerable radio telescope.

On a grand scale

A few miles from Jodrell Bank lies Tatton Park, one of the finest country houses of the North, and built on the decidedly grand scale. Other lesser-known properties to explore include: medieval Raby Castle with its nine towers (near Staindrop, County Durham); the very Victorian Lady Waterford Hall, decorated with murals depicting familiar Bible stories (Ford, Northumberland); Dalemain, a stately home intriguingly adapted from the original pele tower, now home of the Westmorland and Cumberland Yeomanry Museum (Penrith, Cumbria); Burton Constable Hall, an Elizabethan setting for a remarkable collection of scientific instruments (Sproatley, East Riding of Yorkshire); Croxteth Hall, where visitors can join an Edwardian house party or look at an extensive collection of rare breed animals (Liverpool, Merseyside); and Browsholme Hall, full of unusual objects squirrelled by the Parker family, owners of the hall for over 400 years (near Whitewell, Lancashire).

For art's sake

The North Country has a range of arts and music festivals to rival the rest of England. As always, the breadth of entertainment is prodigious. For concerts devoted to early music – and played in some of England's most glorious medieval churches – visit either the York Early Music Festival (July) or, 25 or so miles (40km) further east, the Beverley and East Riding Early Music Festival (May). At the other end of the spectrum, go south to Huddersfield in November for the Contemporary Music Festival. The Lake District hosts jazz, orchestral and chamber concerts at a number of venues as part of its Summer Music festivities (August), while Chester does broadly the same – as well as throwing in a fringe element, too – in July. Bradford (late June and early July) and Harrogate (late July and early August) both add comedy and street theatre to a range of musical concerts. Manchester, meanwhile, devotes three weeks in May to its Streets Ahead festival. Circus events and fireworks provide alternatives to the music, dance and theatre – and everything is free. And, if you thought the Aldborough Festival was exclusive to Suffolk, look closely at the spelling. A village near Boroughbridge, North Yorkshire, holds the Northern Aldborough (not Aldeburgh) Festival each July; classical music is once again the subject.

Fishing villages and golden sands

The coastline of Northumberland, England's north eastern extremity, bears an intriguing resemblance to Cornwall, in the extreme south west. Fine sandy beaches, a history peopled by

Grizedale Sculpture Trail

A walk through Grizedale Forest offers an intriguing trail of discovery in the hunt for 80 or so large-scale sculptures dotted along its pathways. The Sculpture Trail began as an opportunity for sculptors to develop diverse works on the theme of the Forest, and the sculptures are inspired by the materials and forms which naturally occur there: wildlife, rock formations, drystone walls, and, of course, trees. Most are sited on the Silurian Way, a 9½-mile (15km) circular walk starting at the Visitor Centre where maps (that include short-cuts) may be purchased. www.forestry.gov.uk

Lawnmowers on Display

The British Lawnmower Museum is based in the seaside resort of Southport, Merseyside. Prized exhibits include some of the first machines dating from the early 19th century, mowers once belonging to Nicholas Parsons and to Prince Charles, another capable of cutting a 2-inch (5cm) wide strip, and what is believed to be the only hand-powered rotary lawnmower in existence. Also on view is the world's largest collection of toy mowers and one of the oldest surviving racing lawnmowers (built by the curator). www.lawnmowerworld.co.uk

Settle–Carlisle Railway

When the railway between Settle and Carlisle opened in 1876 it had taken over six years to build, cost more than £3.5 million, and claimed the life of one navvy per week. Crossing perhaps the most inhospitable terrain in England, including the summit of Ais Gill (1,169ft, 356m), the line stretched Victorian engineering to the limits. Today it affords passengers views of enormous beauty, and provides opportunities for walking the dramatic scenery along its route. Excursions are available; for general information see www.settle-carlisle.co.uk.

Gondola

Gondola is the National Trust's only steam yacht, and plies up and down Coniston Water in the Lake District for around seven months each year. Described as 'a perfect combination of the Venetian Gondola and the English Steam Yacht', she was launched at Coniston in 1859, remaining in service until 1937, when her hull became a houseboat and her boiler was used for the cutting of timber in a saw mill. In 1977 she was bought by the National Trust, and, restored to former glory, once more ferries visitors the length of the lake.
www.nationaltrust.org.uk

saints and martyrs, and a rural interior characterise both. In Northumberland it is a simple matter to escape the throng, but take a trip to the Farne Islands, and you will be outnumbered by both birds and seals. The golden shores south of Bamburgh and north of Dunstanburgh, two glorious beaches that never seem busy, have the added attraction of offering views of their respective castles. Further south, into the North York Moors national park, the coastline is more for the fossil hunter and the walker – the Cleveland Way here follows the sea – than the sun-seeker.

Many of the picturesque villages, such as Ravenscar, Runswick Bay, Staithes and Robin Hood's Bay, tumble down cliffs that yield an array of fossils. Then come the famous resorts of Scarborough, Filey and Bridlington, each with magnificent golden beaches ideal for family outings. Southport, on the southern Lancashire shores, has endless sand, as does its illustrious neighbour, Blackpool, over the Ribble Estuary. North again is Morecambe Bay, at low tide around 150 square miles (38,850 hectares) of gleaming but potentially treacherous sand. Away from the bustle of Blackpool and the teeming birdlife of Morecambe Bay, try Annaside or Gutterby Spa, two of the region's remoter beaches.

Former glories

Hidden away on Cumbria's westernmost point is an elegant port that, 250 years ago, was busier than Liverpool. Retaining many 17th- and 18th-century buildings, and with pleasure craft bobbing up and down in the old harbour, Whitehaven makes an unusual excursion from the Lake District. The North has countless towns that invite unhurried exploration. One is Hexham, whose focal point is the magnificent abbey, dating largely from the 12th century, but it also has Georgian streets surrounding the Shambles, the shelter for the lively Tuesday market. Others to consider are: Rothbury, in Northumberland, an attractive small market town with a medieval bridge; Barnard Castle (County Durham), where visitors can marvel at the exhibits in the Bowes Museum, then clamber over the ruins of the lofty castle to admire the views of the River Tees; Beverley (East Riding of Yorkshire), a superb mixture of medieval and Georgian architecture; Pickering (North Yorkshire), whose ancient coaching inns reflect its heyday as an important stop on the way to Scarborough and Whitby; Clitheroe (Lancashire), where a diminutive Norman castle watches over the stone-built houses; and Macclesfield (Cheshire), a former weaving centre in the shadow of the southern Pennines with fine 18th-century townhouses.

North Country fare

The region produces a number of edible specialities, confectionery and cheeses in particular. Cumbria, renowned for its coiled, smoky sausage, also produces Cumberland rum butter – originally eaten to celebrate the arrival of a newborn child and still made in Whitehaven – as well as Kendal mint cake, famously taken on expeditions to Mount Everest. Pontefract was once the centre of liquorice cultivation and, although the plant is no longer grown nearby, Pontefract cakes are manufactured in the town. Nantwich Museum devotes a room to Cheshire cheese, while three Yorkshire Dales – Swaledale, Wensleydale and Coverdale – give their names to crumbly cheeses made within the national park. Traditionally, the finest kippers are sold on the quayside at Whitby.

A Northern miscellany

The North Country can also offer many other curiosities. Around Ingleton are a number of cave systems, of which the vast Gaping Ghyll cavern is perhaps the most impressive. Also in North Yorkshire, but west of Masham, is the Druid's Temple, a 19th-century folly built in imitation of a miniature Stonehenge. Hale, just over the Mersey from Runcorn, boasts the grave of John Middleton, a local giant reputedly 9 ft 3 inches (2.8m) tall, while at Lower Heysham, near Morecambe, on a promontory above the sandy beach, are some strange rock 'coffins', perhaps carved by 9th-century missionaries from Ireland. And in one of England's furthest-flung spots, high up in the Pennines where Cumbria and Durham meet, is Cauldron Snout, a magnificent waterfall and series of cataracts.

Some useful web addresses

Lake District National Park	www.lake-district.gov.uk
Yorkshire Dales National Park	www.yorkshiredales.org.uk
North York Moors National Park	http://moors.uk.net
Hadrian's Wall	www.hadrians-wall.org
The Armley Mills Industrial Museum, Leeds	www.leeds.gov.uk/armleymills
Saddleworth Museum and Art Gallery, Uppermill	www.saddleworthmuseum.co.uk
Salts Mill, Bradford	www.saltsmill.org.uk
Paradise Mill, Macclesfield	www.silk-macclesfield.org
Abbeydale Industrial Hamlet, Sheffield	www.simt.co.uk/ham1
Kelham Island Museum, Sheffield	www.simt.co.uk/kel1
Jodrell Bank Science Centre & Arboretum	www.jb.man.ac.uk/scicen
Raby Castle, Staindrop	www.rabycastle.com
Lady Waterford Hall, Ford	www.fordetal.co.uk/ford.asp
Dalemain, Penrith	www.dalemain.com
Burton Constable Hall, Sproatley	www.burtonconstable.com
Croxteth Hall, Liverpool	www.croxteth.co.uk
Browsholme Hall, Whitewell	www.browsholme.co.uk
York Early Music Festival	www.ncem.co.uk/yemf.shtml
Huddersfield Contemporary Music Festival	www.hcmf.co.uk
Lake District Summer Music	www.ldsm.org.uk
Chester Summer Festival	www.chesterfestivals.co.uk
Bradford Festival	www.bethere2002.com
Harrogate International Festival	www.harrogate-festival.org.uk
Manchester International Arts	www.streetsahead.org.uk
Aldborough Festival	www.aldborough.com/festival/Index.asp
Nantwich Museum	www.nantwichmuseum.org.uk

Port Sunlight

Lord Leverhulme employed 30 or so architects to design Port Sunlight, 3 miles (5km) south east of Birkenhead, including a young Edwin Lutyens. Opened on 3 March 1888, Port Sunlight provided high-quality homes at affordable rents for workers at his Lever Brothers' soap factory. Visiting the garden village, with its varied architectural styles, is a fascinating day out. One highlight is the Lady Lever Art Gallery, containing magnificent works by English painters, including some leading pre-Raphaelite artists.
www.portsunlight.org.uk

Berwick-upon-Tweed

Berwick-upon-Tweed, though still in England, is further north than much of the Hebridean island of Islay. Oddly, it is cut off from the county which bears its name, for Berwickshire lies in Scotland. Not surprisingly, Berwick's history is intractably bound up with the struggle between the English and the Scots; between 1147 and 1482, the town changed hands 13 times. The 16th century saw the town walls comprehensively fortified against a Scots-French attack which never materialised, hence their amazing state of preservation. A two-mile (3km) walk around these ramparts gives spectacular views of the historic town.
www.berwickonline.org.uk/guide

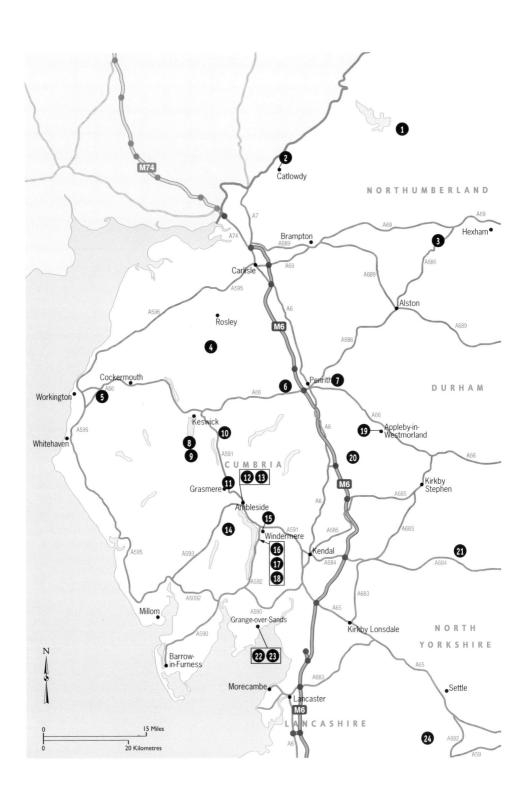

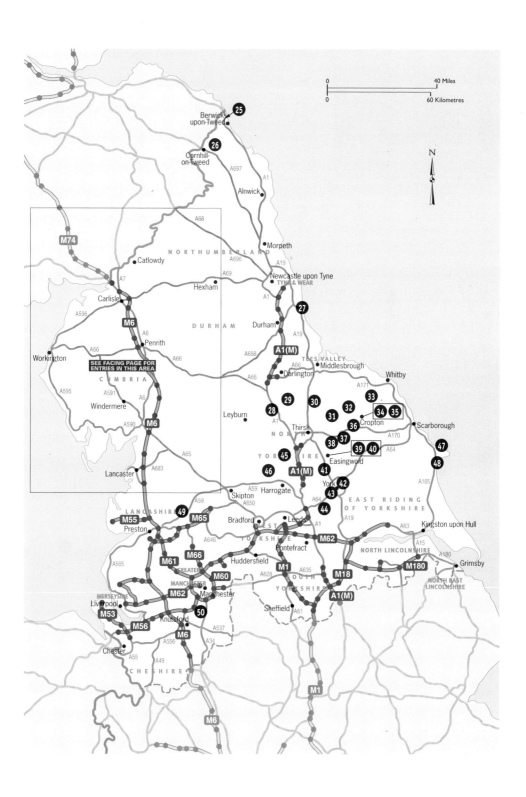

1   The Pheasant Inn (by Kielder Water)   ◆◆◆◆

Stannersburn, Falstone, by Kielder Water, Northumberland NE48 1DD **Tel:** (01434) 240382 **Fax:** (01434) 240382
Web: www.thepheasantinn.com **E-mail:** enquiries@thepheasantinn.com

Traditional 17th-century inn, 380 years old, run by the Kershaw family for the last 18 years. Beamed ceilings, exposed stone walls, centrally heated, open fires provide its cosy atmosphere. An emphasis is maintained on home cooking, using carefully prepared local produce. Eight en-suite bedrooms offer comfortable accommodation with all the modern conveniences you would expect. An ideal location for visiting Kielder Water, Hadrian's Wall, Rothbury (Cragside) and the Scottish Border country.

♿ Accessible Mobility 4

Bed & Breakfast per night: single occupancy from £40.00–£45.00; double room from £65.00–£70.00
Dinner, Bed & Breakfast per person, per night: £48.00–£50.00
Lunch available: 1200–1430

Evening meal: 1900 (last orders 2030)
Bedrooms: 4 double, 3 twin, 1 family
Bathrooms: 8 en-suite
Parking: 30 spaces
Cards accepted: Mastercard, Visa, Switch/ Delta, Eurocard, JCB

Kielder Water and Kielder Forest

Kielder water, the largest man-made lake in Europe, lies at the heart of Kielder Forest. With 150 million trees this is the biggest single wooded area in Britain. Until the mid-20th century visitors to this wild part of Northumberland – and there were few of them – would have had a very different prospect. The area may once have been carpeted with tall Scots pines, but these were felled long ago to make way for the sheep-farming and coal-mining economy of the valley of the River North Tyne. When the first sitka spruces were planted in the late 1940s, the location had been chosen for large-scale afforestation because mining was uneconomic and even hardy sheep struggled in the harsh winter climate.

Nowadays the Kielder area is Northumberland's most popular tourist attraction, drawing upwards of 100,000 visitors a year. The transformation is thanks largely to the controversial construction of the reservoir. Seventy homes were drowned and eight archaeological sites lost. However, a reliable water supply for the homes and industry of the North-East was created, and a host of recreational facilities soon followed Kielder Water's completion in 1982.

Watersports may be the most obvious attraction of the Kielder area, but there is also an imaginative array of activities available within the forest, and a huge range of tastes can now be indulged. Visitors may: fish for trout from bank or boat, or for salmon just downstream from the dam; hire canoes, dinghies, sailboards and motor boats from Leaplish Waterside Park; sail their own craft; receive expert tuition in yachting, windsurfing and rowing; there's even a separate 120-acre area devoted to waterskiing. Alternatively, they can cruise the lake on board the Osprey, complete with commentary, shop, bar and galley. The cruise is highly enjoyable in its own right, but many use the Osprey as a means of reaching the north shore to walk on glorious paths far from the nearest car. Experienced walkers can set aside a full day to complete the Kielder Water Challenge Walk. This strenuous route circumnavigates the reservoir's 27-mile (43.5km) shoreline in just 26 miles (42km) – possible if a few corners are cut – the equivalent of a full marathon. Shorter, waymarked walks, mountain biking, bird-watching (and, if you're lucky, otter-watching), orienteering, horse-riding and a 12-mile (19km) forest drive are land-based options on offer throughout the year.

  Entries are cross referenced by number to the maps on pages 18–19

2 Craigburn

◆◆◆◆

Catlowdy, Longtown, Carlisle CA6 5QP **Tel:** (01228) 577214 **Fax:** (01228) 577014
Web: www.craigburnfarmhouse.co.uk **E-mail:** louiselawson@hotmail.com

A warm and friendly welcome awaits you at Craigburn, peacefully situated on our 150-acre farm which is nestled on the beautiful English/Scottish border. Beautifully appointed en-suite bedrooms, individually designed with lots of personal touches. We are renowned for delicious home-made food using fresh local produce. Special diets are catered for, and we have a well stocked bar. Relax in our comfortable lounge. Ideal for touring or as a stopover for Scotland. Restricted smoking.

Bed & Breakfast per night: single occupancy from £30.00–£35.00; double room from £50.00– £55.00
Dinner, Bed & Breakfast per person, per night: £40.00–£45.00
Evening meal: 1900 (last bookings 1500)

Bedrooms: 3 double, 2 twin, 1 family
Bathrooms: 6 en-suite
Open: February–November
Parking: 20 spaces
Cards accepted: Mastercard, Visa, Switch/ Delta, Eurocard, JCB

3 Langley Castle

★★★★ Silver Award

Langley-on-Tyne, Hexham, Northumberland NE47 5LU **Tel:** (01434) 688888 **Fax:** (01434) 684019
Web: www.langleycastle.com **E-mail:** manager@langleycastle.com

A genuine 14th-century Castle set in an 11-acre woodland estate and converted into a hotel with 18 guest rooms. All rooms have private facilities, some boasting private 'features' such as window seats set into 7ft-thick walls, sauna, spa bath and four-poster beds. The magnificent drawing room, complete with a blazing log fire, complements the intimate Josephine Restaurant. The exclusive nature of the Castle makes Langley the perfect destination for exploring Northumberland, Hadrian's Wall, Bamburgh Castle, Holy Island, the Borders, Kielder Water and the North Pennines.

Bed & Breakfast per night: single occupancy from £94.50–£164.50; double room from £105.00–£215.00
Dinner, Bed & Breakfast per person, per night: £67.50–£114.50 (min 2 nights)
Evening meal: 1900 (last orders 2100)

Bedrooms: 15 double, 3 suites
Bathrooms: 18 en-suite
Parking: 50 spaces
Cards accepted: Mastercard, Visa, Switch/ Delta, Amex, Diners

4 Swaledale Watch

◆◆◆◆ Silver Award

Whelpo, Caldbeck, Wigton, Cumbria CA7 8HQ **Tel:** (016974) 78409 **Fax:** (016974) 78409
Web: www.swaledale-watch.co.uk **E-mail:** nan.savage@talk21.com

Swaledale Watch is a busy sheep farm just outside picturesque Caldbeck and within the Lake District National Park. Enjoy great comfort, excellent food, a warm welcome and peaceful, unspoilt surroundings. A central location for touring, walking or exploring the rolling Northern Fells. All rooms are beautifully decorated, homely, and have private facilities. Chilly evenings mean open fires in the lounges with books for every interest. A magical, memorable walk lies within 150 yards of the house. Your happiness is our priority.

Bed & Breakfast per night: single occupancy from £21.00–£25.00; double room from £38.00–£44.00
Dinner, Bed & Breakfast per person, per night: £31.00–£47.00
Evening meal: 1900

Bedrooms: 2 double, 2 twin, 2 family
Bathrooms: 4 en-suite, 1 private
Parking: 10 spaces

5 The Melbreak Hotel

Winscales Road, Little Clifton, Workington, Cumbria CA14 1XS **Tel:** (01900) 61443 **Fax:** (01900) 606589
Web: www.melbreakhotel.co.uk **E-mail:** enquiries@melbreakie.fsnet.co.uk

The Melbreak Hotel offers an ideal base from which to explore the northern lakes and coast. Situated on the edge of the Lake District, the hotel boasts dramatic views across the countryside to the mountains beyond – including the imposing Melbreak from which the hotel takes its name. All rooms are en-suite and have direct dial telephone, television and tea/coffee making facilities. Special breaks and weekly tarrif available.

Bed & Breakfast per night: single occupancy from £48.00–£58.00; double room from £65.00– £75.00
Dinner, Bed & Breakfast per person, per night: £60.00–£70.00
Lunch available: 1200–1400

Evening meal: 1830 (last orders 2100)
Bedrooms: 14 double, 20 twin, 2 family
Bathrooms: 36 en-suite
Parking: 36 spaces
Cards accepted: Mastercard, Visa, Switch/ Delta, Amex, Diners, Eurocard, JCB

6 Tymparon Hall

Newbiggin, Stainton, Penrith, Cumbria CA11 0HS **Tel:** (01768) 483236 **Fax:** (01768) 483236
Web: www.tymparon.freeserve.co.uk **E-mail:** margaret@tymparon.freeserve.co.uk

Tymparon Hall is easy to find, close to Lake Ullswater and M6 junction 40. A perfect location for the Lakes, Eden Valley, Hadrian's Wall and the Borders. The secluded 18th-century farmhouse in peaceful surroundings is found on the fringe of a quiet village. Enjoy comfortable, spacious accommodation, personal service and good food. Home cooked three-course dinners available most evenings. Relax in the cosy lounge with a real fire on chilly evenings. Many tourist attractions within easy reach.

Bed & Breakfast per night: single occupancy from £25.00–£35.00; double room from £50.00–£55.00
Dinner, Bed & Breakfast per person, per night: £38.00–£40.00
Evening meal: 1830 (last bookings 1630)

Bedrooms: 1 double, 1 twin, 1 family
Bathrooms: 2 en-suite, 1 private
Parking: ample
Open: February–December

7 Hornby Hall Country House

Brougham, Penrith, Cumbria CA10 2AR **Tel:** (01768) 891114 **Fax:** (01768) 891114
Web: www.hornbyhall.co.uk **E-mail:** enquire@hornbyhall.co.uk

Hornby Hall is a 16th-century farmhouse still with its original tower and spiral staircase. The house has been restored to provide comfortable accommodation and quiet country house atmosphere. Meals are served in the Great Hall, using fresh local food. We are ideally situated for trips to the Lakes, Dales, Hadrian's Wall and Carlisle which has an interesting castle and a superb museum. Ride on the famous Carlisle–Settle railway or fish quietly on Hornby's own stretch of water.

Bed & Breakfast per night: single occupancy from £30.00–£45.00; double room from £50.00–£80.00
Dinner, Bed & Breakfast per person, per night: £45.00–£66.00
Evening meal: 1900 (last orders 2100)

Bedrooms: 6 double/twin, 1 family
Bathrooms: 4 en-suite, 1 shared
Parking: 10 spaces
Cards accepted: Mastercard, Visa, Switch/ Delta, Amex,

8 Borrowdale Gates Country House Hotel & Restaurant   ★★★ Silver Award

Grange-in-Borrowdale, Keswick, Cumbria CA12 5UQ **Tel:** (017687) 77204 **Fax:** (017687) 77254
Web: www.borrowdale-gates.com **E-mail:** hotel@borrowdale-gates.com

Borrowdale Gates Hotel nestles peacefully in two acres of wooded gardens on the edge of the ancient hamlet of Grange. This charming Lakeland house is set amidst the breath-taking scenery of the Borrowdale valley with panoramic views of the countryside. The bedrooms, of which ten are on the ground floor, are tastefully decorated and furnished. The award-winning restaurant offers fine food that is complemented by a carefully chosen wine list. Recommended by 'The Good Food Guide'. One of 'The Which? Hotel Guide' hotels of the year 2003.

Bed & Breakfast per night: single room from £45.00–£70.00; double room from £80.00–£133.00
Dinner, Bed & Breakfast per person, per night: £62.50–£91.50
Lunch available: 1215–1330 (last orders)
Evening meal: 1900 (last orders 2045)

Bedrooms: 3 single, 13 double, 12 twin, 1 family **Bathrooms:** 29 en-suite
Parking: 40 spaces
Open: 30 January–December
Cards accepted: Mastercard, Visa, Switch/Delta

---

9 Hazel Bank Country House   ◆◆◆◆◆ Gold Award

Rosthwaite, Borrowdale, Keswick, Cumbria CA12 5XB **Tel:** (017687) 77248 **Fax:** (017678) 77373
Web: www.hazelbankhotel.co.uk **E-mail:** enquiries@hazelbankhotel.co.uk

Award-winning Hazel Bank (RAC 'Little Gem') stands amidst beautiful four-acre grounds overlooking dramatic Borrowdale, with breathtaking views of Great Gable and other central Lakeland peaks. Set in a secluded and tranquil position with direct access to the fells, Hazel Bank has been completely refurbished and provides quality, well-proportioned bedrooms, all with stunning views. Superb meals (AA Top Food Awards, AA Red Rosette for fine cuisine and RAC Two Dining Awards) and fine wines are served in the elegant dining room. Vegetarians by arrangement. Cumbria Tourist Board 'Awards for Excellence' - Winner in 2002, English Tourism Council finalist in 2003.

Dinner, Bed & Breakfast per person, per night: £55.00–£79.50
Evening meal: 1900 (last orders 1900)

Bedrooms: 6 double, 2 twin
Bathrooms: 8 en-suite
Parking: 12 spaces
Cards accepted: Mastercard, Visa, Switch/Delta, Eurocard, JCB

---

10 Dale Head Hall Lakeside Hotel   ★★★ Gold Award

Lake Thirlmere, Keswick, Cumbria CA12 4TN **Tel:** (017687) 72478 **Fax:** (017687) 71070
Web: www.daleheadhall.info **E-mail:** onthelakeside@daleheadhall.info

Dale Head Hall occupies a stunning position on the shores of Lake Thirlmere, one of Cumbria's quietest, most pastoral lakes. It provides an idyllic base for exploring this most beautiful corner of England. The bedrooms at the front of the hotel (three with four-poster beds) offer gorgeous lake views. With roaring log fires in the winter and refined cuisine served in the hotel's oak panelled dining room, it is a most romantic place for a few quiet days away.

Bed & Breakfast per night: single occupancy from £72.50–£82.50; double room from £95.00– £115.00
Dinner, Bed & Breakfast per person, per night: £85.00–£100.00
Evening meal: 1930 (last orders 2000)

Bedrooms: 9 double, 2 twin, 1 family
Bathrooms: 12 en-suite
Open: February–December
Parking: 20 spaces
Cards accepted: Mastercard, Visa, Switch/Delta, Amex, Eurocard, JCB

11 The Grasmere Hotel

★★ Silver Award

Grasmere, Ambleside, Cumbria LA22 9TA **Tel:** (015394) 35277 or 08000 567895 **Fax:** (015394) 35277
Web: www.grasmerehotel.co.uk **E-mail:** enquiries@grasmerehotel.co.uk

An elegant Victorian Lakeland stone-built country house set in the quiet location of Grasmere village, in an acre of secluded natural gardens bordered by the River Rothay. Renowned for our cuisine, our beautiful award-winning restaurant offers a four-course dinner with a varied choice of culinary delights that are imaginatively presented with only fresh produce used. A place for all seasons, The Grasmere Hotel extends a warm welcome and all the comfort you could wish for.

Bed & Breakfast per night: single room from £35.00–£60.00; double room from £70.00–£120.00
Dinner, Bed & Breakfast per person, per night: £47.00–£75.00
Evening meal: 1900 (last orders 1930)

Bedrooms: 2 single, 9 double, 2 twin
Bathrooms: 13 en-suite
Parking: 13 spaces
Open: February–December
Cards accepted: Mastercard, Visa, Switch/Delta, Amex, Eurocard, JCB

The Lake District

To many, the Lake District is a landscape untainted by human hand, a rare example of Nature left gloriously to her own devices. So it may seem, but the reality is different. The breath-taking splendour of the bare mountains, closely cropped turf criss-crossed by drystone walls and lush lowland pasture is as much a product of human activity as the Fens or the Cotswolds. Wind the clock back 5,000 years, and a very different Lakeland scene appears.

The lower slopes were carpeted with mixed oak forest, giving way to birch and pine to a height of about 2,000ft (600m). Above this, only the highest peaks rose above the trees. Down below, the valley bottoms were swamps clogged

with sedge and alder. Then our ancestors ventured inland from the more hospitable coastline and began to transform the terrain, a process that has already lasted perhaps five millennia. These New Stone Age peoples knew the volcanic rocks of the Langdale Pikes made the best axe-heads. And with them they cleared land for the grazing of their animals and the planting of their crops.

They left other signs, too. Castlerigg Stone Circle, near Keswick, is the most marvellously situated Neolithic remain, while Long Meg and her Daughters (shown below), near Salkeld, is even larger. With the advent of the Iron Age, around 500BC, trees disappeared at a faster rate. Settlements grew up on limestone areas, where loose rocks were used for round, drystone huts and hillforts. Again, remains can be seen at Carrock Fell in Mungrisdale and at two separate Castle Crags, one in Borrowdale, the other by Haweswater.

To help subjugate the local tribe, the Romans built an astonishing road, still in use today, over Wrynose and Hardknott Passes. The soldiers (apparently from present-day Croatia) stationed at the spectacularly sited Hardknott Fort marvelled at views stretching to the Isle of Man. Today's visitors can do the same. After the Romans came the shadowy Celts and, in the seventh century, the Angles. They left beautiful carved stone crosses, as at Bewcastle, an isolated hamlet north of Brampton, and place-names ending in -ton, -ham, and -ington.

12 The Old Vicarage

Vicarage Road, Ambleside, Cumbria LA22 9DH **Tel:** (015394) 33364 **Fax:** (015394) 34734
Web: www.oldvicarageambleside.co.uk **E-mail:** the.old.vicarage@kencomp.net

Tucked quietly away in its own grounds in the centre of one of the finest walking areas of the British Isles, the Old Vicarage at Ambleside in the beautiful English Lake District is an elegant Victorian residence, offering pleasant accommodation and a warm welcome. All the bedrooms have a television, video, alarm/clock radio, CD player, hairdryer, mini fridge, private bath/shower and toilet. There is ample parking within the grounds and pets are welcome. Indoor heated swimming pool, sauna and hot tub.

Bed & Breakfast per night: double room from £70.00

Bedrooms: 1 single, 6 double, 2 twin, 2 family
Bathrooms: 10 en-suite
Parking: 16 spaces
Cards accepted: Mastercard, Visa, Switch/ Delta, Eurocard, JCB

The next wave of settlers was the Vikings, a more peaceable lot than often imagined. They too hewed crosses from stone (Gosforth churchyard has a superb tenth-century example) and gave us words to describe the landscape: *fell, gill* and *beck* are all Norse in origin, as is the ubiquitous *-thwaite* place-name element, meaning a forest clearing. Throughout the twelfth century, the Normans, who had ousted the Scots from Lakeland in 1092, established several Cumbrian monasteries, of which Furness Abbey (extensive ruins still stand) was the most important. The Cistercian monks continued deforestation and, through efficient farming methods, increased the prosperity of the area, so encouraging raids by the Scots. To defend themselves, 14th-century landowners built large fortified (pele) towers, some of which have since been incorporated into stately homes. Sizergh Castle (near Kendal), Hutton-in-the-Forest (north west of Penrith) and Muncaster Castle are three open to the public. Other pele towers have been absorbed into farm buildings.

For about 100 years between the mid-17th and 18th centuries, there occurred a significant change in the vernacular architecture. Farmhouses, long constructed with wooden frames, were rebuilt in the durable and abundant local stone. To the modern eye, the results are quintessentially Lakeland – and very beautiful. Townend, owned by the National Trust and dating from 1626, is a fine example standing in the magnificent village of Troutbeck, near Windermere. If the 'Great Rebuilding in Stone' was architecture's major event, the enclosures of the 18th and 19th century had as great an impact on the landscape. Gangs of itinerant craftsmen were kept busy for decades enclosing the open fells with drystone walls.

Around the turn of the 19th century, the first tourists arrived in search of wild beauty. Leading artists such as Gainsborough, Turner and Constable all visited, while the poets tended to stay longer. Wordsworth (whose birthplace at Cockermouth and homes at Grasmere and Rydal all welcome visitors), Coleridge, Southey and De Quincey formed a literary coterie that has inspired millions. Other luminaries to move here included the art critic and social reformer, John Ruskin, and Beatrix Potter. Both their houses (at Brantwood, by Coniston Water, and at Near Sawrey, Hawkshead, respectively) make fascinating outings.

An important arrival in 1847 was the railway. Windermere (or Birthwaite as it was known till the trains steamed into town) was transformed into a thriving Victorian resort above the lakeshore. Ever since, people have idled away endless hours simply messing about in boats, as immortalised in *Swallows and Amazons* by Arthur Ransome, another literary incomer. Or you can take a leisurely ride on the steam yacht *Gondola* (National Trust), which plies the waters of Lake Coniston.

The landscape continues to change. After thousands of years of deforestation, the process is being reversed: at Grizedale, visitors can follow a 9½-mile (15km) sculpture trail – one of the earliest and one of the best – through a new forest. And new lakes have been created too: Thirlmere is an artificial, but beautiful, reservoir designed to slake the thirst of the north west. But over and above all this are the mountains. They may have changed their outward appearance, but their rocks, and their majesty, are timeless.

13   Riverside Hotel

♦♦♦♦

Under Loughrigg, Nr. Rothay Bridge, Ambleside, Cumbria LA22 9LJ **Tel:** (01539) 432395 **Fax:** (01539) 432440
Web: www.riverside-at-ambleside.co.uk **E-mail:** info@riverside-at-ambleside.co.uk

Set in beautiful gardens, Riverside is a stylish Victorian country house that provides high quality bed & breakfast in a wonderful rural location – yet within ten minutes' walk from the centre of Ambleside. All of our bedrooms have en-suite facilities, some with spa baths, and all have either river, fell or garden views. Riverside is situated in the heart of the Lake District and is the perfect location for a peaceful and relaxing holiday.

Bed & Breakfast per night: single occupancy from £29.00–£45.00; double room from £58.00–£90.00

Bedrooms: 5 double, 1 twin, 1 family
Bathrooms: 5 en-suite
Parking: 10 spaces
Cards accepted: Mastercard, Visa, Switch/Delta

14   Borwick Lodge

♦♦♦♦ Silver Award

Outgate, Hawkshead, Ambleside, Cumbria LA22 0PU **Tel:** (015394) 36332 **Fax:** (015394) 36332
Web: www.borwicklodge.com **E-mail:** borwicklodge@talk21.com

A leafy driveway entices you to a rather special 17th-century country house with magnificent panoramic lake and mountain views. Quietly secluded in beautiful gardens. Ideally placed in the heart of the lakes and close to Hawkshead village with its good choice of restaurants and inns. Tastefully decorated en-suite bedrooms with a lounge for guests' own use with a well-stocked 'honesty bar'. Margaret and Malcolm MacFarlane welcome you to this most beautiful corner of England. Totally NON-SMOKING.

Bed & Breakfast per night: single room from £39.00; double room from £66.00–£78.00

Bedrooms: 1 single, 5 double
Bathrooms: 6 en-suite
Parking: 8 spaces

15   Cedar Manor Country Lodge

♦♦♦♦♦ Silver Award

Ambleside Road, Windermere, Cumbria LA23 1AX **Tel:** (015394) 43192 **Fax:** (015394) 45970
Web: www.cedarmanor.co.uk **E-mail:** cedarmanor@fsbdial.co.uk

A charming Gentleman's residence in a country garden setting close to the Village and Lake Windermere. Central for exploring Lakeland. The Lodge has 11 individually furnished bedrooms some with king-sized beds and Spa Bath. Breakfast is a very special occasion, with an emphasis on local produce, freshly baked breads, home-made jams and many other delicacies to enjoy. We offer complimentary afternoon tea with home-baked cakes and biscuits. 'Superior bed and breakfast accommodation with all the comforts of a quality hotel'.

Bed & Breakfast per night: single occupancy from £56.00–£66.00; double room from £80.00– £130.00

Bedrooms: 6 double, 2 twin, 2 family, 1 suite
Bathrooms: 11 en-suite
Parking: 16 spaces
Cards accepted: Mastercard, Visa

16 Crag Brow Hotel and Restaurant   ★★ Silver Award

Helm Road, Bowness-on-Windermere, Cumbria LA23 3BU **Tel:** (015394) 44080 **Fax:** (015394) 46003
Web: www.cragbrow.com **E-mail:** rooms@cragbrow.com

Perfectly situated overlooking the old village of Bowness, the lake and Claife Heights. Within two minutes' walk of the lake shore and with ample car parking. All bedrooms are tastefully furnished and en-suite, with colour television, radio, tea/coffee facilities, hairdryer and telephone. Our restaurant has a reputation locally for excellence and we have an extensive wine list and well-stocked bar where you can relax in warmth by a log fire.

Bed & Breakfast per night: single room from £40.00–£65.00; double room from £50.00–£120.00
Dinner, Bed & Breakfast per person, per night: £42.50–£75.00
Evening meal: 1800 (last orders 2030)

Bedrooms: 1 single, 10 double/twin, 1 family
Bathrooms: 12 en-suite
Parking: 30 spaces
Cards accepted: Mastercard, Visa, Switch/Delta, Amex, Barclaycard

17 Linthwaite House Hotel   ★★★ Gold Award

Crook Road, Windermere, Cumbria LA23 3JA **Tel:** (015394) 88600 **Fax:** (015394) 88601
Web: www.linthwaite.com **E-mail:** admin@linthwaite.com

Country house hotel, 20 minutes from the M6, situated in 14 acres of peaceful hilltop grounds, overlooking Lake Windermere and with breathtaking sunsets. The 26 rooms have en-suite bathrooms, satellite television, radio, telephone and tea/coffee making facilities. The AA 2 Rosette restaurant serves modern British food using local produce complemented by fine wines. There is a tarn for fly-fishing, croquet, golf practice hole and free use of nearby leisure spa. Romantic breaks feature a king-size double bed with canopy, champagne, chocolates and flowers. English Tourist Board 'Hotel of the Year' 1994. Accessible Mobility 1

Bed & Breakfast per night: single room from £99.00–£140.00; double room from £109.00–£315.00
Dinner, Bed & Breakfast per person, per night: £69.00–£181.00
Lunch available: 1200–1330

Evening meal: 1900 (last orders 2100)
Bedrooms: 1 single, 20 double, 3 twin, 1 family, 1 suite **Bathrooms:** 26 en-suite
Parking: 30 spaces
Cards accepted: Mastercard, Visa, Switch/Delta, Amex, Diners, JCB

18 Gilpin Lodge Country House Hotel and Restaurant   ★★★ Gold Award

Crook Road, Windermere, Cumbria LA23 3NE **Tel:** (015394) 88818 **Fax:** (015394) 88058
Web: www.gilpinlodge.com **E-mail:** hotel@gilpinlodge.com

A friendly, elegant, relaxing hotel in 20 tranqil acres of woodland, moors and delightful country gardens, 12 miles from the M6 and 2 miles from Lake Windermere. Opposite Windermere golf course, the hotel offers golf-inclusive breaks. Sumptuous bedrooms – many with split-level sitting areas and four-poster beds; special bathrooms – some with jacuzzi baths; exquisite cuisine (AA 3 Rosettes). Free use of nearby leisure club. Year-round 'Great Little Escapes'. A Pride of Britain hotel.

Dinner, Bed & Breakfast per person, per night: £100.00–£135.00 (min 2 nights at weekends)
Evening meal: 1900 (last orders 2115)

Bedrooms: 9 double, 5 twin
Bathrooms: 14 en-suite
Parking: 40 spaces
Cards accepted: Mastercard, Visa, Switch/Delta, Amex, Diners, JCB

19 Appleby Manor Country House Hotel

★★★ Silver Award

Roman Road, Appleby-in-Westmorland, Cumbria CA16 6JB **Tel:** (017683) 51571 or (017683) 51570 **Fax:** (017683) 52888
Web: www.applebymanor.co.uk **E-mail:** reception@applebymanor.co.uk

Probably the most relaxing and friendly hotel you'll choose. Set amidst breathtaking beauty, you'll find spotlessly clean bedrooms; satellite television and video films; sunny conservatory and terraces; magnificent lounges; log fires; a splendid indoor leisure club with small pool, jacuzzi, steam room, sauna and sunbed; and great food in the award-winning restaurant. With an 18-hole golf course, the mountains and valleys of the Lake District, and the Yorkshire Dales and North Pennine Fells close by, you're certain to enjoy yourselves.

Bed & Breakfast per night: single occupancy from £77.00–£84.00; double room from £114.00–£128.00
Dinner, Bed & Breakfast per person, per night: £67.00–£75.00 (min 2 nights, 2 sharing)
Lunch available: 1200–1400

Evening meal: 1900 (last orders 2100)
Bedrooms: 18 double, 5 twin, 8 family
Bathrooms: 30 en-suite
Parking: 50 spaces
Cards accepted: Mastercard, Visa, Switch/Delta, Amex; Diners; Eurocard; JCB

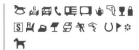

Lady Anne Clifford and Her Monuments

'They that shall be of thee shall build the old waste places' reads the quotation (from Isaiah 58:12) above the door of Outhgill church near Kirkby Stephen. The message, carved at the instigation of Lady Anne Clifford who restored the church in the 17th century, was one which she took to heart. When at the age of 60 she inherited lands in Cumberland, Westmorland and Yorkshire, she embarked upon a frenzy of building, repairs and restoration with a near-religious zeal.

Her enthusiasm was engendered by long years of frustration. She was just 15 in 1605 when her father died and, as his only surviving child, she confidently expected to inherit his extensive northern estates. Instead she found they had been left to his brother and nephew, and she immediately began a long and fruitless campaign to regain her inheritance. In 1643, however, her cousin Henry died without heir, and the estates, at long last, passed to her as his only legitimate successor.

Neglect and the Civil War had taken their toll on her many castles. Those of Appleby, Skipton, Brough, Brougham (shown here), Pendragon and Barden Tower had all fallen into decay, but during the next two decades Lady Anne restored them to their original splendour. She also repaired churches at Skipton, Brough, Brougham and Appleby and built almshouses and monuments, a display of wealth not altogether wise in the puritan atmosphere of Commonwealth England.

To celebrate the restoration of her inheritance Lady Anne commissioned a remarkable painting – depicting herself and all the major characters from her eventful life. Known as the Great Picture, this now hangs in the keep of Appleby Castle. Also in the town she built the St Anne's almshouses and the white pillars at either end of the main street, while her tomb and that of her beloved mother, Margaret, Countess of Cumberland, lie in St Lawrence's church. On the road to Brougham is the Countess Pillar marking the spot where Lady Anne last saw her mother alive.

Skipton Castle, lovingly restored by Lady Anne, remains one of the most complete and best preserved medieval castles in England. But, despite all her efforts, Barden Tower and the castles of Pendragon, Brough and Brougham are all ruins once more. A 100 mile (160km) walk, Lady Anne's Way, takes in all the buildings and monuments associated with this redoubtable lady.

20 Crake Trees Manor

♦♦♦♦♦ Silver Award

Maulds Meaburn, Crosby Ravensworth, Penrith, Cumbria CA10 3JG **Tel:** (01931) 715205 or 07968 744305
Web: craketreesmanor.co.uk **E-mail:** ruth@craketreesmanor.co.uk

Up the track and over the brow of the hill. Look back a moment, the view is forever, home at last... Traditional skills and local materials create a stylish home from the 19th-century barn at the centre of our farm. From the kitchen window I see two hares leaping, peewits dive to protest and a tiny roe deer grazes shyly, her calf hidden in the barley. Three superb bedroom suites are now ready for rest and relaxation. Their windows frame views right over to the Pennines. Footpaths and byways beg to be explored and hidden lanes to be cycled, yet we are only ten minutes from the M6 junction 38. So sink back into that chair, enjoy the afternoon tea tray, farmhouse supper and breakfast spread, all prepared to make the most of good local foods and adventurous recipes.

Bed & Breakfast per night: single room from £35.00–£45.00; double room from £70.00–£80.00
Dinner, Bed & Breakfast per person, per night: £42.00–£57.00

Bedrooms: 1 single, 3 double/twin
Bathrooms: 4 en-suite

21 Helm

♦♦♦♦♦ Gold Award

Askrigg, Leyburn, North Yorkshire DL8 3JF **Tel:** (01969) 650443 **Fax:** (01969) 650443
Web: www.helmyorkshire.com **E-mail:** holiday@helmyorkshire.com

Idyllically situated with 'the finest view in Wensleydale'. Experience the comfort, peace and quiet of this 17th-century hillside Dales farmhouse. Each charmingly furnished bedroom has en-suite facilities and many special little touches. Period furniture, oak beams and log fires create the ideal atmosphere in which to relax and share the owners' passion for really good food. Helm offers a superb choice of breakfasts, home-made bread and preserves, exceptionally good dinners and an inspired selection of wines. Totally non-smoking.

Bed & Breakfast per night: single occupancy from £51.00–£60.00; double room from £67.00– £85.00
Dinner, Bed & Breakfast per person, per night: £53.50–£62.50 (2 sharing room)
Evening meal: 1900

Bedrooms: 2 double, 1 twin
Bathrooms: 3 en-suite
Open: January–November
Parking: 5 spaces
Cards accepted: Mastercard, Visa, Switch/Delta, JCB

22 Mayfields

♦♦♦♦

3 Mayfield Terrace, Kents Bank Road, Grange-over-Sands, Cumbria LA11 7DW
Web: www.accommodata.co.uk/010699.htm

Mayfields is a deceptively spacious, charming, small guest house, highly recommended for the warmth of welcome and exceedingly good home cooking. Situated on the fringe of Grange-over-Sands, adjacent to open countryside, ideally situated for exploring the Lakes, Dales, Cartmel and Furness peninsulas and the magnificent 12th-century Cartmel Priory. Mayfields' bedrooms are very well appointed and individually furnished and the residents' lounge is a cosy room with colour television and a lovely piano. A non-smoking establishment.

Bed & Breakfast per night: single room £27.00; double room £54.00
Dinner, Bed & Breakfast per person, per night: £40.00
Lunch available: 1300 (Sundays)
Evening meal: 1830

Bedrooms: 1 single, 2 double/twin
Bathrooms: 2 en-suite, 1 shared
Parking: 3 spaces

23 Clare House

★ Silver Award

Park Road, Grange-over-Sands, Cumbria LA11 7HQ **Tel:** (01539) 533026 or (01539) 534253
Web: www.clarehousehotel.co.uk **E-mail:** info@clarehousehotel.co.uk

We offer rest and relaxation, a garden to sit in, a promenade to stroll along, wonderful views across the Bay from our family-run hotel and delightful meals for which we hold an AA rosette. If this is what you seek, we would be pleased to hear from you. We offer four-day breaks or weekly stays at advantageous terms.

Dinner, Bed & Breakfast per person, per night: £58.00–£63.00
Evening meal: 1845 (last orders 1915)

Bedrooms: 3 single, 3 double, 11 twin
Bathrooms: 16 en-suite, 1 shared
Open: March–November
Parking: 16 spaces
Cards accepted: Mastercard, Visa, Switch/ Delta, Eurocard, JCB, Solo, Maestro

Piel Island

Just offshore from Barrow in Furness is Piel Island, a small rocky outcrop in the sea surmounted by the brooding ruins of a castle. Tiny and unimportant it may be, but it still has its ferry service, pub – even its own king.

The island has a colourful history. It is separated from the mainland yet remains fairly accessible, so making it a useful haven in troubled times. From the 14th century it was the centre of a lively smuggling trade largely orchestrated by the monks of Furness Abbey. They built the impressive castle as a fortified warehouse to keep their cargoes safe from raiders, and to keep the King's customs men at bay.

The island's most historic moment arrived in June 1487, when Lambert Simnel, pretender to the English throne, landed at Piel with 8,000 men. Simnel was an impostor, a baker's son claiming to be the Earl of Warwick (then imprisoned in the Tower of London) who, backed by Margaret of Burgundy, gathered a force of German mercenaries and Irish recruits, intending to take the throne by force. Leaving Piel, he set off across Furness towards London, but was defeated at the Battle of Stoke on June 16th. In contrast, the 18th century brought more prosperous and settled times to the island, with Piel's busy harbour servicing Furness's thriving shipping and iron industries. The island's pub and its few houses were built at this time.

The Ship Inn continues to flourish, a useful watering-hole for sailors and day trippers from the mainland. The landlord is traditionally known as the 'King of Piel', a reference, it is supposed, to Lambert Simnel's claim to the throne. Anyone who sits in a particular old wooden chair in the pub, becomes a 'Knight of Piel', and must carry out certain gallant duties – such as buying everyone a drink, being a moderate smoker, a lover of the opposite sex, and generally of good character. If shipwrecked, a Knight of Piel has the right to free board and lodging in the pub.

The ferry from Roa runs from April to October, 11am–5pm, weather permitting, making the island an easy day trip. Facilities are minimal (the island has neither electricity nor telephone) but for those wishing to stay longer, camping is permitted anywhere on the island by arrangement, on arrival, with the Ship Inn.

Entries are cross referenced by number to the maps on pages 18–19

24 Middle Flass Lodge

 ◆◆◆◆

Forest Becks Brow, Settle Road, Bolton-by-Bowland, Clitheroe, Lancashire BB7 4NY **Tel:** (01200) 447259 **Fax:** (01200) 447300
Web: www.middleflasslodge.co.uk **E-mail:** info@middleflasslodge.fsnet.co.uk

Set in beautiful countryside within the Forest of Bowland, this peacefully located barn conversion is an ideal base for the Dales, Lakes and walking etc. Neat and cosy rooms all with full facilities. Exposed timbers are featured throughout the property – also in the attractive lounge and dining room/ restaurant. Chef-prepared cuisine using fresh local produce wherever possible. Always personal and professional attention. Table licence, gardens and ample parking.

Bed & Breakfast per night: single occupancy from £35.00–£42.00; double room from £48.00–£64.00
Dinner, Bed & Breakfast per person, per night: £47.00–£55.00
Evening meal: 1730 (last orders 1915)

Bedrooms: 2 double, 2 twin, 1 family
Bathrooms: 5 en-suite
Parking: 12 spaces
Cards accepted: Mastercard, Visa, Switch/ Delta

25 Meadow Hill Guest House

 ◆◆◆◆

Duns Road, Berwick-upon-Tweed TD15 1UB **Tel:** (01289) 306325 **Fax:** (01289) 307466
Web: www.meadow-hill.co.uk **E-mail:** pammewing@onetel.com

Panoramic views over the Tweed, Cheviots and Berwick-Upon-Tweed. All rooms en-suite, dining rooms, bar, lounge and gardens. Two ground floor suites with full disabled facilities. Transport to and from railway station if necessary. Meadow Hill Guest House is situated by the battle site of Halidon Hill where in 1333 Edward III took Berwick from the Scots. A total of six rooms, all en-suite, with television, tea and coffee facilities. Non-smoking except in bar. Off-street parking.  Accessible Mobility 2

Bed & Breakfast per night: single occupancy from £30.00–£35.00; double room from £50.00–£70.00

Bedrooms: 2 double, 2 twin, 2 family
Bathrooms: 6 en-suite
Parking: 10 spaces
Cards accepted: Mastercard, Visa, Switch/ Delta, Amex, JCB

26 Tillmouth Park Country House Hotel

★★★ Silver Award

Cornhill-on-Tweed, Northumberland TD12 4UU **Tel:** (01890) 882255 **Fax:** (01890) 882540
Web: www.tillmouthpark.co.uk **E-mail:** reception@tillmouthpark.f9.co.uk

This secluded country mansion is set in 15 acres of mature parkland gardens. Tillmouth Park boasts 14 fully appointed en-suite bedrooms which are spacious and individually styled with period and antique furniture, an award-winning wood-panelled restaurant, an informal bistro and a well-stocked bar. A perfect venue for golf, fishing and shooting – the hotel is ideally situated for peace and tranquillity. It offers exceptional hospitality, comfort and service. Helicopter landing pad on site. Two AA Rosettes.

Bed & Breakfast per night: single room from £70.00–£140.00; double room from £140.00–£180.00
Dinner, Bed & Breakfast per person, per night: £70.00–£240.00
Lunch available: 1200–1400

Evening meal: 1900 (last bookings 1845)
Bedrooms: 1 single, 6 double, 5 twin, 2 family
Bathrooms: 14 en-suite
Parking: 50 spaces
Cards accepted: Mastercard, Visa, Switch/ Delta

27 Seaham Hall Hotel and Serenity Spa

★★★★ Gold Award

Lord Byron's Walk, Seaham, County Durham SR7 7AG **Tel:** 0191 516 1400 **Fax:** 0191 516 1410
Web: www.seaham-hall.com **E-mail:** reservations@seaham-hall.com

An innovative and stylish hotel combining historical elegance and 21st-century luxury. Set in 30 acres of landscaped grounds and gardens, perched on the clifftop overlooking the North Sea, Seaham Hall is ideally located for visiting Durham, Newcastle upon Tyne and Sunderland. Each suite is individually designed, beds are huge and baths are designed for two. Our restaurant boasts three AA Rosettes and is renowned for its superb food and extensive wine list. The Serenity Spa is unique in Europe, with its combination of Oriental and Western treatments.

Bed & Breakfast per night: single room from £245.00–£550.00; double room from £245.00–£550.00
Dinner, Bed & Breakfast per person, per night: £305.00–£630.00
Lunch available: 1200–1430

Evening meal: 1900 (last orders 2200)
Bedrooms: 19 suites
Bathrooms: 19 en-suite
Parking: 120 spaces
Cards accepted: Mastercard, Visa, Switch/Delta, Amex, Diners, Eurocard, JCB

The Angel of the North

In February 1998 something remarkable happened on the southern edge of Gateshead, one of England's erstwhile industrial centres. On a hilltop visible from both the A1 and the main London–Newcastle railway, a winged figure was sighted. No ordinary angel, this, for reports spoke of it being as high as four double-decker buses and with a span as wide as a jumbo jet. It stood with wings outstretched, suggesting welcome and embrace. Word got out, cameras arrived and a website was devoted to it. More remarkable still, all these reports turned out to be entirely true.

The Angel of the North, to give it its full name, is almost certainly England's most high-profile work of art. The creation of sculptor Antony Gormley, it towers 65ft (20m) above its site at the head of the Team Valley – and is set to become as much a symbol of the North East as the Tyne Bridge. Its history, though, begins back in 1989, when the former bath block at the Team Colliery was reclaimed. This, Gateshead Council decided, would be an ideal location for a 'landmark sculpture'. Once the site had been landscaped, the council asked a shortlist of international artists to pitch for the commission, a competition won in January 1994 by Gormley.

The scale of the design clearly called for considerable funding, but the expense – about £800,000 all told – was met without any contributions from the local council tax. Both the size and the exposed position meant that the 200 ton angel would have to be enormously strong to cope with winds of up to 100mph (160kph). The engineering firm of Ove Arup was called in to advise and, after close consultation with the sculptor, fabrication began at nearby Hartlepool. By September 1997, vast sections of the sculpture, made from a weather-resistant steel designed to mellow to a rich red-brown, were arriving at Team Valley under police escort.

Thanks to its lofty position – it reminds the sculptor of a megalithic mound – more than one person every second will see the angel. This, in theory, works out at 33 million a year. Given that its life is thought to be a hundred years or more, a lot of people are going to witness this arresting apparition.

28 | Little Holtby

◆◆◆◆ Silver Award

Leeming Bar, Northallerton, North Yorkshire DL7 9LH **Tel:** (01609) 748762 **Fax:** (01609) 748822
Web: www.littleholtby.co.uk **E-mail:** littleholtby@yahoo.co.uk

Today's discerning traveller is looking for somewhere special, where the warmth of welcome and attention to comfort will remain a treasured memory. Beams, polished wood floors and antiques all add to the charm of an old farmhouse. All the spacious, period bedrooms have glorious views. One of the double bedrooms has a four-poster bed. Generous country breakfasts with local organic and free range produce, Aga-cooked. Our aim is to give our guests the best. Treat yourself to a really memorable stay.

Bed & Breakfast per night: single occupancy £30.00; double room from £50.00–£55.00
Dinner, Bed & Breakfast per person, per night: £37.50–£40.00

Bedrooms: 2 double, 1 twin
Bathrooms: 1 en-suite, 1 shared
Parking: 10 spaces

---

29 | Lovesome Hill Farm

◆◆◆◆

Lovesome Hill, Northallerton, North Yorkshire DL6 2PB **Tel:** (01609) 772311 **Fax:** (01609) 774715
E-mail: pearsonlhf@care4free.net

Be sure of a friendly welcome upon arrival at Lovesome Hill Farm with home-made biscuits and tea. John will happily show you around our traditional working farm which is set amidst open countryside. The accommodation is in the converted granary and farm house, with a blend of antique and modern furniture and all en-suite. Gate Cottage offers quality accommodation with a half-tester bed and its own patio – a romantic hideaway. Meals are served in the Granary Meal House using our own and fresh local produce whenever possible. The Yorkshire Dales and Moors, York, Durham, Northallerton and Thirsk are all within easy reach.  Accessible Mobility 1

Bed & Breakfast per night: single room from £26.00–£32.00; double room from £48.00–£52.00
Dinner, Bed & Breakfast per person, per night: £40.00–£42.00
Evening meal: 1900 (by arrangement)

Bedrooms: 1 single, 3 double, 1 twin, 1 family
Bathrooms: 6 en-suite
Cards accepted: Mastercard, Visa, Switch/Delta, JCB

---

30 | Churchview House

◆◆◆◆◆ Gold Award

72 High Street, Swainby, Northallerton, North Yorkshire DL6 3DG **Tel:** (01642) 706058
Web: www.churchviewhouse.co.uk **E-mail:** churchviewhouse@aol.com

This elegant mid 19th-century house is in a peaceful village within the North York Moors National Park. Churchview House offers a unique blend of charm, comfort and cuisine, based upon a relentless pursuit of attention to detail and excellence. The newly refurbished house is decorated with original artwork and eclectic furniture from around the world. Luxurious bathrooms, large powerful showers and handmade mosaics provide a welcome end to a day's walking on the moors. The coast and many other places of interest are nearby.

Bed & Breakfast per night: single room from £40.00; double room from £65.00

Bedrooms: 1 double, 1 twin
Bathrooms: 2 en-suite

31 Laskill Grange   ◆◆◆◆

Hawnby, nr Helmsley, York, North Yorkshire YO62 5NB **Tel:** (01439) 798268 **Fax:** (01439) 798498
Web: www.laskillgrange.co.uk **E-mail:** suesmith@laskillfarm.fsnet.co.uk

A delightful country farmhouse with a beautiful one acre garden and lake with ducks and swans. We offer complete relaxation in our lovely en-suite rooms. Emphasis is placed on comfort and food, as characterised on the BBC 'Holiday' programme. Lots to do and see - a walkers' paradise. 'A jewel in the North Yorkshire Moors'. York and the coast are only 40 minutes' drive away.

Bed & Breakfast per night: single room from £30.00–£33.00; double room from £60.00–£70.00

Bedrooms: 1 single, 3 double, 3 twin
Bathrooms: 6 en-suite, 1 private
Parking: 20 spaces

32 Sevenford House   ◆◆◆◆ Silver Award

Thorgill, Rosedale Abbey, Pickering, North Yorkshire YO18 8SE **Tel:** (01751) 417283
Web: www.sevenford.com **E-mail:** sevenford@aol.com

A beautifully appointed vicarage built from the stones of Rosedale Abbey, Sevenford House stands in four acres of lovely gardens in the heart of the beautiful Yorkshire Moors National Park. Three charming en-suite bedrooms with television, radio, and tea/coffee making facilities, offer wonderful views of the surrounding valley and moorland. A relaxing guests' lounge/library with open fire. This is an excellent base for exploring the region. Riding and golf locally. Ruined abbeys, Roman roads, steam railways, beautiful coastline and pretty fishing towns are all within easy reach.

Bed & Breakfast per night: single occupancy from £35.00–£45.00; double room from £50.00–£60.00

Bedrooms: 1 double, 1 twin, 1 family
Bathrooms: 3 en-suite
Parking: 6 spaces

33 Broom House   ◆◆◆◆ Silver Award

Broom House Lane, Egton Bridge, Whitby, North Yorkshire YO21 1XD **Tel:** (01947) 895279 **Fax:** (01947) 895657
Web: www.egton-bridge.co.uk **E-mail:** mw@broom-house.co.uk

Broom House: an excellent place to stay - tucked into a quiet dell in Eskdale is Egton Bridge one of the prettiest villages in the North Yorkshire Moors. Maria and David refurbished this 19th-century farmhouse to provide six charmingly decorated ensuite rooms. A place to stay in all seasons with oak beams, log fires and views of open countryside. Highly recommended for our superb choice of breakfast featuring a variety of local produce. An ideal location from which to explore the east cost and the North York Moors National Park.

Bed & Breakfast per night: single occupancy from £36.00; double room from £49.00– £58.00
Evening meal: 1800–2000 (large parties only)

Bedrooms: 4 double, 1 twin, 1 family
Bathrooms: 6 en-suite
Parking: 7 spaces
Cards accepted: Mastercard, Visa, Switch/ Delta, Eurocard, JCB

34 High Farm

◆◆◆◆ Silver Award

Cropton, Pickering, North Yorkshire YO18 8HL **Tel:** (01751) 417461 **Fax:** (01751) 417807
Web: www.hhml.com/bb/highfarmcropton.htm **E-mail:** highfarmcropton@aol.com

High Farm is an elegant Victorian farmhouse located at the edge of a quiet, unspoilt village, with fine views over the North York Moors National Park. Relax and unwind in the old world charm and sample home baking over an open fire. Enjoy the beautiful two-acre garden planted with trees, shrubs and roses. Ideal base for walkers and nature lovers. Visit nearby Castle Howard, Rievaulx Abbey and Moors Railway. Private parking. A short stroll from the village inn and brewery.

Bed & Breakfast per night: single occupancy £29.00; double room £48.00

Bedrooms: 3 double
Bathrooms: 3 en-suite
Parking: 10 spaces

The 'Mouseman' of Kilburn

In the small town of Kilburn, nestling beneath the southern fringes of the North York Moors, is a furniture-making company of international repute. It was established at the turn of the century by a local carpenter, Robert Thompson, who began his career in his father's business, performing mundane village tasks such as repairing gates or constructing farm wagons. However, inspired by the exquisite medieval wood-carvings in Ripon Cathedral, Thompson determined to revive the craftman's skills, teaching himself to emulate the work of the medieval masters. By the 1920s he was running the family firm and so able to take it in the direction of fine furniture-making.

All Thompson's work was in oak, using wood that was naturally seasoned in the open air, and was carved by hand, often making use of a medieval tool, the adze, to create a hewn look on table-tops and other surfaces. Quality, sturdy durability and loving attention to detail were its hallmarks, characteristics recognised by Father Paul Neville, headmaster of nearby Ampleforth College, who commissioned Thompson to carve a memorial cross for the cemetery there. This was a turning point for Thompson, for the subsequent commission to refurbish the school and make additions to the church both provided him with a steady supply of work and did much to cement and spread his reputation. By the time of his death in 1955 Robert Thompson's carpentry workshop was world-famous.

Now run by his grandsons and great-grandsons, it still operates from the Elizabethan timber-framed cottage which was the Thompson family home, while a visitor centre has been established in the old carpenter's shop. In the local church a memorial chapel to Thompson has been carved in English oak by his own craftsmen in the distinctive Thompson style.

Robert Thompson's reputation as the Kilburn 'Mouse-man' stems from his trademark, a little mouse, symbol of industry in quiet places, which was – and is – carved on every piece of furniture produced by the workshop. According to Thompson, the idea came about when he was working in a church roof with a craftsman who grumbled that they were as poor as church mice. Supposedly Thompson immediately carved a mouse on one of the beams and later adopted it as his trademark. Whether or not the story is true is unknown, for the original church mouse has never been located!

35 Burr Bank

◆◆◆◆◆ Gold Award

Cropton, Pickering, North Yorkshire YO18 8HL **Tel:** (01751) 417777 or 0776 884 2233 **Fax:** (01751) 417789
Web: www.burrbank.com **E-mail:** bandb@burrbank.com

Winner of Yorkshire's 'Guest Accommodation of the Year 2000'.
A quarter mile from the village and set in 80 acres, with wonderful views over Cropton Forest and Moors. Comfortable, spacious ground-floor accommodation and personal attention. An interesting, peaceful holiday with easy access to the coast, Moors, Wolds and York. Much to do and see using Burr Bank as your home for a while. We hope you enjoy our part of Yorkshire as much as we do. No smoking.

Bed & Breakfast per night: single room £29.00; double room £58.00
Dinner, Bed & Breakfast per person, per night: £47.00
Evening meal: 1900

Bedrooms: 1 single, 1 double, 1 twin
Bathrooms: 3 en-suite
Parking: 20 spaces

36 The Cornmill

◆◆◆◆ Silver Award

Kirby Mills, Kirkbymoorside, York, North Yorkshire YO62 6NP **Tel:** (01751) 432000 **Fax:** (01751) 432300
Web: www.kirbymills.demon.co.uk **E-mail:** cornmill@kirbymills.demon.co.uk

This restored 18th-century Watermill and Victorian Farmhouse provides tranquil, well appointed accommodation on the River Dove. Large bedrooms with en-suite baths and/or powerful showers, fluffy towels, king-size beds, themed four-poster rooms, guest lounge, honesty bar, wood-burning stove and bootroom are in the Farmhouse. Our sumptuous breakfasts and pre-booked dinners are served in the Mill with glass viewing panel over the millrace. Near golf, horse riding, abbeys, castles, coast and the North York Moors. See also our self-catering accommodation on page 53. Accessible Mobility 1

Bed & Breakfast per night: double room from £60.00–£75.00
Dinner, Bed & Breakfast per person, per night: £55.00–£62.50
Evening meal: 1930 (last orders 2000)

Bedrooms: 3 double, 2 twin
Bathrooms: 5 en-suite
Parking: 8 spaces
Cards accepted: Mastercard, Visa, Switch/Delta

37 Sproxton Hall

◆◆◆◆

Sproxton, Helmsley, North Yorkshire YO62 5EQ **Tel:** (01439) 770225 **Fax:** (01439) 771373
Web: www.sproxtonhall.co.uk **E-mail:** info@sproxtonhall.demon.co.uk

Relax in the tranquil atmosphere and comfort of our 17th-century Grade II listed farmhouse. Magnificent views over idyllic countryside on a 300 acre working farm, one mile south of the market town of Helmsley. Lovingly and tastefully furnished, giving the cosy elegance of a country home. Restful, oak-beamed drawing room with log fire. Enjoy a hearty breakfast in a most attractive dining room. Extremely comfortable, centrally heated double and twin bedrooms. En-suite or private bathrooms, tea making facilities, remote control colour television. Delightful country garden to relax in. No smoking.

Bed & Breakfast per night: single occupancy from £35.00–£40.00; double room from £56.00–£66.00

Bedrooms: 1 double, 2 twin
Bathrooms: 2 en-suite, 1 private
Parking: 10 spaces
Cards accepted: Mastercard, Visa, Eurocard

38 | Shallowdale House

◆◆◆◆◆ Gold Award

West End, Ampleforth, York, North Yorkshire YO62 4DY **Tel:** (01439) 788325 **Fax:** (01439) 788885
Web: www.shallowdalehouse.co.uk **E-mail:** stay@shallowdalehouse.co.uk

Winner of the 2003 Yorkshire Tourist Board White Rose Award for Guest Accommodation of the Year. Shallowdale House is stunningly situated, in extensive hillside gardens, on the southern edge of the North York Moors National Park (20 miles north of York). Phillip Gill and Anton van der Horst have carefully created a distinctively elegant and restful place to stay, where good food matters and the service is always friendly and attentive. All the rooms enjoy exceptional panoramic views of gorgeous countryside and this is an excellent base for exploring a beautiful area. "They revel in offering tip-top hospitality" The Which? Hotel Guide.

Bed & Breakfast per night: single occupancy from £55.00–£65.00; double room from £75.00–£90.00
Dinner, Bed & Breakfast per person, per night: £65.00–£72.50
Evening meal: 1930 (last bookings 1200)

Bedrooms: 1 double, 2 double/twin
Bathrooms: 2 en-suite, 1 private
Parking: 3 spaces
Open: all year except Christmas/New Year
Cards accepted: Mastercard, Visa, Switch/Delta, Eurocard

39 | The Old Vicarage

◆◆◆◆ Gold Award

Market Place, Easingwold, York, North Yorkshire YO61 3AL **Tel:** (01347) 821015 **Fax:** (01347) 823465
Web: www.oldvicarage-easingwold.co.uk **E-mail:** kirman@oldvic-easingwold.freeserve.co.uk

Standing in the market square, yet surrounded by half an acre of gardens with croquet lawn and ample parking, our 18th-century home provides a tranquil haven easily accessible to York, the Moors and Dales. Tastefully furnished, well-appointed bedrooms are complemented with patchwork quilts and little unexpected extra touches. A traditional English breakfast using local produce is served in the east-facing dining room and the drawing room, with its grand piano, is exclusively for guests' enjoyment.

Bed & Breakfast per night: single occupancy from £40.00–£50.00; double room from £60.00–£75.00

Bedrooms: 3 double, 1 twin
Bathrooms: 4 en-suite
Parking: 6 spaces
Open: February–November

40 | The George at Easingwold

★★ Silver Award

Market Place, Easingwold, York, YO61 3AD **Tel:** (01347) 821698 **Fax:** (01347) 823448
Web: www.the-george-hotel.co.uk **E-mail:** info@the-george-hotel.co.uk

A traditional 18th-century inn overlooking the cobbled Georgian market square, run by owners Kay and Michael Riley and their enthusiastic staff. The George offers discerning guests a warm welcome, real ales and a fine selection of local produce in both the restaurant and bar. All the bedrooms have recently been refurbished to a high standard. Oak beams and open fires in the cooler months add to the character. The inn makes an ideal centre for visiting York, the Dales and North Yorkshire Moors.

Bed & Breakfast per night: single occupancy from £55.00–£65.00; double room from £75.00–£90.00
Dinner, Bed & Breakfast per person, per night: £40.00–£57.50 (min 2 nights)
Lunch available: 1200–1400

Evening meal: 1900 (last orders 2100)
Bedrooms: 8 double, 5 twin, 2 family
Bathrooms: 15 en-suite
Parking: 9 spaces
Cards accepted: Mastercard, Visa, Switch/Delta, Eurocard, JCB

At-a-glance symbols are explained on the flap inside the back cover

41 Skelton Grange Farmhouse

◆◆◆◆

Orchard View, Skelton, York YO30 1YQ **Tel:** (01904) 470780
Web: www.skelton-farm.co.uk **E-mail:** info@skelton-farm.co.uk

Five mews cottage style rooms to rear of this former 18th-century dairy farm. Situated in a quiet village only half a mile away from York Park and Ride. All rooms are en-suite, individually and tastefully decorated and at ground floor level offereing discerning guests homely comfort and freedom of access. Private parking is available. There are many local walks, golf, restaurants and pubs nearby. Visiting our website is a must. www.skelton-farm.co.uk

Bed & Breakfast per night: single occupancy from £37.50–£55.00; double room from £49.00– £69.00; family room from £79.00–£85.00

Bedrooms: 2 double, 1 twin, 2 family
Bathrooms: 5 en-suite
Parking: 5 spaces
Cards accepted: Mastercard, Visa, Switch/ Delta, Eurocard, Solo

Salts Mill

A marvel of its age and pre-eminent among Bradford's textile mills until its closure in the 1980s, Salts Mill was built in 1853 by Titus Salt for his worsted manufacturing business. Now the vast Italianate-style mill is a Grade II listed building, still surrounded by the terraced sandstone houses and community buildings of the village that the visionary Salt planned to cater for his workers' every need. In 1987 it was bought by locally-born Jonathan Silver and since then has been undergoing creative but sympathetic restoration. It is now home to several businesses (employing some 1,400 people in fields such as electronics and manufacturing) and a clutch of cultural enterprises. Of the latter, the most notable are the galleries devoted to the work of artist David Hockney, another of Bradford's sons, a schoolmate of Jonathan Silver and a regular visitor to the mill.

The 1853 Gallery, on the ground floor of the main spinning block, was the first of the three Hockney galleries to open. On its walls hang 350 original works, a permanent exhibition of cartoons, prints, paintings and computer-generated images from Hockney's childhood years to recent times. Here, too, a bookshop displays its wares not on conventional shelves but on tables, chairs and other pieces of furniture, between vases of flowers and local pottery. The mood is set for browsing with strains of Hockney's favourite pieces of music, often from opera, playing in the background. A second gallery is to be found in an old wool-sorting room, next to Salts Diner on the second floor. This is an experimental space and exhibitions change regularly: the past few years have, for example, seen pictures of Hockney's dachshunds and his opera sets. The third and newest gallery, above the Diner, is a more intimate space, displaying images that have a particular meaning for David Hockney personally.

Apart from the galleries, Salts Mill has some fairly upmarket shops, whose goods range from contemporary furniture and high-quality household objects to top designer label clothes. The civilised, relaxed atmosphere that pervades the galleries carries through to Salts Diner, where you can pick up a newspaper to read while you enjoy good, reasonably priced food and drink. Salts Mill is open daily 10am–6pm, admission free. Frequent trains link Saltaire with Bradford and Leeds.

42 Ascot House

◆◆◆◆ Silver Award

80 East Parade, York YO31 7YH **Tel:** (01904) 426826 **Fax:** (01904) 431077
Web: www.ascothouseyork.com **E-mail:** admin@ascothouseyork.com

Ascot House is a family-run 15 bedroomed Victorian villa built in 1869, with en-suite rooms of character – many having four poster or canopy beds. There is a spacious lounge for residents to relax in and delicious traditional English or vegetarian breakfasts are served in the dining room. The historic city centre and York Minster are 15 minutes' walk away and it is only an hours' drive to the Dales, the Moors or the beautiful Yorkshire coast. Residential licence, sauna and private enclosed car park.

Bed & Breakfast per night: single room from £26.00–£60.00; double room from £52.00–£64.00

Bedrooms: 1 single, 8 double, 3 twin, 3 family
Bathrooms: 12 en-suite, 1 private, 1 shared
Parking: 14 spaces
Cards accepted: Mastercard, Visa, Switch/Delta, Diners, Eurocard, JCB, Solo

43 Holmwood House Hotel

◆◆◆◆ Silver Award

114 Holgate Road, York YO24 4BB **Tel:** (01904) 626183 **Fax:** (01904) 670899
Web: www.holmwoodhousehotel.co.uk **E-mail:** holmwood.house@dial.pipex.com

Close to the city walls, an elegant listed Victorian town house offering a feeling of home with a touch of luxury. All the en-suite bedrooms are different in size and decoration, some with four-poster beds and two have spa baths. All rooms are non-smoking and air conditioned rooms are available. Imaginative breakfasts are served to the sound of gentle classical music. There is an inviting sitting room with an open fire. Car park. On the A59. Why not take a look at our web-site?

Bed & Breakfast per night: single occupancy from £50.00–£75.00; double room from £65.00–£110.00

Bedrooms: 13 double/twin, 1 family
Bathrooms: 14 en-suite
Parking: 9 spaces
Cards accepted: Mastercard, Visa, Switch/Delta, Amex, Barclaycard

44 Glebe Farm

◆◆◆◆

Bolton Percy, York, North Yorkshire YO23 7AL **Tel:** (01904) 744228

An elegant family-run Victorian farmhouse on a working farm. Offering excellent accommodation within easy reach of York city. The Moors, Dales and coast can be reached within an hour. Self-contained en-suite annexe, conservatory, garden and ample parking. The farm is in a quiet village with an exceptional 15th-century church. Bolton Percy is four miles from Tadcaster and nine miles from York.

Bed & Breakfast per night: single occupancy from £24.00–£28.00; double room from £48.00– £56.00

Bedrooms: 1 twin
Bathrooms: 1 en-suite
Open: April–October
Parking: 2 spaces

45   Ravencroft B&B

◆◆◆◆ Gold Award

Moorside Avenue, Ripon, North Yorkshire HG4 1TA   **Tel:** (01765) 602543
Web: www.ravencroftbandb.com   **E-mail:** guestmail@btopenworld.com

Enjoy a warm welcome to this traditional family home. Ripon bypass A61 is two minutes away, the cathedral one mile and Fountains Abbey three miles away. Luxury en-suite rooms completed in 2003. Very full hot and cold menu in new facilities. Service quality paramount. Emphasis on relaxed, informal hospitality. Several complimentary services usually include free transport to evening meal in city. Guest comments in 2003: "Five star hotel comfort" (Hants), "Hope to be back" (Canada), "Excellent" (South Africa/New Zealand/Australia/Kansas), "Wonderful" (Netherlands), "Fabulous" (New Zealand), "Best ever" (Norway), "Glad we found you" (Seattle), "Felt like royalty" (Essex).

Bed & Breakfast per night: single occupancy from £40.00–£45.00; double room from £50.00–£59.00

Bedrooms: 1 double, 1 family
Bathrooms: 2 en-suite
Parking: 3 spaces
Cards accepted: Mastercard, Visa, Switch/Delta, Amex, JCB, Solo, Maestro

46   Knottside Farm

◆◆◆◆◆ Gold Award

The Knott, Pateley Bridge, Harrogate, North Yorkshire HG3 5DQ   **Tel:** (01423) 712927   **Fax:** (01423) 712927

Situated within easy reach of York, Harrogate, Dales and North York Moors, this lovingly refurbished house, which nestles into the hillside, has panoramic views over Nidderdale. A very special experience awaits the visitor. An atmosphere of comfort and relaxation pervades the delightful accommodation where attention to detail is second to none. However, what really sets this place apart is the amazing quality of the cuisine. Nigel is Cordon Bleu trained and cooking is obviously the love of his life.

Bed & Breakfast per night: single occupancy £60.00; double room from £68.00–£74.00
Evening meal: 1945

Bedrooms: 3 double
Bathrooms: 2 en-suite, 1 private
Parking: 4 spaces

47   North Star Hotel

★★ Silver Award

North Marine Road, Flamborough, Bridlington, East Riding of Yorkshire YO15 1BL   **Tel:** (01262) 850379 or Freephone 0500 602021
Web: www.puffinsatflamborough.co.uk   **E-mail:** info@puffinsatflamborough.co.uk

The North Star is only a 10-minute drive from the famous RSPB bird sanctuary at Bempton Cliffs and is ideally situated for the many cliff walks in the area. We are within easy travelling distance of many of Yorkshire's finest East Coast attractions including: Bridlington, Whitby, Scarborough, the North Yorkshire Moors ('Heartbeat' Country), the historic city of York, the splendour of Burton Agnes Hall and Gardens, and Sewerby Hall with its children's zoo. Most of our recently-refurbished bedrooms have panoramic sea views. Relax in the charming atmosphere of our Olde Worlde Bar or dine in the more formal setting of our non-smoking restaurant.

Bed & Breakfast per night: single occupancy from £45.00–£55.00; double room from £65.00–£75.00
Lunch available: 1130–1400
Evening meal: 1830 (last orders 2100)

Bedrooms: 2 double, 5 twin
Bathrooms: 7 en-suite
Parking: 30 spaces
Cards accepted: Mastercard, Visa, Switch/Delta, Diners, Eurocard

48 Maryland Bed & Breakfast   ◆◆◆◆

66 Wellington Road, Bridlington, East Riding of Yorkshire YO15 2AZ **Tel:** (01262) 671088
Web: www.maryland.bridlington.co.uk **E-mail:** mills@marylandbandb.fsbusiness.co.uk

Spoil yourself by staying at Maryland, a friendly, caring bed and breakfast in a spacious Victorian house. Come and experience our high standard of hospitality and customer care. The bedrooms are clean, spacious and exceedingly comfortable in our totally non-smoking home. We are placed just ten minutes walk from the historic harbour, spa theatre and the award-winning beaches of Bridlington. With Flamborough Head, RSPB's Bempton Cliffs Reserve and the 19th-century estate and gardens of Sewerby Hall nearby there is truly something for everyone. Why not let us help you plan your next holiday?

Bed & Breakfast per night: single room from £20.00–£25.00; double room from £40.00–£50.00

Bedrooms: 1 single, 2 double, 1 twin, 1 family
Bathrooms: 1 private, 1 shared

---

49 Northcote Manor   ★★★ Silver Award

Northcote Road, Langho, Blackburn BB6 8BE **Tel:** (01254) 240555 **Fax:** (01254) 246568
Web: www.northcotemanor.com **E-mail:** sales@northcotemanor.com

Northcote Manor is a privately owned, 14 bedroom country house hotel situated in the beautiful Ribble Valley in the heart of north-west England. In the capable hands of Craig Bancroft and award-winning chef Nigel Haworth, the Manor is best known for its excellent restaurant and friendly hospitality, awarded a Michelin Star and, in 1999, an independent hotel of the year award. Gourmet one-night breaks available from £90 per person which includes champagne, a five-course gourmet dinner and stunning Lancashire breakfast.

Bed & Breakfast per night: single room from £100.00–£120.00; double room from £130.00–£150.00
Evening meal: 1900 (last orders 2130, Sat & Sun 2200)

Bedrooms: 14 double
Bathrooms: 14 en-suite
Parking: 60 spaces
Cards accepted: Mastercard, Visa, Switch/Delta, Amex

---

50 Stanneylands Hotel   ★★★ Silver Award

Stanneylands Road, Wilmslow, Cheshire SK9 4EY **Tel:** (01625) 525225 **Fax:** (01625) 537282
Web: www.stanneylandshotel.co.uk **E-mail:** sales@stanneylandshotel.co.uk

A strikingly handsome country house hotel set in beautiful gardens. With open fires and oak-panelled dining rooms, hospitality abounds on every hand. Stanneylands offers the very finest of English and International cuisine, prepared and served with pride and care. Ideally located for visiting Styal Mill, Jodrell Bank, Tatton Park and Bramall Hall, and within easy reach of the motorway network and Manchester International Airport.

Bed & Breakfast per night: single room from £69.00–£99.00; double room from £99.50–£120.00
Dinner, Bed & Breakfast per person, per night: £65.00–£80.00
Evening meal: 1900 (last orders 2130)

Bedrooms: 7 single, 11 double, 11 twin, 2 suites
Bathrooms: 31 en-suite
Cards accepted: Mastercard, Visa, Switch/Delta, Amex, Diners

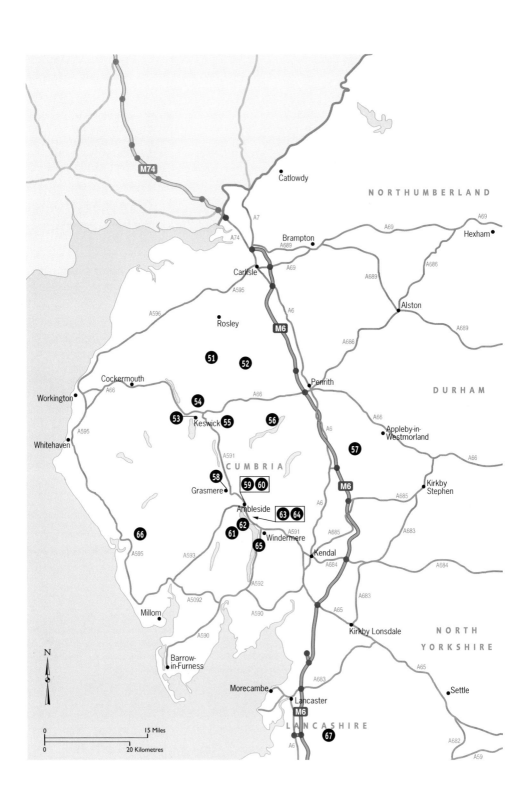

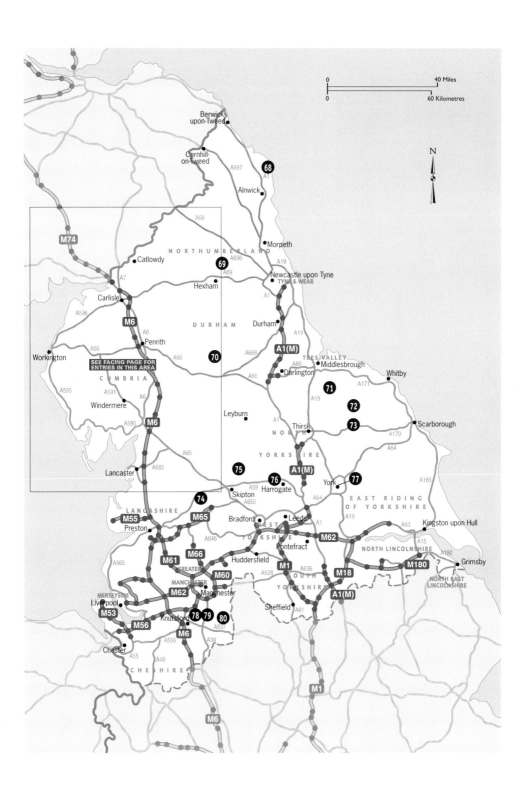

51   The Barn, Manor Cottage ★★★★

Caldbeck, Wigton, Cumbria

Contact: Mrs Wade, Manor Cottage, Fellside, Caldbeck, Wigton, Cumbria CA7 8HA
Tel: (016974) 78214 **E-mail:** walterwade@tiscali.co.uk

The converted barn nestles in the Caldbeck Fells, an unspoilt corner of the Lake District National Park. Retaining its original pine beams and old hay loft (now the upper lounge), it has magnificent views to the distant Pennines. The picturesque village of Caldbeck is only two miles away and there are good places to eat locally. The accommodation provides a spacious split level lounge, double bedroom, well equipped oak fitted kitchen and shower room with toilet.

Low season per week: £140.00–£210.00
High season per week: £240.00–£300.00
Short breaks: from £90.00–£120.00

1 cottage: sleeping 2/3 people

Early Quakers

The England of the 17th century was governed by a combination of the State (with or without a monarch) and the Church. These authoritarian bodies admitted little freedom of expression and discouraged all dissent. Into this society was born George Fox (1624–91), the son of a Leicester weaver. After a series of revelations and visions, he became convinced that he should spread the word of the 'inner light' of Christ's salvation. Eschewing the ritual, rigid framework and labyrinthine power structure of the established Church, Fox travelled the country, preaching his simple message out of doors to all who would listen. In one vision, while on Pendle Hill north of Burnley, he saw a multitude gathered together 'in worship of God in a place by a river'.

In the spring of 1652, he was in Dentdale, in the north-western corner of Yorkshire (now Cumbria) where he was well received by a group called 'the Seekers', a local sect with broadly similar beliefs. On Whit Saturday he stayed the night with a like-minded farmer at Brigflatts, a couple of miles west of Sedbergh, before attending a large gathering of Seekers on the Sunday. This congregation was, according to his diary, the fulfilment of Fox's vision on Pendle Hill. At Sedbergh's Hiring Fair the following week he preached with such conviction that over a thousand congregated on Firbank Fell, a lonely hill not far from Brigflatts. Although not the birthplace of Quakerism (there was no such single event) this was a major step in the setting up of the worldwide movement.

Despite persecution and discrimination which continued for hundreds of years, Fox's powerful message sank home, and the local area has an active group of Friends to this day.

A few years after Fox's preaching, a group of Quakers bought land at Brigflatts where, in 1675, one of the earliest Friends' Meeting Houses was built. It is there now, serenely peaceful and almost unchanged in over 300 years. Quakers and others seek out this whitewashed stone building with its simple, mullioned windows beside the River Rawthey, while the spot (by some jagged rocks) where Fox preached on Firbank Fell – now known as Fox's Pulpit – can also be seen. Kendal, the largest town in the immediate area, has had a Friends' Meeting since 1660. The present 19th-century building is now the permanent home of the Quaker Tapestry Exhibition. The tapestry, created by more than four thousand people in 15 countries, depicts events and beliefs of Quakers since 1652, the year George Fox preached at Firbank.

52 | Carrock Cottages   ★ ★ ★ ★ ★

Carrock House, Howhill, Hutton Roof, Penrith, Cumbria **Web:** www.carrockcottages.co.uk
Contact: Carrock Cottages, Carrock House, Howhill, Hutton Roof, Penrith, Cumbria CA11 0XY
Tel: (01768) 484111 **Fax:** (01768) 488850 **E-mail:** info@carrockcottages.co.uk

Your stepping stone to the Cumbrian Lake District. Carrock Cottages are three characterful stone-built cottages set on the fringe of the Lakeland Fells. A quiet rural location near the lovely villages of Hesket Newmarket with its award-winning brewery, Caldbeck and Greystoke. Explore the beauty of the Lake District National Park or head north to historic Carlisle and on to Hadrian's Wall. Fell walking and other activities close to hand as well as excellent restaurants. Facilities also include on-site games room and spa facilities. A warm welcome guaranteed.

Low season per week: £275.00–£390.00
High season per week: £325.00–£1295.00
Short breaks: from £100.00–£600.00

4 cottages: sleeping 2–14 people
Cards accepted: Mastercard, Visa, Switch/Delta, Amex

---

53 | Bannerdale   ★ ★ ★ ★

Springs Road, Keswick, Cumbria **Web:** www.bannerdale.info
Contact: Ms Hutton, 39 Millfield Gardens, Keswick, Cumbria CA12 4PD
Tel: (01768) 772546 or 07816 824253 **Fax:** (01768) 772546 **E-mail:** hazel@bannerdale.info

Set at the foot of Walla Crag in the heart of the Lake District, Bannerdale offers luxury self-catering accommodation for six people. Situated on a quiet country road and overlooking the surrounding meadows and mountains, peacefully located only 10 minutes walk from the market town of Keswick. Recently refurbished to a very high standard, the house has three bedrooms and a luxurious bathroom and kitchen. French windows lead onto a large elevated patio boasting magnificent uninterrupted views as far as the eye can see.

Low season per week: £340.00–£420.00
High season per week: £470.00–£810.00
Short breaks: from £155.00–£295.00 (low season only)

1 house: sleeping 6 people

---

54 | Underscar   ★ ★ ★ ★ ★

Keswick, Cumbria **Web:** www.heartofthelakes.co.uk
Contact: Heart of the Lakes, Fisherbeck Mill, Old Lake Road, Ambleside, Cumbria LA22 0DH
Tel: (01539) 432321 **Fax:** (01539) 433251 **E-mail:** contactus@heartofthelakes.co.uk

Underscar offers a small number of exclusive holiday homes that occasionally become available for rental and which will appeal to discerning clients looking for something rather special. Properties sleep 2–4+2, or 6+2 in one, two or three bedrooms. Two bathrooms, one en-suite to the main bedroom. Award-winning designers have introduced a feeling of originality and style. All properties have use of the on-site health spa. No pets. Non-smoking. Nearest shops in Keswick, one mile. Excellence in England 2002 Gold winer - self catering holiday of the year.

Low season per week: from £550.00
High season per week: max £1465.00

25 mews-style houses: sleeping 2–8 people
Cards accepted: Mastercard, Visa, Switch/Delta

At-a-glance symbols are explained on the flap inside the back cover

55 | The Studio ★★★★

St Johns-in-the-Vale, Keswick, Cumbria **Web:** www.keswickholidays.co.uk
Contact: Mrs Green, The Studio, Fornside House, St Johns-in-the-Vale, Keswick, Cumbria CA12 4TS
Tel: (01768) 779666 **E-mail:** selfcatering@keswickholidays.co.uk

Fornside is a very pretty area in St Johns-in-the-Vale, seated at the base of the Helvelyn range. Keswick is five miles away. 'The Studio' – formerly the house of an artist, hence the name – was originally a barn adjoining Fornside House and is about 250 years old. It has now been converted into a lovely first-floor apartment and everything is beautifully decorated and furnished. The main open plan living area has glorious views towards Skiddaw. Outside there is private parking and a terraced rock garden for your pleasure.

Low season per week: £125.00–£240.00
High season per week: £240.00–£320.00
Short breaks: from £80.00 (November–end March)

1 apartment: sleeping 2–4 people

56 | Lakefield ★★★★

Watermillock, Ullswater, Penrith, Cumbria **Web:** www.heartofthelakes.co.uk
Contact: Heart of the Lakes, Fisherbeck Mill, Old Lake Road, Ambleside, Cumbria LA22 0DH
Tel: (01539) 432321 **Fax:** (01539) 433251 **E-mail:** contactus@heartofthelakes.co.uk

A large, detached bungalow set on the shores of Ullswater with 500 yards of private lake frontage and with stunning lake and mountain views. Four bedrooms (two doubles, one twin, one child's twin) and two bathrooms. This property offers substanital accommodation and even has its own sundeck verandah which is built over the water. Most main windows have lake views. Plenty of private parking. Nearest shops are in Glenridding which is about four miles away. No pets. Leisure membership included.

Low season per week: from £630.00
High season per week: max £1900.00

1 bungalow: sleeping 8 people
Cards accepted: Mastercard, Visa, Switch/Delta

57 | Harrys Barn ★★★★

Maulds Meaburn, Penrith, Cumbria **Web:** www.harrysbarn.co.uk
Contact: Mrs Hatton, Coat Flatt Mill, Orton, Penrith, Cumbria CA10 3RE
Tel: (01539) 624664 **Fax:** (01539) 624527 **E-mail:** hattonjulie@hotmail.com

Situated in the tranquil East Cumbrian village of Maulds Meaburn – the perfect place to escape from the hassles of the 21st century and ideally located for exploring undiscovered Cumbria. Harrys Barn has recently been converted to provide luxury accommodation for two adults and up to two children. Your well-behaved dogs are also welcome! Downstairs, there is a king-size bedroom, cosy 'bunk room' and small bath with shower. Upstairs is the open plan living area with comfortable sofas, wood-burning stove, beech kitchen and dining area.

Low season per week: £250.00–£275.00
High season per week: £325.00–£350.00
Short breaks: from £50.00–£60.00

1 cottage: sleeping 2+2 people

58 Coachmans Cottage ★★★★

Ryelands, Grasmere, Hawkshead, Ambleside, Cumbria **Web:** www.heartofthelakes.co.uk
Contact: Heart of the Lakes, Fisherbeck Mill, Old Lake Road, Ambleside, Cumbria LA22 0DH
Tel: (01539) 432321 **Fax:** (01539) 433251 **E-mail:** contactus@heartofthelakes.co.uk

Converted from an old coach house, this delightful cottage is situated in peaceful surroundings with views over nearby fields and hills. Built of Lakeland stone and with its own enclosed garden, the accommodation is all at first floor level. Light and sunny L-shaped sitting/dining room. Two en-suite bedrooms, one double and one twin. Well-equipped kitchen. Private parking. No pets. Non smoking. Village shops in Grasmere are within a few hundred yards. Leisure club membership included.

Low season per week: from £287.00
High season per week: max £743.00
Short breaks: from £175.00–£460.00

1 cottage: sleeping 4 people
Cards accepted: Mastercard, Visa, Switch/Delta

59 Loughrigg Suite ★★★★★

Loughrigg Brow, Ambleside, Cumbria **Web:** www.heartofthelakes.co.uk
Contact: Heart of the Lakes, Fisherbeck Mill, Old Lake Road, Ambleside, Cumbria LA22 0DH
Tel: (01539) 432321 **Fax:** (01539) 433251 **E-mail:** contactus@heartofthelakes.co.uk

Luxury apartment is situated within a magnificent Victorian mansion, formerly the Ambleside Vicarage. Reached via either stairs or lift, this property has panoramic views over the countryside. Most attractive sitting/dining room, modern well-equipped kitchen, two bedrooms – one en-suite double room and one single room. Separate shower room. No pets. Non smokers. Shops and village amenities half a mile away. Shared use of tennis court and grounds. Leisure club membership included.

Low season per week: from £330.00
High season per week: max £530.00

1 apartment: sleeping 2/3 people
Cards accepted: Mastercard, Visa, Switch/Delta

60 Overbeck Cottage ★★★★

Rothay Bridge, Ambleside, Cumbria **Web:** www.riversidelodge.co.uk
Contact: Mr & Mrs Rhone, Riverside Lodge, Rothay Bridge, Ambleside, Cumbria LA22 0EH
Tel: (01539) 434208 **Fax:** (01539) 431884 **E-mail:** alanrhone@riversidelodge.co.uk

Overbeck Cottage is a completely independent and private wing of Riverside Lodge, situated in an idyllic riverside setting only 500 yards from the centre of Ambleside. Rooms enjoy superb views across river to Loughrigg Fell. The cottage is furnished and equipped to a high standard and is available to discerning couples only – sorry, no children or pets. The tariff is all-inclusive with no additional charges and reflects the attention to detail in this interesting and unique property. For pictures and testimonials visit www.riversidelodge.co.uk

Low season per week: £300.00–£375.00
High season per week: £400.00–£450.00

1 cottage: sleeping 2 people
Cards accepted: Mastercard, Visa, Switch/Delta

61 The Hideaways Premier Collection   ★ ★ ★ ★ – ★ ★ ★ ★ ★

Hawkshead/Sawrey area **Web:** www.lakeland-hideaways.co.uk
Contact: The Minstrels Gallery, The Square, Hawkshead, Ambleside, Cumbria LA22 0NZ
Tel: (01539) 442435 **E-mail:** bookings@lakeland-hideaways.co.uk

Family-run cottages in and around Hawkshead village. **High Orchard** sleeps 8 people – a detached four-bedroom, Victorian house with stunning views and beautiful gardens. **Ben Fold** sleeps 4/6 people – a detached country cottage with an Aga and open fire, making it the perfect 'hideaway'. **Sawrey Stables** sleeps 7 people – a detached barn conversion complete with whirlpool bath, Aga and open fire. **Sawrey Knotts** sleeps 2/4/5 people – three luxury suites recently converted to the highest standard, with whirlpool baths in some… perfect to relax after a day on the fells.

Low season per week: £240.00–£360.00
High season per week: £600.00–£900.00
Short breaks: from £200.00–£500.00

1 house, 2 cottages and 3 apartments: sleeping 2–8 people

---

62 Chestnuts, Beeches and The Granary   ★ ★ ★ ★

High Wray Bank, Low Wray, Ambleside, Cumbria **Web:** www.accommodationlakedistrict.com
Contact: Mr Benson, High Sett, Sun Hill Lane, Windermere, LA23 1HJ
Tel: (01539) 442731 or (01539) 444618 **Fax:** (01539) 442731 **E-mail:** info@accommodationlakedistrict.com

Two charming cottages and one bungalow converted from a former coach house and corn store. Set in idyllic surroundings overlooking Lake Windermere, with magnificent panoramic views of the Lakeland mountains. All tastefully furnished and equipped to an ETC Four Star rating. Beautiful lawned gardens to wander through which are enclosed, so safe for children to play. Set in the hamlet of HIgh Wray with its quiet unspoilt beauty, between the idyllic village of Hawkshead and the larger town of Ambleside, making this the ideal base for walkng and touring. Use of private boathouse by prior arrangement.

Low season per week: £200.00–£500.00
High season per week: £250.00–£500.00
Short breaks: from £200.00–£250.00

2 cottages and 1 bungalow: sleeping 1–6 people

---

63 Holbeck Ghyll Lodge   ★ ★ ★ ★

Windermere, Cumbria **Web:** www.holbecklodge.com
Contact: Mrs M Kaye, Holmdene, Stoney Bank Road, Holmfirth HD9 7SL
Tel: (01484) 684605 **Fax:** (01484) 689051 **E-mail:** info@holbecklodge.com

Extremely comfortable Lakeland stone lodge situated half a mile from Lake Windermere between Troutbeck and Ambleside. Has an enclosed garden suitable for children and dogs. One double-bedded room and en-suite. Two twin-bedded rooms. Dining/living room with open fire. Oak-fitted dining kitchen with all appliances. Bathroom with bath/shower etc. Good walking area and excellent pubs nearby. Water sports available on Lake Windermere. Available Easter to end October.

Low season per week: max £410.00
High season per week: max £490.00

1 cottage: sleeping 6/8 people
Open: Easter–end October

64 Hodge Howe ★★★★★

Windermere, Cumbria **Web:** www.heartofthelakes.co.uk
Contact: Heart of the Lakes, Fisherbeck Mill, Old Lake Road, Ambleside, Cumbria LA22 0DH
Tel: (01539) 432321 **Fax:** (01539) 433251 **E-mail:** contactus@heartofhtelakes.co.uk

Delightfully renovated cottage only 300 yards from Lake Windermere in a lovely, peaceful, woodland setting. Cosy sitting room with log-burning stove. Gallery-style kitchen leads to dining room with its floor-to-ceiling windows and access to the courtyard garden. Three bedrooms – double room with en-suite, a further double and a twin. Separate bathroom. Courtyard garden has table and chairs. Ample parking. Non-smoking. Local shops and pub, 2–3 miles. Leisure club membership included.

Low season per week: from £330.00
High season per week: max £774.00

1 cottage: sleeping 6 people
Cards accepted: Mastercard, Visa, Switch/Delta

65 Gavel Cottage ★★★★

Storrs Park, Bowness-on-Windermere, Windermere, Cumbria **Web:** www.screetons.co.uk
Contact: Screetons, 25 Bridgegate, Howden, Goole, East Yorkshire DN14 7AA
Tel: (01430) 431201 **Fax:** (01430) 432114 **E-mail:** howden@screetons.co.uk

A secluded period cottage situated south of the village, close to the marina. Full of character and tastefully furnished, Gavel Cottage offers a comfortable holiday retreat situated in a quiet location overlooking its own private grounds. The fully equipped accommodation has gas central heating and comprises entrance hall, open plan living area including cosy lounge with open fire, dining area and kitchen, two bedrooms, bathroom, gardens and summer house. Membership of Burnside Leisure Complex is included.

Low season per week: £235.00–£295.00
High season per week: £335.00–£475.00
Short breaks: from £175.00

1 cottage: sleeping 4 people

66 Old Brantrake ★★★★

Eskdale, Holmrook, Cumbria
Contact: Mr Tyson, Brant Rake, Eskdale, Holmrook, Cumbria CA19 1TT
Tel: (01946) 723340 **Fax:** (01946) 723340 **E-mail:** tyson@eskdale1.demon.co.uk

Old Brantrake is a 17th-century listed farmhouse, restored to a high standard, one and a half miles from Eskdale Green at SD148987. It is ideal for the central fells or exploring the quiet Western Lake District. The sitting room has a woodfire and Sky television, whilst the kitchen/dining room has fully modern facilities. The three bedrooms sleep up to six. There is a bathroom and a shower room, both with lavatory. Dogs by arrangement. Non-smoking. Short breaks, November to March only. Brochure available.

Low season per week: £275.00–£365.00
High season per week: £375.00–£460.00
Short breaks: from £115.00–£200.00

1 cottage: sleeping 5–6 people

67 Higher Lee ★★★★

Abbeystead, Lancaster, Lancashire
Contact: Mrs S T Entwistle, Lentworth Farm, Abbeystead, Lancaster, Lancashire LA2 9BE
Tel: (01524) 791287

A perfect English country house set in two acres of delightful walled gardens providing privacy amd peaceful seclusion. This beautiful house, dating from 1671, has open fireplaces and wooden floors complemented by traditional-style furniture and fabrics. Sleeps ten. Booking through Hoseasons (01502) 501515, Ref E1977.

Low season per week: £601.00–£601.00
High season per week: £727.00–£1227.00
Short breaks: from £339.00–£810.00

1 house: sleeping 10 people

68 Link House Farm ★★★★

Newton-by-the-Sea, Alnwick, Northumberland
Contact: Mrs J Hellmann, The Granary, Link House Farm, Newton-by-the-Sea, Alnwick, Northumberland NE66 3DF
Tel: (01665) 576820 **Fax:** (01665) 576821 **E-mail:** jayne.hellmann@virgin.net

A group of five individual holiday cottages, skillfully created from the quality conversion of old stone-built farm buildings. Situated on a farm in the village of Newton-by-the-Sea, only yards from National Trust sand dunes and sandy beaches of Beadnell Bay. Each cottage completely self-contained with own garden/sitting area. All furnished, decorated and equipped to high standard. Excellent for bird watching. Also children's playground and grass area. Local pubs half a mile. Shops in the next village which is just two miles away.

Low season per week: £220.00–£450.00
High season per week: £300.00–£910.00
Short breaks: from £110.00–£330.00

5 cottages: sleeping 2–10 people

69 The Old Church ★★★★

Chollerton, Hexham, Northumberland **Web:** http://chollerton.urscene.net
Contact: Mrs M Framrose, Old Chuch Cottage, Chollerton, Hexham, Northumberland NE46 4TF
Tel: (014343) 681930 **E-mail:** oldchurch@supanet.com

Old Church, Chollerton has three beautiful, peaceful apartments set in tranquil Northumberland countryside. We welcome our visitors as friends and aim to provide a holiday home-from-home, with comfortable rooms and spacious gardens to relax in. Six miles north of Hexham and close to Hadrian's Wall in the picturesque North Tyne Valley. You can walk, watch birds, or visit historic sites and houses, beauitful gardens and inexpensive restaurants serving superb food. There is also easy access to Newcastle, Alnwick and the Scottish Borders.

Low season per week: £130.00–£270.00
High season per week: £200.00–£420.00
Short breaks: from £95.00–£250.00 (low and mid-season only)

3 apartments: sleeping 2/4/5 people

70 Laneside ★★★★

Forest-in-Teesdale, Barnard Castle, County Durham **Web:** www.rabycastle.com
Contact: Upper Teesdale Estate, Raby Estates Office, Middleton-in-Teesdale, Barnard Castle, County Durham DL12 0QH
Tel: (01833) 640209 **Fax:** (01833) 640963 **E-mail:** teesdaleestate@rabycastle.com

Laneside, a haven of absolute tranquillity, combines the best features of traditional Dales life with modern facilities. The former farmhouse is spacious yet cosy, with a wood-burning stove. Occupying an elevated position, it enjoys stunning south-facing panoramic views of Upper Teesdale. It is an ideal base for walking, cycling, bird watching or simply to relax and enjoy the scenery and countryside of Teesdale. Local attractions are plentiful and the market towns of Barnard Castle and Middleton-in-Teesdale are within easy reach.

Low season per week: £220.00–£270.00
High season per week: £350.00–£450.00
Short breaks: from £110.00–£400.00

1 cottage: sleeping 8 people

71 | Ingleby Manor

★★★★

Ingleby Greenhow, Great Ayton, North Yorkshire **Web:** www.inglebymanor.co.uk
Contact: Mrs C Bianco, Ingleby Manor, Ingleby Greenhow, Great Ayton, North Yorkshire TS9 6RB
Tel: (01642) 722170 **Fax:** (01642) 722170 **E-mail:** christine@inglebymanor.co.uk

The Essence of England. Your own comfortable apartment in an historic Grade II* manor house, once the home of a courtier of Henry VIII. Peaceful acres of gardens, woodland and open countryside around, views of green hills and purple moors from the window. Sweet peas from the gardens, fresh farm eggs and a home-made cake waiting on the kitchen table. A stroll down the tree-tunnel avenue to the 12th Century church and then coffee and a freshly-baked scone in the Servants Hall in front of the Aga. 4 apartments and a 4-bedroom detached house in the grounds. TeessideAirport 30 minutes, York/Durham 1 hour.

Low season per week: £235.00–£415.00
High season per week: £358.00–£895.00
Short breaks: from £111.00–£338.00
4 apartments: sleeping 3–6 people
Detached house: sleeping 8 people

Cards accepted: Mastercard, Visa, Switch/Delta

Yorkshire Dales Barns

The beauty of the Yorkshire Dales derives in large part from the natural magnificence of the landscape: nature generously gave this central stretch of the Pennine chain dramatic limestone outcrops and clear, fast-running rivers. But man too has added to the splendour of the Dales. The trees may have been cleared long ago, but in their stead on the lower slopes came hay-meadows full of as many as 40 species of herb, bounded by drystone walls of simple beauty. In the northern Dales such as Swaledale and Arkengarthdale, almost every field has its own barn, each one adding to the glorious impression these valleys create.

These barns – it is estimated that there are over a thousand in Swaledale and Arkengarthdale alone – are a sign of a vanishing form of agriculture. In the 17th, 18th and 19th centuries, when most of these barns were built, farms were small and numerous. Many who tended the land also worked in the local lead and coal mines, and so had little time to devote to farming. The summer harvest of the hay crop was the most labour-intensive time of year, and the hard-pressed farmers evolved an agricultural system which allowed a more even spread of work. They built their barns – almost all using the drystone method of construction with stones sloping outwards to take the rain away – in the fields where the hay was growing. Storing the hay in the nearby barns was therefore a simple task. Since the cows spent the winter in the same barn as their foodstuff, it was easy both to feed the cattle and to fertilise the same field with their manure. The quid pro quo was that the farmer had to walk to each of his barns in the winter months – not too arduous if there were only a few barns on the round.

Modern employment practices and the quest for efficiency have meant that farms are now few and large. This no longer fits in with the traditional system, and many outlying field barns have become redundant. In Swaledale and Arkengarthdale a conservation scheme run by the national park has saved countless from dereliction; some are still used by their owners while others have found new life as 'bunkhouse barns'. These offer basic accommodation to walkers and are often on or near long-distance footpaths. At Hazel Brow, Low Row, visitors may go inside a traditional Dales barn as part of the open farm scheme.

72 Appledore Cottage ★★★★

Appledore, Thorgill, Pickering, North Yorkshire **Web:** www.appledorecottage.eu
Contact: Mr D Glover, St Margaret's Rectory, South Street, Durham DH1 4QP
Tel: (0191) 384 3623 **E-mail:** david@glover.u-net.com

Completely restored in 1999, Appledore enjoys glorious views over beautiful Rosedale in the heart of the Yorkshire Moors. Light and airy by day, with easy access to the spacious garden, an open fire makes this extremely comfortable cottage cosy in the evening. Equipped to the highest standards – four large bedrooms, bathroom, shower room, sitting room, living room/kitchen with dishwasher, microwave, washing machine etc. Lovely Rosedale Abbey nearby with shops, pubs and restaurants. Many local attractions including walking, golf, steam railway, beaches and historic houses.

Low season per week: £375.00–£475.00
High season per week: £575.00–£675.00

1 cottage: sleeping 8/9 people

73 The Cornmill ★★★★

Kirby Mills, Kirkbymoorside, York **Web:** www.kirbymills.demon.co.uk
Contact: Mr & Mrs Tinkler, The Cornmill, Kirby Mills, Kirkbymoorside, York YO62 6NP
Tel: (01751) 432000 **Fax:** (01751) 432300 **E-mail:** cornmill@kirbymills.demon.co.uk

Sensitively converted into two well-appointed mews holiday cottages, the Old Stable Block now sleeps two adults in each, with an additional single sofa-bed, with spring mattress, in the lounge. On the ground floor is the large double bedroom and a bathroom with bath and power shower. On the upper floor is an open plan living room with a dining area and a kitchenette equipped with a refridgerator, microwave, electric oven and gas hob. One cottage has the option of twin beds or king-size double. See also our serviced accommodation on page 36.

Low season per week: from £250.00
High season per week: max £325.00

2 cottages: sleeping 2/4 people
Cards accepted: Mastercard, Visa, Switch/Delta

74 Tewit and Badger Cottages ★★★★

Rimington, Clitheroe, Lancashire **Web:** www.ruralcottage.co.uk
Contact: CS Smith Properties, No1 Howcroft Cottages, Rimington, Clitheroe, Lancashire BB7 4EJ
Tel: (01200) 445598 **Fax:** (01200) 444188

In a delightful rural setting, these semi-detached cottages have been sympathetically converted from a barn, which dates back to the 1700s, and retains many original features. Enjoying long-reaching views over the Ribble Valley and Pendle Hill. Each cottage has spacious yet cosy accomodation consisting of an open plan lounge/dining kitchen with flag floors and log burning stoves for those colder evenings, well-appointed bedrooms and bathrooms. Ideally situated for the Lake District, Yorkshire Dales or Blackpool.

Low season per week: £220.00–£250.00
High season per week: £350.00–£400.00

2 cottages: sleeping 4–5 people

75 | Low Laithe Barn ★ ★ ★ ★ ★

Bolton Abbey, Skipton, North Yorkshire **Web:** www.beechhousebarns.co.uk
Contact: Mrs S Gray, Beech House Farm, Langbar, Ilkley, West Yorkshire LS29 0EP
Tel: (01943) 609819 **Fax:** (01943) 609337 **E-mail:** info@beechhousebarns.co.uk

Stylish, luxurious and unusually well equipped detached 'field barn'. A unique place where old meets new and both win. Sleeps 2–7 and cot in four beds (king-size or single). Three baths (two en-suite). All power showers. Large open plan kitchen-dining room-living room. Fully automatic central heating and hot water. Set admidst acres of breathtaking Yorkshire Dales countryside with uninterrupted views and absolute privacy. Three miles from Bolton Abbey and Ilkley. 30 minutes by car to Harrogate, Leeds and Bradford and one hour to York, Manchester and the Lake District. Exlcusive Devonshire Club membership.

Low season per week: £480.00–£570.00
High season per week: £590.00–£1120.00

1 barn conversion: sleeping 2–7 people + cot
Cards accepted: Mastercard, Visa, Switch/Delta, Amex, Diners, Eurocard, JCB

76 | Mount Pleasant Farm Holiday Cottages ★ ★ ★ ★

Killinghall, Harrogate, North Yorkshire
Contact: Mrs L Prest, Mount Pleasant Farm, Skipton Road, Killinghall, Harrogate, North Yorkshire HG3 2BU
Tel: (01423) 504694

These converted farm buildings, situated just two miles from the spa town of Harrogate, are immaculately maintained and fully equipped and sleep from three to six people. Set in rolling countryside, they are ideal for exploring the Dales and nearby historic points of interest such as Bolton and Fountains Abbey and the ancient cities of York and Ripon. With a family pub/restaurant only 200 yards away, the cottages are suitable for couples and families alike.

Low season per week: £195.00–£250.00
High season per week: £290.00–£410.00

2 cottages and 1 bungalow: sleeping 3–6 people

77 | Bishopgate Pavilion - Bishops Wharf ★ ★ ★ ★ ★

Postern Close, York **Web:** www.johnkgraham.com
Contact: Mr Graham, 31 Falcon Way, Clippers Quay, London E14 9UP
Tel: (0207) 538 8980 or 07973 857187 **Fax:** (0207) 538 8980 **E-mail:** john@johnkgraham.com

Luxurious and spacious 3rd-floor apartment (with lift) with one bedroom accommodating two adults. Spectacular views of the city, York Minster, Clifford's Tower and the river. Walk to all of York's attractions. Enjoy a glass of wine on the balcony overlooking the river. Private parking. Quiet location. Luxuriously furnished and equipped to the highest standards. Bookings taken on a nightly basis with no fixed starting day or number of nights. Finalist in the 2002 and 2003 Self-Catering Holiday of the Year awards. Direct-dial telephone and modem socket.

Low season per week: £339.00–£410.00
High season per week: £410.00–£469.00
Short breaks: from £198.00–£269.00

1 apartment: sleeping 2 people
Cards accepted: Mastercard, Visa, Switch/Delta, Eurocard

78 6 The Sycamores & 7 The Cedars   ★ ★ ★ ★

Warford Park, Faulkners Lane, Mobberley, Knutsford, Cheshire **Web:** www.interludes-uk.com
Contact: Jenny Dawson, Interludes, Croft Cottage, Hough Lane, Alderley Edge, Cheshire SK9 7JE
Tel: (01625) 599802 or 07968 594036 **Fax:** (01625) 599802 **E-mail:** info@interludes-uk.com

Peaceful and relaxing with crisp cotton bed linen, fluffy white towels and robes, Molton Brown toiletries and membership of the on-site leisure club. These special new apartments, with lift and secure entry, are surrounded by beautiful countryside. Each has a living/dining room, fully equipped dining kitchen and two double bedrooms, one having an en-suite shower. Manchester Airport and the motorway network are within easy reach, as are Knutsford (Tatton RHS Show), Manchester, Chester, the Peak District and North Wales.

Low season per week: from £450.00
High season per week: max £550.00
Short breaks: from £130.00–£195.00

2 apartments: sleeping 4 people
Cards accepted: Mastercard, Visa, Switch/Delta, Amex

Cheshire Salt

Everyone knows that coal – in the main – comes from the North, while tin comes from Cornwall, but what about salt? The answer is the Cheshire Plain, that area of flat, fertile farmland between Chester and Macclesfield. Most of us may not know, for example, that one mine at Winsford supplies all the salt used to clear snow and ice from the United Kingdom's roads. But the Romans, those industrious plunderers of England's natural resources, knew all about the estimated 400 billion tons of salt lying beneath the rich soil – and they were here almost 2,000 years ago to tap the wealth of the area. Indeed the Latin name for Middlewich, 'Salinae', can be roughly translated as 'saltworks'.

The Cheshire Plain, 200 million years ago, was at the bottom of a shallow, salty sea. As the water evaporated, the salt formed into vast deposits of solid sodium chloride – or rock salt. Water flowing through this layer of rock salt reaches the surface as brine, and it was these brine springs that attracted the Romans.

In the 17th century, coal began to be used to evaporate the brine in large iron pans, and the efficiency of salt production was hugely improved. The biggest headache then became transport, of coal to the works and salt from them. To this end the navigable stretch of the River Weaver was extended to Winsford, and the Trent and Mersey Canal completed in 1777, allowing salt works to open at Northwich, Middlewich, Wheelock and Lawton. Larger, deeper salt beds were soon discovered, and by the late 19th century over 1 million tons of white salt were sailing down the Weaver Navigation each year.

Workers clogs and mine bucket at the Lion Salt Works

Today there are three commercial plants producing white salt for a range of uses (from food storage to soap and plastic manufacture). These (and others) adopted the 'vacuum evaporation process' at the turn of the century, but one, the Lion Salt Works at Marston, near Northwich, stuck with the traditional 'open pan' system of evaporation, largely unchanged since Roman times. In 1986 it eventually closed, but the local council bought the fascinating site, now open to the public in the afternoons. Together with the Salt Museum in the old Northwich Workhouse, it makes an intriguing exploration of Cheshire's industrial past – although perhaps the most fascinating site of all is the Anderton Boat Lift, a vast monument to the engineering achievements of the Victorian era. For over a century this 'wonder of the waterways' just north of Northwich, built in 1875, hauled boats from the Weaver Navigation up 50ft (15m) and into the Trent and Mersey Canal above. Closed in 1982, the Boat Lift may yet work again if a local restoration group is successful.

79 The Hayloft ★★★★

Alderley Edge, Cheshire **Web:** www.interludes-uk.com
Contact: Interludes, Croft Cottage, Hough Lane, Alderley Edge, Cheshire SK9 7JE
Tel: (01625) 599802 **Fax:** (01625) 599802 **E-mail:** info@interludes-uk.com

The Hayloft, situated in the grounds of the owners' home, is in a quiet and peaceful location in three quarters of an acre of gardens with uninterrupted views of the surrounding countryside, yet only minutes from the village. The Edge (National Trust) is the perfect place to walk and be at peace with the world. The cosy accommodation has a living room and compact kitchen with everything you need. A shower room with Molton Brown toiletries leads off the bright and sunny dual aspect double bedroom.

Low season per week: from £350.00
High season per week: max £375.00
Short breaks: max £180.00

1 apartment: sleeping 2 people
Cards accepted: Mastercard, Visa, Switch/Delta, Amex

80 Higher Ingersley Barn ★★★★★

Bollington, Macclesfield, Cheshire **Web:** www.higheringersleyfarm.co.uk
Contact: Higher Ingersley Farm, Oakenbank Lane, Bollington, Macclesfield, Cheshire SK10 5RP
Tel: (01625) 572245 **Fax:** (01625) 574231 **E-mail:** bw.peacock@ntlworld.com

This old stone-built barn, sympathetically converted in 2001, features impressive oak beams throughout and occupies an elevated position on the edge of the Peak District. Located off a quiet lane, with its own private landscaped garden, truly a secret hideaway! Three double bedrooms, all with en-suite bathrooms, plus a sofa bed in the lounge for two additional guests. Beautiful large lounge, dining room and a fully equipped kitchen and utility room. Stunning countryside, yet within five minutes of the unspoilt silk town of Bollington.

Low season per week: £380.00–£480.00
High season per week: £520.00–£800.00

1 cottage: sleeping 6+2 people

England's Heartland

The Malvern Hills

Looking from the east, the Malverns, rising from the Severn Plain, seem to belie their modest height. What they lack in altitude, however, they more than make up for in age, beauty and the panoramas they offer. On a clear day the views from the top stretch to far-distant horizons. The best way to explore these glorious hills – they stretch roughly 8 miles (13km) in a north–south direction – is on foot, but several roads cross the Malverns affording magnificent views for the less mobile.

Eyam and the Plague

In September 1665 a journeyman tailor lodging in the village of Eyam in the Derbyshire Peak opened a parcel of cloth sent from London where bubonic plague was then raging. Within four days he was dead – and plague had descended on Eyam. The young rector, William Mompesson, persuaded the whole village to make a courageous act of self-sacrifice and Eyam was sealed off from the outside world for a year. But Eyam paid dearly for its bravery: out of an estimated population of 350, some 250 died. An exhibition in Eyam Museum recounts the full story.
www.eyammuseum.demon.co.uk

Away from the throng

From East Anglia's fertile plains to the rugged border country of the Welsh Marches, from the Home Counties' prosperous market towns to the dark, stone-built communities of the Peaks, the great swathe of counties that forms England's Heartland has it all. And for the most part you can have the elegance, the raw beauty, the culture and the history to yourself. Yes, the Peak District National Park is deservedly popular and yes, Stratford-upon-Avon is rightly a stop on most visitors' itineraries, but choose your moment wisely and even these can be enjoyed at a leisurely pace, the madding crowd left far behind.

In the steps of literary giants

Whatever your particular bent, there's ample opportunity to indulge it. Keen to follow in the footsteps of the famous? Try Lichfield, whose sons include three major figures from the 18th-century flowering of the arts: Joseph Addison, David Garrick and Dr Johnson. The last has his own museum, based in the house of his birth in Breadmarket Street. Other places of literary pilgrimage are D H Lawrence's Eastwood and Lord Byron's gothic Newstead Abbey (both Nottinghamshire, though at opposite ends of the social scale), Shaw's comfortable Corner in Ayot St Lawrence (Hertfordshire), A E Housman's much wilder Wenlock Edge (Shropshire) and Samuel Pepys' urbane Brampton (Cambridgeshire).

Lanes for walking, cycling or pootling

But if meandering lazily along English backwaters on a limpid afternoon is more your taste, consider a few of the following. Add a couple more ingredients – a half-decent road map and nothing to hurry back for – and you

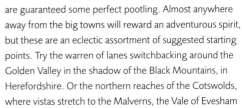

are guaranteed some perfect pootling. Almost anywhere away from the big towns will reward an adventurous spirit, but these are an eclectic assortment of suggested starting points. Try the warren of lanes switchbacking around the Golden Valley in the shadow of the Black Mountains, in Herefordshire. Or the northern reaches of the Cotswolds, where vistas stretch to the Malverns, the Vale of Evesham and Stratford-upon-Avon. There's the little-known but savagely beautiful countryside around the Clee Hills south and west of Bridgnorth, or the gentler, undulating farmland of Suffolk between Diss and Southwold. Norfolk's north coast offers sleepy villages – a pair are appropriately called Little and Great Snoring – and unspoilt coastline. And there are the Lincolnshire Wolds west of Louth, where few visitors discover the distinct charms of Bag Enderby or Normanby le Wold.

Striking out

But if the narrowest of lanes still has too much of the hurly-burly, swap the car for a pair of boots, the road atlas for a walking map. Strike out along the footpaths and bridleways. A good place to start is on one of England's many long-distance paths. Almost all have circular walks of anything from two to

20 miles (3–30km) sharing their waymarks, so don't be put off by the "long-distance" element. Running down the western edge of the region, and criss-crossing in and out of Wales is Offa's Dyke Path, which roughly follows the route of the 8th-century earthwork constructed by the Mercian king to keep the Welsh at bay. Also oriented north–south, but stretching from Staffordshire to the Cotswolds, is the Heart of England Way. Rural in character for most of its length, it follows the Birmingham and Fazeley Canal to the east of the city, before dropping down to Chipping Campden (where it joins the Cotswold Way). Two more long-distance paths explore East Anglia's many sandy beaches. The first, the Peddars Way and Norfolk Coast Path, was, as its name suggests, once two separate routes. It starts in the flinty fields near Thetford and follows the course of a Roman road (the Peddars Way) till it reaches the coast near Holme. From here until Cromer – the Norfolk Coast Path – you will have as company the varied birdlife that throngs the dunes and marshes. Meanwhile, the Suffolk Coast Path between Lowestoft and Felixstowe involves a couple of ferries, and skirts the cliffs that once supported the lost medieval village of Dunwich.

Art for all

One highlight of the Suffolk Coast Path is Snape Maltings, home of the Aldeburgh Festival (June), devoted in part to the music of Sir Benjamin Britten. The welcome proliferation of literary and musical festivals ensures a huge number of events, catering for every taste. By way of a small sample, you can now choose your venue from: Cheltenham (jazz in April, music – and cricket – in July, literature in October), Chelmsford Cathedral (jazz, classical and art exhibitions, May), Solihull (folk music, May), Thaxted (classical and jazz, weekends in June and July), Ludlow (music, drama and dance, June), Warwick and Leamington Spa (classical music, July), Ledbury (poetry, July), Oundle (organ recitals, July), Buxton (opera, July), Three Choirs Festival (August) and Ross-on-Wye (dance, comedy and theatre, August).

Narrow streets and imposing townhouses

Such events are frequently based in attractive, historical market towns, the sort of town that specialises in medieval higgledy-piggledyness, Elizabethan and Jacobean sturdiness, Georgian elegance or a combination of these and countless other architectural styles. Some are well-known, others less so. Tewkesbury, for example, is a fine medieval town that has long been blessed by – and suffered from – its position at the confluence of the rivers Severn and Avon. A magnificent row of 15th-century shops and the memorably named House of the Nodding Gables are a couple of venerable survivors of the regular flooding. Bewdley is a thoroughly gracious former river port higher up the Severn. Since 1798, the centrepiece has been Thomas Telford's elegant bridge, but as well as the myriad streets ideal for strolling, there is a station on the scenic Severn Valley Railway. Bromyard, by contrast, has a striking hill setting, two old coaching inns

Birmingham Pre-Raphaelites

Birmingham's City Museum and Art Gallery houses the largest (and arguably finest) collection of Pre-Raphaelite art in the world, including Holman Hunt's The Last of England, The Blind Girl by Millais and Rossetti's Beata Beatrix, together with a vast number of other paintings, drawings and crafts.
www.bmag.org.uk
Near by, Wightwick Manor, just outside Wolverhampton is entirely furnished and decorated by some of the most prominent Pre-Raphaelite artists, while in Birmingham Cathedral may be found some superb stained-glass designed by Edward Burne-Jones, Pre-Raphaelite and native of the city.
www.nationaltrust.org.uk

Kilpeck

At Kilpeck, eight miles (13km) south-west of Hereford, is the tiny sandstone church of Sts Mary and David. Its size may be modest, but its stone-carvings are the most glorious example of the exuberant work of the 12th-century Herefordshire School of stonemasons. The south door in particular, long protected by a wooden porch, displays a magnificent array of carvings – of beasts, fishes, foliage, fruit – in an almost pristine state. Similar work may be found in churches at Fownhope and Rowlstone (both in Herefordshire) and at Ruardean in the Forest of Dean, all set in glorious countryside.

Slimbridge

When the naturalist and painter Peter Scott founded the Wildfowl & Wetlands Trust at Slimbridge, Gloucestershire, in 1946, he operated from two derelict cottages and used wartime pill-boxes as hides. Today the organisation is internationally recognised for its research into wetland conservation and, at Slimbridge, offers visitors a superb opportunity to watch a vast range of birds. In winter up to 8,000 migrants fly in to the 800 acre (323 hectare) reserve, forming possibly the world's largest collection of ducks, geese and swans. Slimbridge is also the only place in Europe where all six species of flamingo can be seen! www.wwt.org.uk/visit/slimbridge

Dunmow Flitch

The once-common phrase 'to eat Dunmow bacon' means to live in conjugal bliss, and refers to an ancient custom still practised in Great Dunmow, near Bishop's Stortford in Essex. In order to win a flitch (or side) of bacon, a couple must prove that in the first twelve months and a day of their marriage they have not exchanged a word of anger, and certainly never repented of the day they wed. The trial, held every four years before a bewigged judge, is conducted with the utmost (mock) seriousness. www.sparkle.co.uk/flitch

and a clutch of timber-framed houses, not to mention sweeping views from the nearby Bromyard Downs. Uppingham is crammed full of 17th-, 18th- and 19th-century buildings all made from the glorious, mellow Rutland stone of the area. Southwold has the pleasing air of a town ignored by most aspects of the 20th century. The Suffolk port enjoyed something of a renaissance when it became fashionable with Victorian holidaymakers, but otherwise just the right amount of nothing has entertained locals and visitors ever since the bustling medieval harbour silted up. Melton Mowbray's cattle market was established over 900 years ago. Not much in the town is quite as old, but 14th-century Anne of Cleves' House is now witnessing its eighth century.

Pies and produce

Melton's real fame derives from its associations with pork pies and Stilton cheese, both of which are still made and sold here. Bakewell, in Derbyshire, is synonymous with a delicious upside-down pudding, widely available in the area, but the town is also worth visiting for an agricultural show in August and its fine stone architecture. Heacham, in Norfolk, has long been the English headquarters of lavender growing; tours are available. Spalding, over the border into Lincolnshire, draws thousands in early May to its annual flower parade, while asparagus takes centre stage at the Fleece Inn at Bretforton in Worcestershire. The ancient pub, owned by the National Trust, runs an auction devoted to asparagus on the evening of the last Sunday in May.

Homes and gardens

The Trust owns and manages a vast range of properties throughout the region, from Mr Straw's House in Worksop – a modest hundred-year-old semi – to the working Theatre Royal in Bury St Edmunds. A random sample of other historic houses – most still privately owned – includes: Weston Park (Palladian mansion with gardens by 'Capability' Brown, Staffordshire); Eastnor Castle (Georgian castle with Gothic interiors, Ledbury, Herefordshire); Woburn Abbey (18th-century mansion with considerable art collection, Bedfordshire); Audley End (17th-century house with Adam touches, Essex); Stanford Hall (riverside William and Mary house with notable ballroom, Swinford, Leicestershire); Burghley House (Elizabethan palace with baroque interiors, Stamford, Lincolnshire); Kentwell Hall (Tudor mansion with garden maze, Long Melford, Suffolk); and Sulgrave Manor (ancestral home of George Washington, Northamptonshire). All these properties run special events of one form or another in high season.

Look East

The region's coastline runs from Essex to Lincolnshire. Essex has a mixture of lonely marsh and fine beach, while Suffolk alternates sand and shingle. Norfolk's golden shores, though, stretch for mile after mile, and Lincolnshire

– after a marshy section around the Wash – boasts more excellent beaches. Naturally, there are the famous seaside resorts, with their quintessentially English attractions and their cheerful brashness, but there is another side to the coastline. For a quieter maritime excursion try Frinton (Essex), Covehithe (Suffolk), Happisburgh – pronounced 'Haysborough' – Holkham and Hunstanton (all Norfolk) and Anderby Creek (Lincolnshire). Unique amongst east coast resorts, Hunstanton has the distinction of facing west. Watch the sun go down over the waves in the knowledge that no one else within 150 or so miles (240km) is doing the same...

Divine inspiration

And, of course, there are the region's countless churches. The medieval stone-carvers of Herefordshire honed their skills to perfection at Kilpeck. Distinctive round towers stand out against the gentle Norfolk landscape, as at Sedgeford. The warm, honey-coloured stone that characterises so many of the unsung Northamptonshire villages was used on consecrated ground, too; Brixworth is a marvellous Saxon church in an imposing setting. In Suffolk and northern Essex, the locally abundant flint was the main material in such opulent churches as Long Melford and Dedham, both villages of remarkable beauty aside from their churches.

Some useful web addresses

Samuel Johnson Birthplace Museum, Lichfield	www.lichfield.gov.uk/sjmuseum
D H Lawrence Birthplace, Eastwood	www.broxtowe.gov.uk/dhlawrence/dhlawbirth.htm
Newstead Abbey, Newstead	www.newsteadabbey.org.uk
Shaw's Corner, Ayot St Lawrence	www.nationaltrust.org.uk
Cheltenham International Jazz Festival	www.cheltenhamfestivals.co.uk
Cheltenham Festival of Literature	www.cheltenhamfestivals.co.uk
Cheltenham International Festival of Music	www.cheltenhamfestivals.co.uk
Thaxted Festival	www.thaxted.co.uk/festival.htm
Warwick and Leamington Festival	www.warwickarts.org.uk
Ledbury Poetry Festival	www.poetry-festival.com
Oundle International Festival	www.oundlefestival.org.uk
Buxton Festival	www.buxtonfestival.co.uk
Three Choirs Festival	www.3choirs.org
Ross-on-Wye International Festival	www.rossonwye-intfestival.co.uk
Bakewell Agricultural Show	www.bakewellshow.demon.co.uk
Norfolk Lavender, Heacham	www.norfolk-lavender.co.uk
Spalding Flower Parade	www.springfields.mistral.co.uk/page4.htm
Fleece Inn, Bretforton	www.nationaltrust.org.uk
Mr Straw's House, Worksop	www.nationaltrust.org.uk
Theatre Royal, Bury St Edmunds	www.theatreroyal.org
Weston Park, Shifnal	www.weston-park.com
Eastnor Castle, Ledbury	www.eastnorcastle.co.uk
Woburn Abbey	www.woburnabbey.co.uk
Audley End	www.english-heritage.org.uk
Stanford Hall, Swinford	www.stanfordhall.com
Burghley House, Stamford	www.burghley.co.uk
Kentwell Hall, Long Melford	www.kentwell.co.uk
Sulgrave Manor	www.sulgravemanor.org.uk

Westonbirt

Robert Holford was just 21 when he began the outstanding collection of tree specimens that now forms Westonbirt Arboretum. Almost 170 years

later, visitors can see the spectacular culmination of his life's work. The arboretum covers 600 acres (240 hectares) of woodland with 17 miles (27km) of paths and 18,000 listed specimens of plants. Some 4,000 species flourish here, many as exotic as the Chilean firebush or the handkerchief tree, all arranged in a landscape of great beauty. www.forestry.gov.uk

Bakewell Puddings

The story of Bakewell's famous puddings is one of triumph over adversity. In 1860 a cook at the White Horse Inn (now the Rutland Arms) preparing a strawberry tart for some dignitaries mistakenly placed egg mixture intended for the pastry base on top of the jam. The resulting 'disaster' was nevertheless

cooked up and promptly declared a culinary masterpiece. The puddings (those in the know never call them 'tarts') have been served in the town ever since.

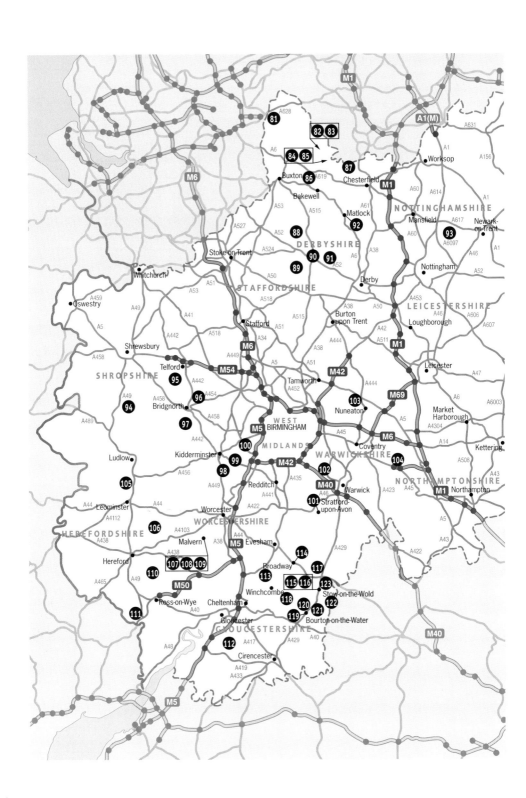

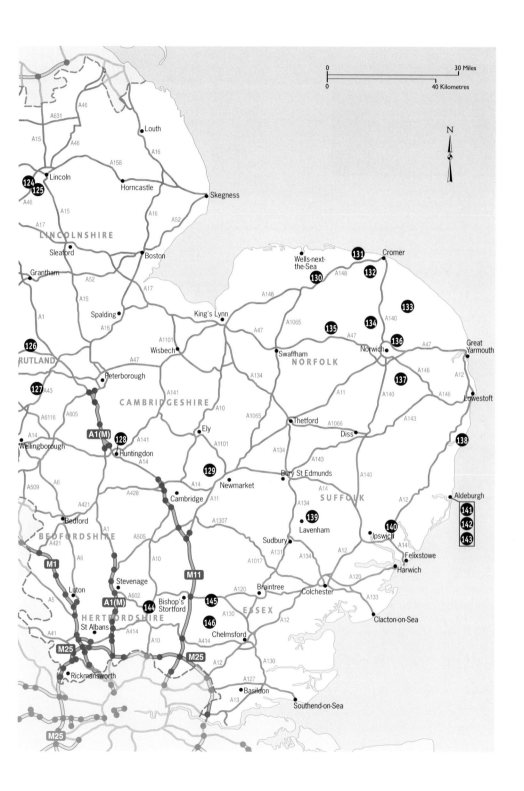

81 Wind in the Willows Hotel ★★ Silver Award

Derbyshire Level, off Sheffield Road (A57), Glossop, Derbyshire SK13 7PT **Tel:** (01457) 868001 **Fax:** (01457) 853354
Web: www.windinthewillows.co.uk **E-mail:** info@windinthewillows.co.uk

The Wind in the Willows is a family-owned, early Victorian country house hotel set in five acres, amidst unspoilt views of the Peak District National Park, nestling in the heather-clad hills of the Pennines. The 12 traditionally styled en-suite bedrooms, oak-panelled rooms, open log fires, antiques, conference rooms and adjacent golf course ensure a memorable stay. The dining room offers fine English traditional cooking, all freshly prepared.

Bed & Breakfast per night: single occupancy from £85.00–£100.00; double room from £110.00–£140.00
Dinner, Bed & Breakfast per person, per night: £80.00–£90.00
Evening meal: 1930 (last orders 1945)

Bedrooms: 12 double/twin
Bathrooms: 12 en-suite
Parking: 20 spaces
Cards accepted: Mastercard, Visa, Switch/Delta, Amex, Diners, Barclaycard

Blue John

The Derbyshire town of Castleton lies in the White Peak, a rolling limestone plateau carved into steep gorges and valleys by the last ice age. As glaciers melted they forced tremendous volumes of water downwards through joints in the limestone to form turbulent underground rivers, gouging out the rock into an impressive network of caverns. Castleton boasts four separate cave systems in its immediate vicinity.

Two of these, Treak Cliff Cavern and Blue John Cavern, contain deposits of Britain's rarest mineral, a beautifully veined fluorspar known as blue john, found nowhere else in the world. The origin of its name is uncertain, but it may derive from the French bleu-jaune (blue-yellow), two of the mineral's predominant colours (much of the stone found its way to French workshops). Its use for ornamental purposes may date back to Roman times, but it was not until the 18th century that blue john was commercially mined and worked on a large scale. The architect Robert Adam used the mineral to decorate fireplaces in the music room at Kedleston Hall in 1762, and also created the famous Chatsworth Tazza, the largest bowl ever constructed from a single piece of blue john.

The caverns provided useful access to many of the deposits of the valuable mineral. Extracting it, however, was no easy matter. Blue john occurs in two distinct formations, either as cylindrical nodules completely buried by clay, or as flat veins sandwiched

between hard layers of limestone. In the past, the deposits were extensive; the mines yielded over 20 tons annually at their peak of production, and the size of individual formations was correspondingly impressive; some nodules measured more than a foot (30cm) in diameter. Today only about half a ton is produced and few large formations are ever found. Consequently most is used for small items of jewellery, cutlery handles and small bowls, on sale in Castleton's souvenir shops.

Guided tours of Blue John Cavern and Treak Cliff Cavern provide a fascinating insight into a unique Peak District industry, while the massive scale of the caves and the superb formations of stalactites cannot fail to impress by their sheer natural grandeur.

82 The Rising Sun Hotel ◆◆◆◆

Thornhill Moor, Near Bamford, Hope Valley S33 0AL **Tel:** (01433) 651323 **Fax:** (01433) 651601
Web: www.the-rising-sun.org **E-mail:** info@the-rising-sun.org

The Rising Sun, an 18th-century inn situated in the heart of the Peak District National Park, is privately owned and family run. The hotel has been sympathetically restored with 12 individually-designed de luxe bedrooms, yet maintains its authentic country inn atmosphere. Fresh flowers in abundance and antiques, together with friendly and efficient staff make this the place to stay. Quality fresh food, real ales and fine wines served daily in a relaxed and comfortable bar. This is not just another hotel – this is an experience.

Bed & Breakfast per night: single room from £49.50–£69.50; double room from £60.00–£130.00
Lunch available: 1200–1500

Bedrooms: 2 single, 8 double/twin, 2 family
Bathrooms: 4 en-suite, 1 shared
Parking: 100 spaces
Cards accepted: Mastercard, Visa, Switch/Delta, Barclaycard

83 Underleigh House ◆◆◆◆◆ Silver Award

Edale Road, Hope, Hope Valley, Derbyshire S33 6RF **Tel:** (01433) 621372 or (01433) 621324 **Fax:** (01433) 621324
Web: www.underleighhouse.co.uk **E-mail:** underleigh.house@btinternet.com

A stunning, tranquil setting and delightful garden set the scene for this charming extended cottage and barn conversion (dating from 1873). Nestling under Lose Hill, one mile from Hope village centre, Underleigh is in the heart of magnificent walking country. Each room is furnished to a high standard with many thoughtful extras included. Delicious breakfasts in the flag-stoned dining hall feature local and homemade specialities. The welcoming beamed lounge offers log fires on chilly evenings.

Bed & Breakfast per night: single occupancy from £40.00–£49.00; double room from £64.00–£69.00

Bedrooms: 4 double, 1 twin, 1 suite
Bathrooms: 6 en-suite
Parking: 10 spaces
Open: February–December
Cards accepted: Mastercard, Visa, Switch/Delta, JCB, Solo

84 Maynard Arms Hotel ★★★ Silver Award

Main Road, Grindleford, Derbyshire S32 2HE **Tel:** (01433) 630321 or **Fax:** (01433) 630445
Web: www.maynardarms.co.uk **E-mail:** info@maynardarms.co.uk

Established in 1898 in the heart of the Peak National Park, the Maynard Arms is an idyllic location for pleasure or business. Superior bedrooms have views over the Derwent Valley. The best local produce is served for both lunch (1200–1400) and dinner (1900–2130) accompanied by our extensive wine list, in the Padley Restaurant overlooking the hotel gardens. The Longshaw Bar satisfies the heartiest of appetites between 1200–1400 and 1800–2130, also serving traditional hand-pulled beers.

Bed & Breakfast per night: single occupancy from £69.00–£89.00; double room from £79.00–£99.00
Dinner, Bed & Breakfast per person, per night: £49.50–£59.50
Evening meal: 1800 (last orders 2130)

Bedrooms: 6 double, 2 twin, 2 suites
Bathrooms: 10 en-suite
Parking: 60 spaces
Cards accepted: Mastercard, Visa, Switch/Delta, Amex, Diners, Eurocard

At-a-glance symbols are explained on the flap inside the back cover

85 The Plough Inn

♦♦♦♦ Silver Award

Leadmill Bridge, Hathersage, Hope Valley, Derbyshire S32 1BA **Tel:** (01433) 650319 or (01433) 650180 **Fax:** (01433) 651049
E-mail: theploughinn@leadmillbridge.fsnet.co.uk

Situated in nine acres of grounds, the 16th-century Plough Inn has recently been restored to give visitors every modern facility and comfort. It is an idyllic location close to the meandering River Derwent and surrounded by magnificent countryside. Cosy and tastefully decorated, the inn provides an ideal environment in which to unwind or visit the many heritage sites of the Peak District National Park. Food at The Plough Inn is a real star attraction.

Bed & Breakfast per night: single occupancy from £55.00–£79.50; double room from £79.50–£120.00
Lunch available: 1130–1430
Evening meal: 1830 (last orders 2130)

Bedrooms: 3 double, 2 suites
Bathrooms: 5 en-suite
Parking: 40 spaces
Cards accepted: Mastercard, Visa, Switch/Delta

86 Cressbrook Hall

♦♦♦♦

Cressbrook, Buxton, Derbyshire SK17 8SY **Tel:** (01298) 871289 or 0800 3583003 **Fax:** (01298) 871845
Web: www.cressbrookhall.co.uk **E-mail:** stay@cressbrookhall.co.uk

A period piece with pedigree! Cressbrook Hall is a fine William IV residence, built 1835 and enjoying a spectacular hillside location. The formal gardens designed by Edward Kemp are currently under restoration. Self-catering cottages, together with elegant serviced accommodation in the Hall are available for weekends or longer visits and ideal for reunions, wedding receptions, management training/team building and special family celebrations. Hall 'home catering' gives you more free time to enjoy this idyllic place. Accommodation which is decidedly, delightfully different!

Bed & Breakfast per night: single occupancy from £55.00–£75.00; double room from £75.00–£105.00

Bedrooms: 1 double, 1 twin, 1 family
Bathrooms: 3 en-suite
Parking: 45 spaces
Cards accepted: Mastercard, Visa, Switch/Delta

87 Horsleygate Hall

♦♦♦♦

Horsleygate Lane, Holmesfield, Derbyshire S18 7WD **Tel:** (01142) 890333 **Fax:** (01142) 890333

Horsleygate Hall is secreted down a country lane in the scenic Cordwell Valley and surrounded by magnificent sprawling gardens - of special interest for keen gardeners. There is a comfortable, old fashioned feel to the house with rugs and flagstones, country oak furniture and old pine fittings. The sitting room and bedrooms, decorated with rich fabrics and colours are comfortable and homely with lovely views out across the gardens and Peak District. Free range eggs, Derbyshire oatcakes and garden fruit are on offer. Ten minutes from Chatsworth.

Bed & Breakfast per night: single occupancy from £32.00–£37.00; double room from £53.00–£57.00

Bedrooms: 1 double, 1 twin, 1 family
Bathrooms: 1 en-suite, 2 shared
Parking: 8 spaces
Open: all year except Christmas

88 Stanshope Hall ◆◆◆◆

Stanshope, Ashbourne, Derbyshire DE6 2AD **Tel:** (01335) 310278 **Fax:** (01335) 310470
Web: www.stanshope.net **E-mail:** naomi@stanshope.demon.co.uk

Seven miles from Ashbourne, between Dovedale and the Manifold Valley in the southern Peak District, Stanshope Hall offers peace and quiet, comfortable licensed en-suite accommodation and home cooking. The rooms have been decorated by theatre artists and the result is a mixture of the theatrical, the humorous and the indulgent. Fruit and vegetables served at dinner are, whenever possible, from our own kitchen garden.

Bed & Breakfast per night: single occupancy from £30.00–£45.00; double room from £60.00–£80.00
Dinner, Bed & Breakfast per person, per night: £52.00–£77.00
Evening meal: 1900 (last orders 1930)

Bedrooms: 2 double, 1 twin
Bathrooms: 3 en-suite
Parking: 3 spaces
Cards accepted: Mastercard, Visa, Switch/Delta

89 Manor House Farm ◆◆◆◆ Silver Award

Prestwood, Denstone, Uttoxeter, Staffordshire ST14 5DD **Tel:** (01889) 590415 **Fax:** (01335) 342198
Web: www.4posteraccom.com **E-mail:** cm_ball@yahoo.co.uk

An oak-panelled, four-postered Tudor retreat, two miles from Alton Towers. An enchanting, rambling farmhouse, the kind of time capsule you can't simulate. Oak timbers, stone, tapestry drapes, curios, pewter and books galore. There are georgous lawned grounds, full of bird song. A summerhouse, tennis and croquet. Rare breed cattle graze peacefully. Rooms have majestic four-poster beds and great views. Chris and Margaret are busy, informal people and the attitude here is 'stay as friends'.

Bed & Breakfast per night: single occupancy from £30.00–£34.00; double room from £50.00–£56.00

Bedrooms: 2 double, 1 family
Bathrooms: 3 en-suite
Parking: 4 spaces
Cards accepted: Mastercard, Visa, Delta

90 Omnia Somnia ◆◆◆◆◆ Gold Award

The Coach House, The Firs, Ashbourne, Derbyshire DE6 1HF **Tel:** (01335) 300145 **Fax:** (01335) 300958
Web: www.omniasomnia.co.uk **E-mail:** alan@omniasomnia.co.uk

A private house, formerly a Victorian coach house, nestling amongst mature trees in a quiet location near Ashbourne town centre. Our rooms are very different, each one special in its own way: Oriens – a room with every facility and many, many pictures, and the superb bathroom has a bath big enough for two! Occidens – enter into your own sitting room, then climb the stairs to a romantic hideaway bedroom. Meridies – a sumptuous, panelled room with a hand-crafted, fully draped four-poster bed.

Bed & Breakfast per night: single occupancy from £52.00–£55.00; double room from £80.00–£90.00
Dinner, Bed & Breakfast per person, per night: £64.00–£79.00
Evening meal: from 1900

Bedrooms: 2 double, 1 suite
Bathrooms: 3 en-suite
Parking: 3 spaces
Cards accepted: Mastercard, Visa, Switch/Delta, JCB, Solo

At-a-glance symbols are explained on the flap inside the back cover

91   Holly Meadow Farm ◆◆◆◆

Bradley, Ashbourne, Derbyshire DE6 1PN   **Tel:** (01335) 370261   **Fax:** (01335) 370261
Web: www.hollymeadowbandb.freeserve.co.uk

Located on the edge of the Peak District and Dovedale, Holly Meadow Farm is a peaceful retreat, yet only three miles from Ashbourne. Two spacious double rooms offer a high degree of comfort and superb views over unspoilt countryside. Hearty farmhouse breakfasts include home-made preserves and local produce. Guests are welcome to explore our 260-acre farm, stroll along the brook, walk through old and new woodland, and watch songbirds, hares, foxes and badgers in their natural habitat. Ideal for exploring Derbyshire's scenery and heritage.

Bed & Breakfast per night: double room from £50.00–£56.00

Bedrooms: 2 double
Bathrooms: 2 en-suite
Parking: 4 spaces

92   Riber Hall ★★★ Silver Award

Matlock, Derbyshire DE4 5JU   **Tel:** (01629) 582795   **Fax:** (01629) 580475
Web: www.riber-hall.co.uk   **E-mail:** info@riber-hall.co.uk

Renowned historic country manor house set in tranquil rolling Derbyshire hills. Gourmet cuisine – AA two rosettes. Many stately homes nearby including Chatsworth. Recommended by all major guides. Two day breaks available. M1 exit 28, twenty minutes.

Bed & Breakfast per night: single occupancy from £97.00–£112.00; double room from £136.00–£182.00
Dinner, Bed & Breakfast per person, per night: £97.50–£118.00 (2 persons sharing)
Lunch available: 1200–1330

Evening meal: 1900 (last orders 2130)
Bedrooms: 12 double, 2 twin
Bathrooms: 14 en-suite
Parking: 45 spaces
Cards accepted: Mastercard, Visa, Switch/Delta, Amex, Diners, Eurocard, JCB

93   Ashdene ◆◆◆◆

Radley Road, Halam, Southwell, Nottinghamshire NG22 8AH   **Tel:** (01636) 812335
E-mail: david@herbert.newsurf.net

'Ashdene' is situated in the small village of Halam, one mile from Southwell Minster, and is a 16th-century yeoman farmhouse with extensive gardens which open several times a year under the 'National Garden Scheme'. Visitors have their own sitting room which has an open log fire. Plenty of off-road parking. An ideal situation for exploring the Dukeries, the Vale of Belvoir, the Derbyshire Dales and Lincolnshire Wolds.

Bed & Breakfast per night: single room from £30.00–£40.00; double room from £50.00–£55.00

Bedrooms: 1 single, 1 double, 1 twin
Bathrooms: 1 en-suite, 1 private, 1 shared
Parking: 7 spaces

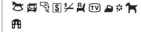

94 Field House ◆◆◆◆

Cardington Moor, Cardington, Church Stretton, Shropshire SY6 7LL **Tel:** (01694) 771485
Web: www.virtual-shropshire.co.uk/fieldhouse **E-mail:** fieldhouse@cardington.fsworld.co.uk

Located in one of the most beautiful valleys in the South Shropshire Hills. A designated environmentally sensitive area offering unsurpassed peace and tranquillity, yet within 25 minutes of Shrewsbury and the Welsh Marches - O/S Explorer 217. Accommodation comprises a friends/family suite of double/twin bedded rooms with inter-connecting bathroom and ground floor en-suite with twin beds.

Bed & Breakfast per night: single occupancy from £25.00; double room from £50.00

Bedrooms: 1 double, 2 twin
Bathrooms: 2 en-suite
Parking: 6 spaces

The Shropshire Hills

The 'Shropshire Alps' and 'Little Switzerland' are not altogether fanciful names for that dramatically hilly part of the county sandwiched between the Welsh border and the River Severn. Here, ancient earth movements have tilted up great layers of different rock strata, each now forming its own ridge of hills stretching in a roughly south-westerly to north-easterly direction.

Most easterly of the ridges are the Clee Hills, formed of rich red sandstone, topped with basalt, and consisting of two separate ridges, Brown Clee Hill (1,792ft, 546m) and Titterstone Clee Hill (1,749ft, 533m). To their west the River Corve flows through a gentle wooded valley, before the land rises again to Wenlock Edge, a well-defined and steep-sided ridge of limestone flanked with trees. West of the Edge the hump of Caer Caradoc (1,506ft, 459m) dominates the Caradoc Hills around Church Stretton, and beyond rises the forbidding plateau of the Long Mynd (1,696ft, 517m). This 10 mile (16km) ridge of moorland, composed of heather-covered grit and shale, is a favourite launch point for gliders, and also some of the best walking country in Shropshire. An ancient path of unknown age, the Port Way, runs the entire length of the crest, commanding magnificent views of the Wrekin (1,335ft, 407m), which protrudes dramatically from the Shropshire Plain, its volcanic rocks the oldest in England. The eastern flank of the Long Mynd is eroded by streams into a series of deep ravines, of which the popular Carding

Mill Valley (shown above) is considered the most beautiful; two others are Callow Hollow and Ashes Hollow. Westward again are the Stiperstones, a sombre rocky outcrop where devils are believed to gather on Midwinter Night and, at 1,731ft (528m), a dramatic vantage point.

Aside from its superb scenery the area is rich in other attractions, with appealing towns, such as Shrewsbury, Bridgnorth, Bewdley and Ludlow all within easy reach. It boasts a string of impressive castles and fortified manors (Ludlow, Clun and Stokesay are three of many), some fine ecclesiastical ruins (Buildwas and Wenlock), and a fascinating industrial heritage (Ironbridge). At the heart of the hills is Church Stretton, an appealing little town which became something of a land-locked resort in the 19th century, a perfect base, then and now, from which to explore the slopes. Contact Church Stretton Tourist Information Centre (tel: 01694 723133, April–October only) for details of sights and walks (guided hikes are available) throughout the region.

95 The Swan ♦♦♦♦

The Wharfage, Ironbridge, Telford, Shropshire TF8 7NH **Tel:** (01952) 432306 **Fax:** (01952) 432994
Web: www.malthousepubs.co.uk

Sister pub to the adjacent Malthouse. An 18th-century malthouse, on the banks of the River Severn, just 250 yards from the bridge and main visitor centre. Developed this year with a contemporary flavour, but still with an eye to the traditional, the pub has eight en-suite, non-smoking rooms that are light, clean and airy – most with a river view. One of our doubles features a glass floor revealing the original hop drying room. To complement the accommodation we offer freshly cooked, great tasting food in a restaurant or bar atmosphere.

Bed & Breakfast per night: single room from £50.00–£65.00; double room from £60.00–£70.00
Dinner, Bed & Breakfast per person, per night: £75.00–£95.00
Lunch available: 1200–1430

Evening meal: 1800 (last orders 2130)
Bedrooms: 3 single, 3 double/twin, 3 family
Bathrooms: 8 en-suite
Parking:
Cards accepted: Mastercard, Visa, Switch/Delta, Amex

96 Old Vicarage Hotel ★★★ Gold Award

Worfield, Bridgnorth, Shropshire WV15 5JZ **Tel:** (01746) 716497 **Fax:** (01746) 716552
Web: www.oldvicarageworfield.com **E-mail:** admin@the-old-vicarage.demon.co.uk

An Edwardian vicarage set in two acres of grounds on the edge of a conservation village in glorious Shropshire countryside, close to Ironbridge Gorge, Severn Valley Railway and Welsh border towns. With an award-winning (AA 3 Rosettes) dining room and cellar, the Old Vicarage is personally run by David and Sarah Blakstad. Two-night leisure breaks available at any time of the year.

Bed & Breakfast per night: single occupancy from £60.00–£110.00; double room from £95.00–£165.00
Dinner, Bed & Breakfast per person, per night: £75.00–£102.50 (min 2 nights)
Lunch available: 1200–1400

Evening meal: 1900 (last orders 2100)
Bedrooms: 7 double, 6 twin, 2 family
Bathrooms: 14 en-suite
Parking: 30 spaces
Cards accepted: Mastercard, Visa, Switch/Delta

97 Bulls Head Inn ♦♦♦♦

Chelmarsh, Bridgnorth, Shropshire WV16 6BA **Tel:** (01746) 861469 **Fax:** (01746) 862646
Web: www.virtual-shropshire.co.uk/bulls-head-inn **E-mail:** dave@bullshead.fsnet.co.uk

Charming 17th-century Inn in the village of Chelmarsh with views over the Severn valley offering excellent accommodation. Four miles from historic Bridgnorth and set in the beautiful Shropshire countryside. All bedrooms are individually and tastefully furnished (one with a four-poster bed). There are ground floor bedrooms/apartments (situated around the well-stocked, pretty gardens) that are equipped for people with disabilities. There is a choice of delightfully furnished cottages for self-catering breaks. Ideally located to explore the many places of interest.

Bed & Breakfast per night: single room from £35.00–£48.00; double room from £52.00–£73.00
Lunch available: 1200–1400
Evening meal: 1830 (last orders 2130)

Bedrooms: 1 single, 3 double, 2 twin, 3 family
Bathrooms: 9 en-suite
Parking: 60 spaces
Cards accepted: Mastercard, Visa, Switch/Delta, Amex, Eurocard, Solo

98 Yew Tree House

◆◆◆◆ Silver Award

Norchard, Crossway Green, Hartlebury, Kidderminster, Worcestershire DY13 9SN **Tel:** 0800 093 5423 or (01299) 250921
Web: www.yewtreeworcester.co.uk **E-mail:** yewtreehouse1@btopenworld.com

An elegant Georgian farmhouse and 'cider house' cottage, both with a wealth of beams and shrouded in history. Built in 1754, stepping over the threshold of Yew Tree House is a fascinating mix of elegance and atmosphere. Peacefully tucked away but convenient to all motorway systems and sightseeing. Beautifully appointed en-suite rooms with television and hospitality tray. Tennis on-site by arrangement. Golf course and many good eating establishments nearby. Splendid breakfasts are provided.

Bed & Breakfast per night: single occupancy from £35.00–£45.00; double room from £55.00–£60.00
Dinner, Bed & Breakfast per person, per night: £50.00–£60.00 (by arrangement only)

Bedrooms: 2 double, 2 twin, 1 family
Bathrooms: 5 en-suite
Parking: 7 spaces

99 Brockencote Hall

★★★ Gold Award

Chaddesley Corbett, Kidderminster, Worcestershire DY10 4PY **Tel:** (01562) 777876 **Fax:** (01562) 777872
Web: www.brockencotehall.com **E-mail:** info@brockencotehall.com

Nestling in the heart of the Worcestershire countryside, Brockencote Hall is set in seventy acres of private parkland with its own lake. It is the perfect place for relaxation. Proprietors Alison and Joseph Petitjean have created a charming Gallic oasis in the heart of England, combining traditional French comfort and friendliness with superb French cuisine. The hotel offers a choice of seventeen magnificent en-suite bedrooms, including one that has been especially designed to make stays comfortable for disabled guests.

Bed & Breakfast per night: single occupancy from £96.00–£140.00; double room from £116.00–£180.00
Dinner, Bed & Breakfast per person, per night: £85.50–£123.50
Lunch available: 1200–1330

Evening meal: 1900 (last orders 2030)
Bedrooms: 17 double/twin
Bathrooms: 17 en-suite
Parking: 50 spaces

100 St. Elizabeth's Cottage

◆◆◆◆

Woodman Lane, Clent, Stourbridge, West Midlands DY9 9PX **Tel:** (01562) 883883 **Fax:** (01562) 885034
E-mail: st_elizabeth_cot@btconnect.com

A beautiful country cottage in a tranquil setting, with six acres of landscaped garden plus outdoor heated swimming pool. Lovely country walks. Accommodation includes television in all rooms, plus tea/coffee making facilities. Residents' lounge available. Plenty of pubs and restaurants nearby. Easy access to the M5, M6, M42 and M40. 25 minutes from the NEC and Birmingham Airport. Destinations within easy reach include the Symphony Hall and Convention Centre in Birmingham, the Black Country Museum, Dudley, Stourbridge, Crystal factories and the Severn Valley Railway. No smoking. Pets welcome. Open all year.

Bed & Breakfast per night: single room from £30.00–£32.00; double room from £58.00–£62.00

Bedrooms: 2 double, 1 twin
Bathrooms: 3 en-suite
Parking: 6 spaces

101 Broadlands Guest House

23 Evesham Place, Stratford-upon-Avon, Warwickshire CV37 6HT **Tel:** (01789) 299181 **Fax:** (01789) 551382
Web: www.stratford-upon-avon.co.uk/broadlands.htm **E-mail:** broadlands.com@virgin.net

Located just five minutes walk from the centre of the beautiful and historic market town of Stratford-upon-Avon, Broadlands offers an exemplary standard of accommodation to enhance your stay, whether your purpose is business, the theatre or that you merely wish to escape for a while. In a relaxed and friendly atmosphere, the comfort and elegance of the Edwardian era is evident in the dining room and in each of our bedrooms, which have either en-suite or private facilities, television and refreshments.

Bed & Breakfast per night: single room from £35.00–£45.00; double room from £56.00–£70.00

Bedrooms: 2 single, 3 double, 1 twin
Bathrooms: 5 en-suite, 1 private
Parking: 4 spaces
Cards accepted: Mastercard, Visa, Switch/Delta

Packwood Yew Garden

There is something rather surreal about the famous yew garden at Packwood House. On the manicured green lawn, smooth and flat as a billiard table, immaculately clipped yew bushes stand to attention. Seen from a distance they are strangely people-like, resembling a gathering of hooded figures, poised waiting, listening, ready to hurry off about their business. It is no wonder that a human symbolism has been attributed to them; the arrangement of 100 trees with its single large yew, 'the Master', standing atop a mound, surrounded by a 'multitude' of others, is said to represent the Sermon on the Mount. Further refinements to the scheme include a row of twelve on a raised terrace called 'the Apostles'.

Whether the original designer of the garden intended such a scheme is unknown, for references to the Sermon on the Mount idea do not appear in documents until the late 19th century, some 200 years after the first trees were planted. All that is known about the origins of the yew garden is that John Fetherston, who inherited Packwood in 1634, laid out at least part of it between 1650 and 1670, but it is possible that many of the trees were planted some time later.

It was probably John Fetherston's father, another John, who began the fine timber-framed mansion which still forms the core of the present house. Though less famous than the garden, this too is of considerable interest. During the course of the Fetherston family's ownership the original Tudor building underwent considerable alterations, in particular the addition of fine stables and outbuildings in the 1670s. Packwood left the Fetherston family in 1869 and was eventually bought by Alfred Ash, a wealthy industrialist, in 1905. Ash's son, Graham Baron Ash, lavished meticulous care on it, restoring it to match his vision of the perfect Tudor mansion. He was a punctiliously correct and obsessively tidy man who kept everything, including the gardens, in perfect order. The restoration of his house became his passion – until he tired of it and bought a moated castle in Sussex. Donating Packwood to the National Trust, he hoped it would be kept forever as he created it, and so it has been. It remains the kind of museum piece it always was in his lifetime, a perfect monument to the Tudor age. Packwood House is 2 miles (3km) east of Hockley Heath on the A3400.

102 Northleigh House

◆◆◆◆ Silver Award

Five Ways Road, Hatton, Warwick, Warwickshire CV35 7HZ **Tel:** (01926) 484203 or 07774 101894 **Fax:** (01926) 484006
Web: www.northleigh.co.uk **E-mail:** sylviafen@amserve.com

You will find peace, quiet, comfort and a friendly welcome at this rambling 100-year old cottage set amidst gardens and open fields. Its seven individually designed en-suite rooms include many thoughtful extras. Your breakfast will be freshly cooked to your personal tastes. Nearby are some excellent country pubs and also the historic towns of Warwick and Stratford-upon-Avon and the National Exhibition Centre. Please contact Sylvia Fenwick for brochures. No Smoking.

Bed & Breakfast per night: single room from £38.00–£46.00; double room from £58.00–£68.00

Bedrooms: 1 single, 5 double, 1 twin
Bathrooms: 7 en-suite
Open: February–mid December
Parking: 10 spaces
Cards accepted: Mastercard, Visa, Switch/Delta, JCB

103 Leathermill Grange Country Guest House

◆◆◆◆◆ Gold Award

Leathermill Lane, Caldecote, Nuneaton, Warwickshire CV10 0RX **Tel:** (01827) 714637 **Fax:** (01827) 716422
Web: www.leathermillgrange.co.uk **E-mail:** davidcodd@leathermillgrange.co.uk

A beautifully refurbished 19th-century Victorian farmhouse in five acres of grounds with landscaped gardens and lake, surrounded by farmland. Spacious and elegant interior with high quality decor and furnishings. Bedrooms (one with four-poster bed) have en-suite shower rooms. Using our home-grown produce, Aga-cooked dinners are served in the candlelit dining room and there is a guest lounge and conservatory. An ideal base for touring and business, with Stratford-upon-Avon, Warwick Castle, Bosworth, the Belfry, Tamworth, Coventry, NEC, NAC Birmingham and Leicester all within a 30 minute drive.

Bed & Breakfast per night: single occupancy from £60.00–£70.00; double room from £80.00– £90.00
Evening meal: 1930 (with 24 hours notice)

Bedrooms: 2 double, 1 twin
Bathrooms: 3 en-suite, 1 shared
Parking: 20 spaces
Cards accepted: Mastercard, Visa, Switch/Delta, JCB, Solo

104 Village Green Hotel

◆◆◆◆ Silver Award

The Green, Dunchurch, Rugby, Warwickshire CV22 6NX **Tel:** (01788) 813434 **Fax:** (01788) 814714
Web: www.vghrugby.co.uk **E-mail:** info@ughrugby.co.uk

Situated in the centre of this historic and picturesque old coaching village in the heart of Shakespeare's county. The village has no less than five excellent eating houses all within one hundred yards of the hotel. Refurbished in 1997, our speciality is first class accommodation with bedrooms appointed to the highest specification, including our Princess Victoria room which has a four-poster bed. Complete your stay by enjoying one of our traditional English breakfasts.

Bed & Breakfast per night: single room from £44.50–£62.50; double room from £49.50–£79.50

Bedrooms: 3 single, 17 double, 1 twin, 1 family, 2 suites
Bathrooms: 24 en-suite
Parking: 8 spaces
Cards accepted: Mastercard, Visa, Switch/Delta, Amex

At-a-glance symbols are explained on the flap inside the back cover

105   Rosecroft   ◆◆◆◆ Silver Award

Orleton, Ludlow, Shropshire SY8 4HN   **Tel:** (01568) 780565   **Fax:** (01568) 780565
Web: www.stmem.com/rosecroft   **E-mail:** gailanddavid@rosecroftorleton.freeserve.co.uk

Situated in the middle of the picturesque village of Orleton, Rosecroft offers a peaceful retreat in the heart of the countryside. We are close to historic Ludlow, with its castle, listed buildings and excellent food. We are also in close proximity to a number of interesting and exciting gardens for garden lovers. For walkers there is the Mortimer Trail and many others, including Offas Dyke for the very keen. For history lovers there are several National Trust and English Heritage properties within easy striking distance.

Bed & Breakfast per night: single occupancy from £40.00–£45.00; double room from £60.00–£65.00

Bedrooms: 2 double
Bathrooms: 1 en-suite, 1 private
Parking: 5 spaces
Open: all year except Christmas/New Year

---

106   The Steppes   ◆◆◆◆◆ Silver Award

Ullingswick, Hereford HR1 3JG   **Tel:** (01432) 820424   **Fax:** (01432) 820042
Web: www.steppeshotel.co.uk   **E-mail:** info@steppeshotel.co.uk

This award-winning country house hotel with an intimate atmosphere abounds in antique furniture, inglenook fireplaces, oak beams and flag-stoned floors. The old dairy now houses a magnificent cobbled bar with Dickensian atmosphere, and a restored timber-framed barn and converted stable accommodate six large luxury en-suite bedrooms. Outstanding cordon bleu cuisine is served by candle light, and highly praised breakfasts come with an imaginative selection. Leisure breaks from £59.00 (minimum of 2 nights).

Bed & Breakfast per night: single occupancy from £50.00–£55.00; double room from £80.00–£90.00
Dinner, Bed & Breakfast per person, per night: £66.00–£73.00
Evening meal: 1930

Bedrooms: 4 double, 2 twin
Bathrooms: 6 en-suite
Parking: 6 spaces
Open: February–November
Cards accepted: Mastercard, Visa, Switch/Delta

---

107   Colwall Park   ★★★ Silver Award

Colwall, Malvern, Worcestershire WR13 6QG   **Tel:** (01684) 540000   **Fax:** (01684) 540847
Web: www.colwall.com   **E-mail:** hotel@colwall.com

Situated on the sunny western side of the breathtaking Malvern Hills, we provide an ideal setting for a relaxing break in unspoilt countryside on the edge of the Cotswolds. Winners of the prestigious AA Courtesy & Care Award and the highly acclaimed Restaurant of the Year Award – Birmingham Evening Mail (Michelin, Egon Ronay, AA etc.) Our friendly and popular Lantern Bar, a meeting place for locals and residents, offers real ales, superb house wines and an exciting menu of home-made meals and snacks.

Bed & Breakfast per night: single room from £65.00–£80.00; double room from £110.00–£150.00
Dinner, Bed & Breakfast per person, per night: £75.00–£85.00 (min 2 nights)
Lunch available: 1230–1400 (prior reservation)

Evening meal: 1930 (last orders 2100)
Bedrooms: 3 single, 10 double, 7 twin, 1 family, 1 suite **Bathrooms:** 22 en-suite
Parking: 30 spaces
Cards accepted: Mastercard, Visa, Switch/Delta

---

108 The Cottage in the Wood Hotel　　★★★ Silver Award

Holywell Road, Malvern Wells, Malvern, Worcestershire WR14 4LG **Tel:** (01684) 575859 **Fax:** (01684) 560662
Web: www.cottageinthewood.co.uk **E-mail:** reception@cottageinthewood.co.uk

Stunningly set high on the Malvern Hills, looking across thirty miles of the Severn Plain to the horizon formed by the Cotswold Hills. Owned and run by the Pattin family for sixteen years, the aim is to provide a relaxing and peaceful base from which to tour this area of outstanding natural beauty. The restaurant provides exceptional food backed by an extensive wine list of over six hundred bins. The daily half board price is based on a minimum two-night stay, and the weekly price offers seven nights for the price of six. Special breaks all week, all year. AA 2 Rosettes.

Bed & Breakfast per night: single occupancy from £79.00–£99.00; double room from £99.00–£170.00
Dinner, Bed & Breakfast per person, per night: £70.00–£117.00 (min 2 nights)
Lunch available: 1230–1400

Evening meal: 1900 (last orders 2130)
Bedrooms: 23 double, 8 twin
Bathrooms: 31 en-suite
Parking: 40 spaces
Cards accepted: Mastercard, Visa, Switch/Delta, Amex, Eurocard, JCB

109 Holdfast Cottage Hotel　　★★ Silver Award

Marlbank Road, Little Malvern, Malvern, Worcestershire WR13 6NA **Tel:** (01684) 310288 **Fax:** (01684) 311117
Web: www.holdfast-cottage.co.uk **E-mail:** enquiries@holdfast-cottage.co.uk

Pretty wisteria-covered country house hotel, set in two acres of gardens and private woodland, tucked into the foot of the Malvern Hills. Highly recommended for its freshly-prepared menu which changes daily and uses the best local and seasonal produce. Delightful dining room and bar. Cosy lounge with log fire. Enchanting en-suite bedrooms are individually furnished. A personal welcome plus care and attention throughout your stay is assured by the resident proprietors.

Bed & Breakfast per night: single room £50.00; double room from £84.00–£98.00
Dinner, Bed & Breakfast per person, per night: £64.00–£72.00 (min 2 nights)
Lunch available: 1200–1400 by prior reservation only

Evening meal: 1830 (last orders 2100)
Bedrooms: 1 single, 5 double, 2 twin, 1 family
Bathrooms: 8 en-suite, 1 private
Parking: 25 spaces
Cards accepted: Mastercard, Visa, Switch/Delta

110 The Bowens Country House　　♦♦♦♦

Fownhope, Hereford HRI 4PS **Tel:** (01432) 860430 **Fax:** (01432) 860430
Web: www.thebowenshotel.co.uk **E-mail:** thebowenshotel@aol.com

Delightful Georgian house set in the peaceful Wye Valley village of Fownhope, an Area of Outstanding Natural Beauty situated between Hereford and Ross-on-Wye (B4224). Large, well-maintained garden with a grass tennis court (summer months only) and a 9-hole putting green. Perfect centre for walking and touring the Wye Valley, Welsh Marches, Malverns, Brecon Beacons, Black and White villages. Superb home-cooked meals, morning coffee and cream teas. Vegetarians are welcome. Fully licensed with an extensive wine list. Ample parking. Bargain breaks available.

Bed & Breakfast per night: single room £35.00; double room £70.00
Dinner, Bed & Breakfast per person, per night: from £51.00
Evening meal: 1930

Bedrooms: 2 single, 3 double, 3 twin, 2 family
Bathrooms: 10 en-suite
Parking: 10 spaces
Cards accepted: Mastercard, Visa, Switch/Delta

111 Thatch Close ◆◆◆◆

Llangrove, Ross-on-Wye, Herefordshire HR9 6EL **Tel:** (01989) 770300
Web: www.thatchclose.com **E-mail:** thatch.close@virgin.net

A secluded, peaceful and comfortable Georgian farmhouse, yet convenient for the A40, M4 and M50. Our three lovely bedrooms, each with its own bath and shower room (two en-suite), have magnificent views over unspoilt countryside. Relax in the visitors' lounge; sit in the shade of mature trees or on the patio in our colourful gardens – or walk in our fields. You may be greeted by our friendly dog, or our free-flying parrot!

Bed & Breakfast per night: single occupancy from £28.00–£32.00; double room from £48.00–£55.00
Dinner, Bed & Breakfast per person, per night: £41.50–£47.50
Evening meal: 1900

Bedrooms: 2 double, 1 twin
Bathrooms: 2 en-suite, 1 private
Parking: 8 spaces

112 Cardynham House ◆◆◆◆

The Cross, Painswick, Stroud, Gloucestershire GL6 6XX **Tel:** (01452) 814006 **Fax:** (01452) 812321
Web: www.cardynham.co.uk **E-mail:** info@cardynham.co.uk

Cardynham House is a 15th-century Cotswold merchant's house located in historic Painswick village. The beautiful countryside is ideal for walking, yet very close to Gloucester, Cheltenham and Cirencester. The house itself has nine rooms all featuring four-poster beds, each decorated in its own style. Choose from Medieval Garden, Palm Beach, Old Tuscany, Highlands, Dovecote, New England, Cottage Rose, Arabian Nights and the Pooolroom. The Poolroom features its own private patio and heated pool with wave machine. Visit our website for complete details.

Bed & Breakfast per night: single occupancy from £47.00–£75.00; double room from £69.00– £89.00
Dinner, Bed & Breakfast per person, per night: £59.00–£69.00 (min 2 nights at weekends)

Lunch available: Sunday only 1200–1700
Evening meal: 1900 (last orders 2130)
Bedrooms: 6 double, 3 family
Bathrooms: 8 en-suite, 1 private
Cards accepted: Mastercard, Visa, Switch/ Delta, Amex, Eurocard, JCB

113 Alstone Fields Farm ◆◆◆◆◆ Gold Award

Teddington Hands, Stow Road, Tewkesbury, Gloucestershire GL20 8NG **Tel:** (01242) 620592
Web: www.smoothhound.co.uk/hotels/alstone.html **E-mail:** rogers@alstone.fields.fsnet.co.uk

Enjoy the friendliest of welcomes at our beautifully appointed family farm, set in lovely gardens and surrounded by hills and fields. All bedrooms individually and tastefully decorated with every modern facility. Ground floor rooms and access for disabled people.

Bed & Breakfast per night: single occupancy from £40.00–£50.00; double room from £50.00–£60.00

Bedrooms: 6 double/twin
Bathrooms: 5 en-suite, 1 shared
Parking: 6 spaces

114 Broadway Hotel

★★★ Silver Award

The Green, Broadway, Worcestershire WR12 7AA **Tel:** (01386) 852401 **Fax:** (01386) 853879
Web: www.cotswold-inns-hotel.co.uk **E-mail:** info@broadwayhotel.info

The Broadway Hotel is the essence of quintessential England. Used as a retreat by the Abbots of Pershore 600 years ago, it has a feeling of tranquillity still enjoyed by today's visitors. The excellent courtyard restaurant, complete with Ebony Minstrels gallery, serves the freshest local produce from the Vale of Evesham. Ideal for visiting Stratford-upon-Avon, Cheltenham Spa and Oxford.

Bed & Breakfast per night: single room from £75.00–£95.00; double room from £125.00–£159.00
Dinner, Bed & Breakfast per person, per night: £65.00–£80.00
Evening meal: 1900 (last orders 2130)

Bedrooms: 20
Bathrooms: 20 en-suite
Cards accepted: Mastercard, Visa, Switch/Delta, Amex, Diners, Eurocard, JCB

115 The Royalist Hotel

★★★ Silver Award

Digbeth Street, Stow-on-the-Wold, Cheltenham, Gloucestershire GL54 1BN **Tel:** (01451) 830670 **Fax:** (01451) 870048
Web: www.theroyalisthotel.co.uk **E-mail:** info@theroyalisthotel.co.uk

The Royalist Hotel is set right in the centre of the Cotswolds in the market town of Stow-on-the-Wold. Authenticated in the Guiness Book of Records as the oldest inn in England, the building dates from 947AD. The Royalist is privately owned by Alan and Georgina Thompson and Alan is the head chef. Within the Royalist are two fabulous restaurants – the 3-Rosette 947AD Restaurant and the adjoining brasserie/pub named the Eagle and Child, which has been voted England's 8th best pub by The Independent newspaper. Eight individually designed bedrooms, full of Cotswold charm.

Bed & Breakfast per night: single occupancy from £50.00–£60.00; double room from £90.00–£140.00
Dinner, Bed & Breakfast per person, per night: £67.00–£92.00
Lunch available: 1200–1430

Evening meal: 1900 (last orders 2200)
Bedrooms: 7 double/twin, 1 family
Bathrooms: 8 en-suite
Parking: 12 spaces
Cards accepted: Mastercard, Visa, Switch/Delta, Amex, Barclaycard

116 South Hill Farmhouse

◆◆◆◆

Fosseway, Stow-on-the-Wold, Cheltenham, Gloucestershire GL54 1JU **Tel:** (01451) 831888 **Fax:** (01451) 832255
Web: www.southhill.co.uk **E-mail:** info@southhill.co.uk

Sian and Mark Cassie welcome you to the heart of the Cotswolds. South Hill Farmhouse is a friendly, family-run bed and breakfast, situated on the ancient Roman Foss Way on the outskirts of Stow-on-the-Wold. The house is a listed Cotswold stone farmhouse (no longer a working farm). There is ample parking for guests and it is only 10 minutes walk from the centre of Stow-on-the-Wold.

Bed & Breakfast per night: single room from £38.00; double room from £52.00

Bedrooms: 1 single, 3 double, 1 twin, 1 family
Bathrooms: 5 en-suite, 1 private
Parking: 12 spaces
Cards accepted: Mastercard, Visa, Switch/Delta, Eurocard, JCB

117 Neighbrook Manor ◆◆◆◆◆

Near Aston Magna, Moreton-in-Marsh, Gloucestershire GL56 9QP **Tel:** (01386) 593232 **Fax:** (01386) 593500
Web: www.neighbrookmanor.com **E-mail:** info@neighbrookmanor.com

Neighbrook Manor was originally a church on the site of an extinct medieval village mentioned in the Domesday Book 1086 and converted in 1610 with Georgian additions set in 37 acres with half a mile of river. The gardens are glorious with a trout lake and wonderful views. Centrally positioned between Moreton-in-Marsh and Chipping Campden to visit the Cotswolds, Stratford-upon-Avon, Warwick and Sudely Castles together with Hidcote Manor and Kiftsgate Gardens.

Bed & Breakfast per night: single room £48.00; double room £85.00
Dinner, Bed & Breakfast per person, per night: £24.00

Bedrooms: 1 single, 2 double/twin
Bathrooms: 2 en-suite, 1 shared
Parking: 6 spaces
Cards accepted: Mastercard, Visa, Switch, Barclaycard

The Cotswolds

At the heart of England lie the Cotswolds. And at the very soul of the Cotswolds lies stone: oolitic limestone to be precise. This glorious, rich material, laid down beneath ancient seas, has formed the very essence of the area from the neolithic (New Stone Age) period until the present day. Our distant ancestors revered the strong, workable blocks they hewed from their quarries. They created circles of mystical importance – such as the Rollright Stones near Long Compton – and long barrows for their noble dead. Hetty Pegler's Tump, near Stroud, and Belas Knap, south of Winchcombe, are fine examples of the 70 or so within the Cotswolds.

Later generations have lived on, in and beside the stone. The Romans used it to construct majestic roads (much of the Foss Way, Ermin Way and Akeman Street are now quiet lanes ideal for unhurried exploration) that radiated from Corinium (Cirencester), then the second most important town in this outpost of empire. Now it offers quality shopping, convivial dining and, at the Corinium Museum, edification for the mind. Some Romans lived in style, as visitors to the museum and to Chedworth Roman villa, complete with central-heating system and mosaic floors, can see. The Saxons founded many of today's towns and villages. Winchcombe and Malmesbury, where part of the once-glorious abbey still stands, were important settlements with much of interest for the modern-day visitor.

But what we think of as quintessential Cotswolds – mellow honey-coloured cottages huddling round a grand church and with a perfect manor – owes most to medieval times. Almost every village has reminders of the period. A surprising number of buildings date back to the 13th, 14th and 15th centuries, when the region's prosperity, founded on the hardy Cotswold sheep, was at its height. Farmhouses became bigger and grander, and tithe barns – often a perfect fusion of grace and function, as at Great Coxwell, near Faringdon, and Bredon – were needed for storage. But most importantly, churches were enlarged or built anew on the grand scale. The best of these marvellous 'wool' churches includes Chipping Campden, Northleach, Cirencester (shown above), Fairford and Lechlade. A beautifully pinnacled tower, an especially fine collection of memorial brasses, a porch which is a stonemason's tour de force, the most complete medieval stained-glass in Britain, and a marvellous setting by the infant Thames are, respectively, individual highlights.

118 Guiting Guesthouse   ◆◆◆◆◆ Silver Award

Post Office Lane, Guiting Power, Cheltenham, Gloucestershire GL54 5TZ **Tel:** (01451) 850470 **Fax:** (01451) 850034
Web: www.guitingguesthouse.com **E-mail:** info@guitingguesthouse.com

The house is a delightful and carefully-restored 16th-century Cotswold stone farmhouse. Everywhere there are exposed beams, inglenook fireplaces, open fires and polished solid elm floors from the Wychwood forest. Three rooms have four-poster beds and most are en-suite. Television and generously-filled hospitality tray in each room. Access to the guesthouse is available at all times. Delicious evening meals, served by candle light, are prepared and presented by the hosts (with the exception of Sunday). 2 AA Egg Cups.

Bed & Breakfast per night: double room from £70.00
Dinner, Bed & Breakfast per person, per night: £60.00–£65.00
Evening meal: 1900

Bedrooms: 1 single, 6 double/twin
Bathrooms: 5 en-suite, 1 private
Parking: 2 spaces
Cards accepted: Mastercard, Visa, Switch/Delta, Barclaycard

Then, in the 16th century, Henry VIII dissolved the monasteries and redistributed their wealth to his cronies' coffers. One result was the rise of the country house. If the area has the architecture of the modest cottage to a fine art, it is no surprise that on a larger canvas the results are even more stupendous. Owlpen Manor (near Dursley) and Chavenage House (near Tetbury) date from the Elizabethan era, while Chastleton House (recently acquired by the National Trust, near Moreton-in-the Marsh) and Stanway (north-east of Winchcombe) are both the epitome of Jacobean taste. Late 17th-century style lives on at Dyrham Park (another National Trust property, north of Bath). One of the most singular of all houses is Sezincote, at Bourton-on-the-Hill. This eye-opening extravaganza was remodelled in 1800 in Indian style, complete with dome, and was the inspiration for the Indianisation of the Brighton Pavilion.

Many of these magnificent properties are set off by sumptuous gardens, another Cotswold speciality. Two nestling together in the north of the region are Hidcote Manor, where the gardens are conceived as a series of separate outdoor rooms, and Kiftsgate Court, at its best in June when the myriad roses impart their heady scent to the summer breeze. Further south are the world-famous Arboretum at Westonbirt (best in late October for blazing autumnal shades), Barnsley House Garden for herbaceous borders to die for, and Painswick, where the Rococo garden is a magnet for those with a bent for horticultural history. If you're here on the Sunday on or following 19 September, you could join in the Clipping Ceremony, when the

congregation, holding hands, encircles the church. At Westbury Court (Westbury-on-Severn) is a 17th-century formal Dutch water garden.

In the late 19th century, William Morris, won over by the Cotswolds, set up home at Kelmscott Manor (occasionally open, near Bibury). An influential proponent of craftsmanship rather than the mass production of the Victorian age, he attracted like-minded artists and artisans to join him. The nearby village of Kelmscot has many reminders of the Arts and Crafts movement they began, while at Selsley the church is a monument to their achievements and to those of the allied Pre-Raphaelite Brotherhood.

For Morris, Bibury was 'the most beautiful village in England'. He may have been right, though many another Cotwold village would fancy its chances too. And so, beyond all the magnificent scenery that lies between them – the blustery tops of Cleeve and Bredon Hills, the ancient woodland near Sapperton, the Devil's Chimney (a rock pinnacle jutting out of Leckhampton Hill, near Cheltenham) – it is the villages that we love. Shaped by the centuries, carved out of the living stone, encrusted with the patina of time and a golden lichen, they are the embodiment of all that is right in the land. Spend a decade exploring them and there will be more to admire tomorrow. A list of ten, unscientifically selected, is: Bibury, Bourton-on-the-Water, Broadway, Burford, Castle Coombe, the Colns, the Duntisbournes, the Slaughters and Stanton.

The Cotswolds extend eastward into Oxfordshire – see feature on page 160.

119 The Dial House Hotel

★★ Silver Award

The Chestnuts, Bourton-on-the-Water, Gloucestershire GL54 2AN **Tel:** (01451) 822244 **Fax:** (01451) 810126
Web: www.dialhousehotel.com **E-mail:** info@dialhousehotel.com

The Dial House was taken over in September 2000 by Adrian and Jane Campbell-Howard. Since then it has been completely re-furbished to a very high standard to combine a wonderful mix of old and new. Some rooms have fantastic four-poster beds with views over the village, whilst others still have sumptuously large beds of a very elegant design. It is worth noting that the food here is of a very high standard. There is a surprisingly large garden as well. Private Parking. Highly recommendable.

Bed & Breakfast per night: single occupancy from £57.00–£89.00; double room from £90.00–£150.00
Dinner, Bed & Breakfast per person, per night: £66.00–£96.00 (min 2 nights)
Lunch available: 1200–1415

Evening meal: 1830 (last orders 2100)
Bedrooms: 11 double, 2 twin, 1 family
Bathrooms: 13 en-suite
Parking: 20 spaces
Cards accepted: Mastercard, Visa, Switch/Delta, JCB

120 Lords of the Manor Hotel

★★★ Gold Award

Upper Slaughter, Bourton-on-the-Water, Cheltenham, Gloucestershire GL54 2JD **Tel:** (01451) 820243 **Fax:** (01451) 820696
Web: www.lordsofthemanor.com **E-mail:** enquiries@lordsofthemanor.com

In the heart of the Cotswolds, in one of England's most unspoilt and picturesque villages, stands the Lords of the Manor Hotel. Built in the 17th century of honeyed Cotswold stone, the house enjoys splendid views over the surrounding meadows, stream and parkland. The heart of this country house is the dining room where truly memorable dishes, made from the best local ingredients, are served. Nearby are Blenheim Palace, Warwick Castle and Shakespeare country.

Bed & Breakfast per night: single room from £99.00; double room from £155.00–£305.00
Dinner, Bed & Breakfast per person, per night: £94.50–£184.50
Lunch available: 1230–1345
Evening meal: 1900 (last orders 2115)

Bedrooms: 2 single, 13 double, 9 twin, 3 suites
Bathrooms: 27 en-suite
Parking: 50 spaces
Cards accepted: Mastercard, Visa, Switch/Delta, Amex, Diners, Eurocard, JCB

121 Hope Lodge

♦♦♦♦♦

Wyck Rissington, Stow-on-the-Wold, Cheltenham, Gloucestershire GL54 2PN **Tel:** (01451) 822466
Web: www.hopelodge.com **E-mail:** hopelodge@btopenworld.com

Hope Lodge is a traditional Cotswold stone house, originally two cottages with parts dating back to 1680. Recently fully refurbished and extended to provide a house full of character and charm but with all the necessary modern facilities. A lounge for relaxing, one king-size double with large en-suite bath/shower. One twin with large en-suite bath/shower. Full English breakfast with good local produce is served in the country kitchen. Hope Lodge has direct access to the village green with stunning views to the south in the quiet, peaceful setting of Wyck Rissington.

Bed & Breakfast per night: single occupancy from £50.00–£60.00; double room from £70.00–£80.00

Bedrooms: 1 double, 1 twin
Bathrooms: 2 en-suite
Open: March–November

122 Kings Head Inn and Restaurant

◆◆◆◆ Silver Award

The Green, Bledington, Oxford, Gloucestershire OX7 6XQ **Tel:** (01608) 658365 **Fax:** (01608) 658902
Web: www.kingsheadinn.net **E-mail:** kingshead@orr-ewing.com

History comes hot buttered at this quintessential 15th-century Cotswold inn which nestles on the village green, complete with brook and attendant ducks. The inn has always served as a hostelry and indeed Prince Rupert of the Rhine supposedly lodged here prior to the battle of Stow in 1642. To this day much of the medieval character remains with exposed stone walls, an inglenook fireplace, settles and pews. Delightful bedrooms complement with full facilities and thoughtful extras. Our award-winning restaurant offers bar fayre, table d'hôte and à la carte. Excellent value and ideal for exploring many attractions – Blenheim, Warwick, Stratford, Oxford etc.

Bed & Breakfast per night: single occupancy from £50.00–£85.00; double room from £65.00–£90.00
Lunch available: 1200–1400
Evening meal: 1900 (last orders 2200)

Bedrooms: 10 double, 2 twin
Bathrooms: 12 en-suite
Parking: 60 spaces
Cards accepted: Mastercard, Visa, Switch/ Delta, Amex, Eourocard

123 Aston House

◆◆◆◆ Silver Award

Broadwell, Moreton-in-Marsh, Gloucestershire GL56 0TJ **Tel:** (01451) 830475 or 07773 452037
Web: www.netcomuk.co.uk/~nmfa/aston_house.html **E-mail:** fja@netcomuk.co.uk

Guests are welcomed to our home in this quiet village, just 1.5 miles from Stow-on-the-Wold and central for touring the Cotswold villages and surrounding towns. All rooms (one on the ground floor) are comfortably furnished and have tea/coffee making facilities, radio, colour television, armchairs and electric blankets for those colder nights. Bedtime drinks and biscuits are provided. Good English breakfast. No smoking. Pub within walking distance. Internet access available.

Bed & Breakfast per night: double room from £50.00–£54.00

Bedrooms: 2 double, 1 twin
Bathrooms: 2 en-suite, 1 private
Parking: 3 spaces
Open: March–November

124 Damon's Motel

◆◆◆◆

997 Doddington Road, Lincoln, LN6 3SE **Tel:** (01522) 887733 **Fax:** (01522) 887734

Damon's is a beautiful, superior-grade motel, conveniently situated on the Lincoln by-pass. All rooms have either a king-size double bed, or two single beds, all with en-suite facilities. Each room has satellite television, tea/coffee making facilities, direct dial telephone and hairdryer. Enjoy the indoor family swimming pool, gym and solarium. The motel is adjacent to the celebrated Damon's American Restaurant and Lounge Bar which serves food from breakfast through to dinner. Accessible Mobility 2

Bed & Breakfast per night: single occupancy from £51.25–£54.25; double room from £57.40–£60.40

Bedrooms: 27 double, 20 twin/family
Bathrooms: 47 en-suite
Parking: 47 spaces
Cards accepted: Mastercard, Visa, Switch/ Delta, Amex, Diners, Solo

At-a-glance symbols are explained on the flap inside the back cover

125 Welbeck Cottage

◆◆◆◆

19 Meadow Lane, South Hykeham, Lincoln, LN6 9PF **Tel:** (01522) 692669 **Fax:** (01522) 692669
E-mail: mad@wellbeck1.demon.co.uk

Margaret and Philip extend a warm welcome to their 120 year old cottage set in a quiet village six miles from Lincoln city centre, castle and cathedral. South Hykeham old village is surrounded by unspoilt countryside, close to Whisby Nature Park and historic Doddington Hall. Enjoy the comfort of your en-suite bedroom or join us in the conservatory, cottage garden, or in the family sitting room with real open fire in the winter. Home cooked evening meals are available by arrangement.

Bed & Breakfast per night: single occupancy £22.00; double room £40.00
Dinner, Bed & Breakfast per person, per night: £30.00
Evening meal: by arrangement

Bedrooms: 2 double, 1 twin
Bathrooms: 3 en-suite
Parking: 3 spaces

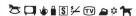

126 Barnsdale Lodge Hotel & Restaurants   ★★★ Silver Award

The Avenue, Exton, Oakham, Leicestershire LE15 8AH **Tel:** (01572) 724678 **Fax:** (01572) 724961
Web: www.barnsdalelodge.co.uk **E-mail:** reservations@barnsdalelodge.co.uk

Set in the heart of Rutland's beautiful countryside overlooking Rutland Water, this 17th-century farmhouse welcomes you with luxury and warmth. Traditional English fayre, using fresh, locally-grown produce, is served in an Edwardian dining room. International wines complement the menus. Afternoon tea, elevenses and buttery lunches are available in the conservatory. Our 46 en-suite bedrooms are filled with antique furniture. The ideal retreat from everyday life. Come and discover the tranquillity of Rutland.
 Accessible Mobility 2

Bed & Breakfast per night: single room from £75.00; double room from £99.50
Dinner, Bed & Breakfast per person, per night: from £75.00 (min 2 nights)
Lunch available: 1200–1415 (hot) and 1200–1430 (cold)

Evening meal: 1900 (last orders 2145)
Bedrooms: 8 single, 24 double, 9 twin, 2 family, 5 suites **Bathrooms:** 46 en-suite
Parking: 250 spaces
Cards accepted: Mastercard, Visa, Switch/Delta, Amex, Diners, Eurocard, JCB

127 Spanhoe Lodge   ◆◆◆◆ Gold Award

Harringworth Road, Laxton, Corby, Northamptonshire NN17 3AT   **Tel:** (01780) 450328 **Fax:** (01780) 450328
Web: www.spanhoelodge.co.uk **E-mail:** jennie.spanhoe@virgin.net

Jennie and Steve assure you of a very warm welcome at their home in picturesque, rural East of England. Set in the Welland Valley in the heart of Rockingham Forest, we are the only GOLD awarded establishment in the area. All our luxuriously appointed rooms are en-suite with television/video, a wide range of toiletries and a full hospitality tray. Our popular gourmet breakfasts are tailored to your specific requirements. We are conveniently situated for Uppingham, Oundle, Corby, Rutland Water and Stamford. You will not be disappointed!

Bed & Breakfast per night: single occupancy from £45.00–£60.00; double room from £60.00–£70.00

Bedrooms: 2 double, 2 twin
Bathrooms: 4 en-suite
Parking: 12 spaces
Cards accepted: Mastercard, Visa, Switch/Delta, Solo

128 The Old Bridge Hotel   ★★★ Silver Award

1 High Street, Huntingdon, Cambridgeshire PE29 3TQ **Tel:** (01480) 458410 **Fax:** (01480) 411017
Web: www.huntsbridge.com **E-mail:** oldbridge@huntsbridge.co.uk

A handsome 18th-century building overlooking the River Ouse, and yet only 500 yards from the town centre. The atmosphere of a beautiful luxurious hotel, yet also a busy meeting place for the local community. All rooms are individually decorated, with satellite televisions, power showers, air conditioning and CD-stereos. An eclectic, modern menu (AA 2 Rosettes), winner of the AA Wine Award 1999 (for the UK's best wine list) and real ales highly acclaimed by CAMRA. Privately owned and personally run by Martin and Jayne Lee and John Hoskins.

Bed & Breakfast per night: single room from £90.00–£120.00; double room from £120.00–£180.00
Dinner, Bed & Breakfast per person, per night: £75.00–£120.00
Lunch available: 1200–1430

Evening meal: 1800 (last orders 2200)
Bedrooms: 6 single, 16 double, 2 twin
Bathrooms: 24 en-suite
Parking: 75 spaces
Cards accepted: Mastercard, Visa, Switch/Delta, Amex, Diners

129 The Meadow House

2A High Street, Burwell, Cambridge, Cambridgeshire CB5 0HB **Tel:** (01638) 741926 or (01638) 741354 **Fax:** (01638) 741861
Web: www.themeadowhouse.co.uk **E-mail:** hilary@themeadowhouse.co.uk

The Meadow House, Burwell is an exceptional, modern property set in two acres of wooded grounds. King-size luxury beds, suite of rooms with balcony available. Large car park. No smoking. Close to Cambridge, Newmarket racecourse, Ely and the Fens. Please look on our website for more colour pictures inside and out and for our exact location.

Bed & Breakfast per night: single occupancy from £25.00–£30.00; double room from £48.00–£52.00

Bedrooms: 2 double, 2 twin, 2 family, 1 suite
Bathrooms: 4 en-suite, 3 shared
Parking: 16 spaces

130 Holly Lodge ◆◆◆◆◆ Gold Award

The Street, Thursford Green, Fakenham, Norfolk NR21 0AS **Tel:** (01328) 878465 **Fax:** (01328) 878465
Web: www.hollylodgeguesthouse.co.uk **E-mail:** hollyguestlodge@btopenworld.com

'Highly Commended B&B/Guesthouse of the Year' as judged by the East of England Tourist Board in the regional England in Excellence Awards 2002. A warm and welcoming atmosphere awaits you at our 18th-century house and private guest cottages. Set in beautiful landscaped gardens with a fruit orchard and outdoor guest sundeck overlooking wildlife pond/water gardens and open farmland. Each cottage offers individual period charm – stylish and comfortably furnished with many thoughtful touches. A fine home-cooked breakfast is served in the sumptuous main dining room. Private conservatory guest lounge. Ideally located for the stunning North Norfolk coast and countryside.

Bed & Breakfast per night: single occupancy from £50.00–£70.00; double room from £60.00–£80.00

Bedrooms: 2 double, 1 twin
Bathrooms: 3 en-suite
Parking: 4 spaces
Open: March–December, excluding October

131 Priestfields ◆◆◆◆ Silver Award

6B North Street, Sheringham, Norfolk NR26 8LW **Tel:** (01263) 820305 **Fax:** (01263) 820125
E-mail: david.phillips10@which.net

Overlooking a long, south-facing lawn, this Edwardian gentleman's residence has been recently renovated to provide exclusive and interesting accommodation on a quiet residential street close to the sea and town centre. The two en-suite double bedrooms are luxuriously appointed with armchairs, colour teletext televisions, radio/alarms and hot beverage facilities. Guests may relax in the sun lounge or sit outside in the lovely garden. Sorry there are no facilities for children or pets and the house is non-smoking throughout. Off road and garage parking available.

Bed & Breakfast per night: double room from £50.00–£60.00

Bedrooms: 2 double
Bathrooms: 2 en-suite
Parking: 2 spaces

132 Felbrigg Lodge

◆◆◆◆◆ Gold Award

Aylmerton, Norfolk NR11 8RA **Tel:** (01263) 837588 **Fax:** (01263) 838012
Web: www.felbrigglodge.co.uk **E-mail:** info@felbrigglodge.co.uk

Set in beautiful countryside two miles from the coast, Felbrigg Lodge is hidden in eight acres of spectacular woodland gardens. Great care is taken to preserve an atmosphere of peace and tranquillity. Large en-suite rooms are all luxuriously decorated with every facility. Indoor heated pool and small gym. Copious breakfasts. Michelin recommended. WHG recommended. Johansen recommended.

Bed & Breakfast per night: single room from £65.00–£100.00; double room from £84.00–£116.00; suite £148.00

Bedrooms: 2 double/twin, 1 suite
Bathrooms: 3 en-suite
Parking: 6 spaces
Open: February–November
Cards accepted: Mastercard, Visa, Switch/Delta, Debit/Connect

Norfolk Lavender

The Romans used lavender daily. They used it as a healing agent and as an insect repellent, in massage oils and to scent their bath water. Indeed, the name of the genus to which all species of lavender belong, *Lavandula*, derives from the Latin word meaning 'for washing'. Whether the Romans brought lavender to England or whether it was already growing here is uncertain, but Roman soldiers settling here would certainly have planted it as part of their herbal first-aid kit. Similarly, lavender was grown for medicinal uses in medieval monastic gardens. The dried flowers were used in Tudor times to scent chests and closets and to keep bedbugs at bay. Its cleansing properties were particularly valued during the plague of 1665, when the street cries of lavender sellers were part of everyday urban life. Victorian women used lavender perfume lavishly to scent themselves, their linen and their clothes.

In Victorian days there were a number of famous lavender fields in the south of England but in the early years of this century the bushes were attacked by a deadly disease, shab, and very little has been commercially grown since.

However, Norfolk Lavender at Heacham in Norfolk, which was founded in 1932, still grows seven varieties of lavender – five for distilling and two for drying. The fields are harvested – mechanically – from about mid-July, roughly one third of the crop being used as flowers for potpourris and sachets, two thirds for distilling. The flowers for drying are packed loosely into sacks through which warm air is blown for several days. The flower heads are then removed from the stalks and sifted. The distilling process is an ancient one. Lavender's fragrance is contained in the oil stored in glands at the base of each floret and this oil is extracted by steam distillation. About 500lb (230kg) of flowers, stalks and all, are loaded into each still while one of the workers stands in it treading them down. Steam is then passed through the still and the mixture of steam and oil vapour passes to the condenser. The pure essential oil then collects in the separator and is drawn off, at the rate of about half a litre per still-load. The oil is matured for a year before being blended with other oils and fixatives.

133 Pheasant Cottage

Long Common Lane, Swanton Abbott, Norwich, Norfolk NR10 5BH **Tel:** (01692) 538169 **Fax:** (01692) 538169
E-mail: melanie@pheasantcottage.freeserve.co.uk

In a particularly beautiful corner of North Norfolk, on the edge of a quiet village, this 17th-century detached cottage has been lovingly transformed to create a home of exceptional quality. Boasting oak beams, attractive furnishings, and stunning views across fields to the church. Delicious breakfasts, homemade bread and preserves served in our spacious dining room in the rennovated old stables with high beamed ceilings overlooking open fields and pretty patio garden. Private gardens featuring orchard, log cabin and many sitting out areas with patio and decking terraces, available to guests. Colour brochure available.

Bed & Breakfast per night: single room from £55.00–£65.00; double room from £60.00–£79.00

Bedrooms: 1 single, 2 double, 1 twin
Bathrooms: 2 en-suite
Parking: 5 spaces

134 Marsham Arms Inn

Holt Road, Hevingham, Norwich NR10 5NP **Tel:** (01603) 754268
Web: www.marshamarms.co.uk **E-mail:** nigelbradley@marshamarms.co.uk

Set in peaceful countryside on the B1149 north of Horsford. Located within 15 miles of the Broads and the coast and five miles from Norwich. Comfortable garden rooms all set on ground floor with plentiful parking. Real ales and an extensive wine list complement the traditionally styled menu featuring fresh fish, steak and kidney pie and many homemade specialities. Non smoking dining area and cheerful staff offer relaxed and friendly service.

Bed & Breakfast per night: single occupancy from £48.00–£55.00; double room from £70.00–£85.00
Lunch available: 1130–1430
Evening meal: 1800 (last orders 2130)

Bedrooms: 8 double/twin, 2 family
Bathrooms: 10 en-suite
Parking: 80 spaces
Cards accepted: Mastercard, Visa, Switch/Delta

135 Frogs Hall Farm

      ◆◆◆◆ Silver Award

Woodgate, Swanton Morley, East Dereham, Norfolk NR20 4NX **Tel:** (01362) 638355 or (07879) 885136 **Fax:** (01362) 638355
Web: www.frogs-hall.fsnet.co.uk **E-mail:** accommodation@frogs-hall.fsnet.co.uk

Luxurious comfort and tranquillity await you at Frogs Hall Farm – delightfully secluded, yet easily accessible. Wander throughout the 20 acres of paddocks and enjoy the wildlife in and around the lake and ponds. Guests are welcome to use the drawing room at anytime or make use of the covered swimming pool and jacuzzi (seasonal). Enjoy the friendly, relaxed atmosphere. Dereham is at the heart of Norfolk, an ideal touring base, with excellent meals served in local pubs. All rooms have tea/coffee-making facilities and colour television.

Bed & Breakfast per night: double room from £50.00–£60.00

Bedrooms: 1 double, 1 twin, 1 family
Bathrooms: 2 en-suite, 1 private
Parking: Unlimited

136 Marriott Sprowston Manor Hotel & Country Club ★★★★ Silver Award

Sprowston Park, Wroxham Road, Norwich, Norfolk NR7 8RP **Tel:** 0870 400 7229 **Fax:** 0870 400 7329
Web: www.marriott.co.uk/nwigs **E-mail:** sprowston.manor@marriotthotels.co.uk

This beautiful manor house comes into view as you approach down the tree lined drive. Set in 170 acres of mature parkland, Sprowston Manor is Norfolk's premier golf and leisure resort surrounded by its own 18-hole championship golf course, host venue to the PGA Europro tour in 2004. An idyllic retreat offering La Fontana health spa which is complemented by a stunning tropical feel pool area plus gym. Dine in the AA Rosette Manor restaurant offering fine cuisine and attentive service or new Zest Café Bar Restaurant open early 2004. A real treat!

Bed & Breakfast per night: single occupancy from £105.00–£210.00; double room from £130.00–£260.00
Dinner, Bed & Breakfast per person, per night: £87.00–£165.00
Lunch available: 1230–1400

Evening meal: 1900 (last orders 2130)
Bedrooms: 42 double, 31 twin, 21 suites
Bathrooms: 94 en-suite
Parking: 150 spaces
Cards accepted: Mastercard, Visa, Switch/Delta, Amex, Diners

137 The Old Vicarage ◆◆◆◆ Silver Award

48 The Street, Brooke, Norwich, Norfolk NR15 1JU **Tel:** (01508) 558329

Situated in the award-winning village of Brooke in a peaceful and secluded situation with extensive gardens. Within seven miles of the centre of Norwich, on the B1332 Norwich–Bungay road, and within easy reach of the Suffolk heritage coast and Norfolk Broads. One large four-poster room with adjoining private bathroom and one twin bedroom with en-suite shower room. Private sitting room with television available for guests' use. We are a no smoking house. No children under 15 years.

Bed & Breakfast per night: double room £50.00
Dinner, Bed & Breakfast per person, per night: £40.50
Evening meal: 1900

Bedrooms: 2 double
Bathrooms: 2 en-suite
Parking: 4 spaces

138 Swan Hotel ★★★ Silver Award

Market Place, Southwold, Suffolk IP18 6EG **Tel:** (01502) 722186 **Fax:** (01502) 724800
Web: www.adnams.co.uk **E-mail:** swan.reception@adnams.co.uk

The Swan has stood in the Market Place since medieval times and remains one of Southwold's prized buildings. Undoubtably the most important and thriving inn in Southwold, The Swan has the reputation of being the historic centre of gossip, entertainment and local politics. Local produce is at the heart of creating sumptuous menus for The Swan's 2 AA Rosette dining room. Exciting renovations in 2003 have seen the addition of two new 'show case' rooms – 'Mr Crisps' and 'The Admirals' – which offer that extra special touch ensuring your visit to The Swan shall not be your last.

Bed & Breakfast per night: single room from £70.00–£85.00; double room from £130.00–£210.00
Dinner, Bed & Breakfast per person, per night: £75.00–£105.00 (winter only, min 2 nights, Sunday Thursday)

Lunch available: 1200–1430
Evening meal: 1900 (last orders 2130)
Bedrooms: 3 single, 23 double, 14 twin, 2 suites **Bathrooms:** 42 en-suite
Cards accepted: Mastercard, Visa, Switch/Delta

139 The Old Convent

♦♦♦♦

The Street, Kettlebaston, Ipswich IP7 7QA **Tel:** (01449) 741557
Web: www.kettlebaston.fsnet.co.uk **E-mail:** holidays@kettlebaston.fsnet.co.uk

A warm and friendly welcome awaits you at our Grade II listed 17th-century thatched house, situated within the tranquillity of a small Suffolk village. Our three bedrooms (one twin and two double), all have en-suite facilities; one with whirlpool bath. Hairdryer available on request. We are centrally situated to explore the many treasures of East Anglia, including Lavenham, Long Melford and Constable Country. Recently refurbished to a fine standard. Seasonal log fire. Guests' television/ video lounge. Colour brochure available. We aim to treat our guests as we ourselves expect to be treated.

Bed & Breakfast per night: single occupancy from £30.00–£45.00; double room from £50.00–£65.00

Bedrooms: 3 double/twin
Bathrooms: 3 en-suite
Parking: 4 spaces

Brasses of East Anglia

East Anglia has a plethora of superb churches that house a wealth of medieval art. One branch of this is that of the monumental brass. Created to mark a grave and to glorify the dead person, brasses are now a lesson in medieval life. The inscriptions provide information on local families, the coats of arms give genealogical material, the depictions of the men, women and children are a source book for costume.

The earliest brasses date from the late 13th and early 14th centuries. In Isleham church in Cambridgeshire, for instance, Sir Geoffrey Bernard is dated to 1275 by the type of tailed surcoat he wears over his armour. Many soldiers are shown lying with a dog as a foot-rest – as at Trumpington, another Cambridgeshire church. This brass is in memory of Sir Roger Trumpington, who died in 1289, and here his dog bites the scabbard of his sword. Sir Roger was a Crusader – a fact indicated by his crossed legs. The most famous military brass in England, however, is that of Sir Robert de Bures in Acton, Suffolk, dated to 1302. He, too, was a Crusader and wears a splendid set of chainmail, with decorative knee-pieces of cuir-bouilli (boiled leather), pryck spurs and a surcoat whose folds are gathered with a waist-girdle.

Other brasses show husband and wife side by side, sometimes with rows of children too. John Daye, the printer, is commemorated in Little Bradley, Suffolk, with a wife, six sons and five daughters, plus two babies under the table. Weston Colville, Cambridgeshire has two good brasses: one to Sir Robert Leverer (1427), depicted in armour and surrounded by flowers, beside his wife in flowing head dress. In the same church, a brass in a much later style (1636) to Abraham Gates shows him with his wife at a prie-dieu and surrounded by cherubs, skulls and an angel with trumpet flying off to tell St Peter of his arrival. The earliest known brass of a priest in a cope is found in East Anglia, at Fulbourn, Cambridgeshire.

Since they are floor monuments, brasses have always been subjected to heavy wear and their conservation is now of great concern. The best places to take rubbings are brass-rubbing centres such as that in St Mary's Church, Bury St Edmunds, the Cambridge Brass Rubbing Centre, or Ely Cathedral, where replicas from all over Britain include the elegant Lady Margaret Peyton II of Isleham.

140 Seckford Hall Hotel

★★★ Silver Award

Woodbridge, Suffolk IP13 6NU **Tel:** (01394) 385678 **Fax:** (01394) 380610
Web: www.seckford.co.uk **E-mail:** reception@seckford.co.uk

A romantic Elizabethan mansion set in 32 acres of landscaped gardens and woodlands. Personally supervised by the owners, Seckford Hall is a haven of seclusion and tranquillity. Oak panelling, beamed ceilings, antique furniture, four-poster bedrooms, suites, leisure club with indoor pool, beauty salon, gym and spa bath and adjacent 18-hole golf course. Two restaurants featuring fresh lobster and game from local farms, extensive wine cellar. Picturesque Woodbridge with its tide mill, antique shops and yacht harbour is a short walk away. 'Constable Country' and Suffolk coast nearby.

Bed & Breakfast per night: single room from £85.00–£130.00; double room from £130.00–£200.00
Lunch available: 1200–1430
Evening meal: 1915 (last orders 2130)

Bedrooms: 3 single, 14 double, 10 twin, 4 family
Bathrooms: 32 en-suite
Cards accepted: Mastercard, Visa, Switch/Delta, Amex, Diners, Eurocard, JCB

141 Wentworth Hotel

★★★ Silver Award

Wentworth Road, Aldeburgh, Suffolk IP15 5BD **Tel:** (01728) 452312 **Fax:** (01728) 454343
Web: www.wentworth-aldeburgh.com **E-mail:** stay@wentworth-aldeburgh.co.uk

With the comfort and style of a country hotel, Wentworth Hotel sits facing the sea on the Suffolk coast. Two comfortable lounges with antique furniture and open fires provide ample space to relax. Each bedroom has colour television, telephone, radio, hairdryer, tea making facilities and many have sea views. The AA Rosette restaurant serves a variety of fresh produce, including local seafood. Choose a light lunch from the bar menu and, weather permitting, eat outside in the sunken terrace garden. Year-round bargain get-aways available.

Bed & Breakfast per night: single room from £69.00–£76.00; double room from £112.00–£160.00
Dinner, Bed & Breakfast per person, per night: £66.50–£90.00
Evening meal: 1900 (last orders 2100)

Bedrooms: 4 single, 10 double, 21 twin
Bathrooms: 35 en-suite
Parking: 30 spaces
Open: 9 January–27 December
Cards accepted: Mastercard, Visa, Switch/Delta, Amex, Diners, Eurocard

142 White Lion Hotel

★★★ Silver Award

Market Cross Place, Aldeburgh, Suffolk IP15 5BJ **Tel:** (01728) 452720 **Fax:** (01728) 452986
Web: www.whitelion.co.uk **E-mail:** whitelionaldeburgh@btinternet.com

Located in the centre of Aldeburgh, an historic fishing town on the Suffolk Heritage coast. Some bedrooms overlook the beach where fresh fish is sold from traditional wooden huts lining the shore. The White Lion offers the highest levels of quality and service, and the bedrooms provide every comfort. Four-poster rooms are available for special occasions. Restaurant 1563, named after the year the hotel was built, is ideal for elegant dining with oak-panelled walls and a roaring log fire in winter. Informal meals are also served in the welcoming bar.

Bed & Breakfast per night: single room from £61.00–£86.00; double room from £96.00–£160.00
Dinner, Bed & Breakfast per person, per night: £53.00–£98.00 (min 2 nights, 2 sharing)
Lunch available: 1200–1400
Evening meal: 1900 (last orders 2100)

Bedrooms: 4 single, 19 double, 14 twin, 1 family
Bathrooms: 38 en-suite
Parking: 15 spaces
Cards accepted: Mastercard, Visa, Switch/Delta, Amex, Diners, Eurocard

At-a-glance symbols are explained on the flap inside the back cover

143 The Brudenell Hotel

★★★ Silver Award

The Parade, Aldeburgh, Suffolk IP15 5BU **Tel:** (01728) 452071 **Fax:** (01728) 454082
Web: www.brudenellhotel.co.uk **E-mail:** info@brudenellhotel.co.uk

The newly refurbished Brudenell Hotel is just a step away from the beach in Aldeburgh. 42 bedrooms including superior and de luxe rooms – several enjoying views of the sea, river or marshlands. Our AA Rosette restaurant, with its panoramic views, offers the very best of fresh local produce, with seafood and grills a speciality, and is open for lunch and dinner. The terrace is ideal for al fresco dining during the summer months. Our new bar also serves morning coffee and afternoon teas.

Bed & Breakfast per night: single room from £61.00–£91.00; double room from £96.00– £186.00
Dinner, Bed & Breakfast per person, per night: £56.00–£110.00 (min 2 nights, 2 sharing)
Lunch available: 1200–1430

Evening meal: 1800 (last orders 2145)
Bedrooms: 6 single, 27 double, 7 twin, 1 family, 1 suite **Bathrooms:** 42 en-suite
Parking: 15 spaces
Cards accepted: Mastercard, Visa, Switch/ Delta, Amex, Diners, Eurocard

144 Marriott Hanbury Manor Hotel & Country Club

★★★★★ Gold Award

Ware, Hertfordshire SG12 0SD **Tel:** (01920) 487722 **Fax:** (01920) 487692
Web: www.hanbury-manor.com **E-mail:** guestrelations.hanburymanor@marriotthotels.co.uk

'London's Favourite Hotel and Country Club' provides the perfect location for every occasion. Set in 200 acres of Hertfordshire countryside, yet just 25 miles from Central London and 16 miles from Stansted Airport. Hanbury Manor combines luxurious accommodation with exemplary service and a choice of award-winning cuisine in either the traditional fine dining Zodiac Restaurant or the more contemporary-style Oakes Grill. All this is complemented by a PGA championship golf course and an excellent health and beauty spa.

Room only per night: from £139.00

Bedrooms: 105 double, 56 twin
Bathrooms: 161 en-suite
Cards accepted: Mastercard, Visa, Switch/ Delta, Amex, Diners

145 Canfield Moat

 ◆◆◆◆◆ Gold Award

High Cross Lane West, Little Canfield, Dunmow, Essex CM6 1TD **Tel:** (01371) 872565 or 07811 165049 **Fax:** (01371) 876264
Web: www.canfieldmoat.co.uk **E-mail:** falk@canfieldmoat.co.uk

A peaceful Georgian rectory set among eight acres in the heart of the Essex countryside yet only ten minutes from the M11 and Stansted Airport and within easy reach of London, Cambridge and 'Constable Country'. The large, elegant en-suite bedrooms are supplied with almost every conceivable luxury. Breakfasts include our own eggs and produce from our vegetable garden, and guests are welcome to use the tennis court, croquet lawn and, in season, heated outdoor pool. There is a good selection of pubs and restaurants nearby.

Bed & Breakfast per night: single occupancy from £40.00–£50.00; double room from £60.00– £70.00

Bedrooms: 1 double, 1 twin
Bathrooms: 2 en-suite
Parking: 8 spaces
Open: all year except Christmas/New Year

146 Garnish Hall

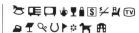 ◆ ◆ ◆ ◆ Silver Award

Margaret Roding, Dunmow, Essex CM6 1QL **Tel:** (01245) 231209 **Fax:** (01245) 231224
E-mail: anna@garnishhall.fsnet.co.uk

Garnish Hall is the home of Anna, a nurse, Peter a surgeon and Bruno the Jack Russell. Parts of the Hall date back to the 14th century. There is a partially walled back garden and two ponds with fish. The peace is only disturbed by bantams, the black swans and geese. There is a Norman church, with reputedly the finest doorway in Essex, adjacent to the grounds. Recommended by "Which?"

Bed & Breakfast per night: single occupancy from £40.00–£55.00; double room from £80.00– £100.00
Dinner, Bed & Breakfast per person, per night: £75.00

Lunch available: soup and sandwiches anytime by agreement, £10 per person
Evening meal: by prior arrangement
Bedrooms: 2 double, 1 family
Bathrooms: 2 en-suite, 1 private
Parking: ample

Greensted's Log Church

St Andrew's Church, Greensted, near Chipping Ongar in Essex, has long been famed as the oldest wooden building in Europe, and the oldest wooden church in the world. In 1995, however, its nave timbers were submitted to dendrochronological examination, a method of dating wood by examining the spacing of its tree rings. Embarrassingly, given that the church's fame lay in part in its antiquity, the tests revealed that the oldest sections of the building were 220 years younger than had previously been thought. Instead of dating from Saxon times (around 845AD) the church could not have been built earlier than 1066, the date of the Norman conquest.

The new date also threw into doubt one of the most significant events in the church's history: its rôle as a resting place for the body of the martyred King Edmund on its way from London to Bury St Edmunds. The church makes much of this claim, with a stained glass window dedicated to the saint, a picture of his martyrdom, and a finely carved beam depicting one of the legends surrounding his death. But Edmund's body was transported in 1013, some half century before the present church was built. Though it is likely that there were earlier buildings on the site, this particular structure clearly never housed the saint.

The claims of being the oldest wooden building, however, still stand. The primitive wooden church now forms the nave of the present building and is constructed from huge logs, split in half and joined with wooden wedges; the rounded sides of the logs form the exterior wall, while the smooth sides face the interior. The original church had no windows and was lit by oil lamps, and it is thought that dark patches in the wood may be scorch marks.

The early church has undergone a gradual transformation, with substantial additions in Tudor and Victorian times, and now has every appearance of a pretty English parish church, lovingly cared for in neatly manicured surroundings. Only its heavy wooden walls hark back to a darker age, when religion and civilisation maintained a tenuous footing in wild, forested lands. Greensted church is now one of the most visited in the country, attracting some 100,000 visitors every year.

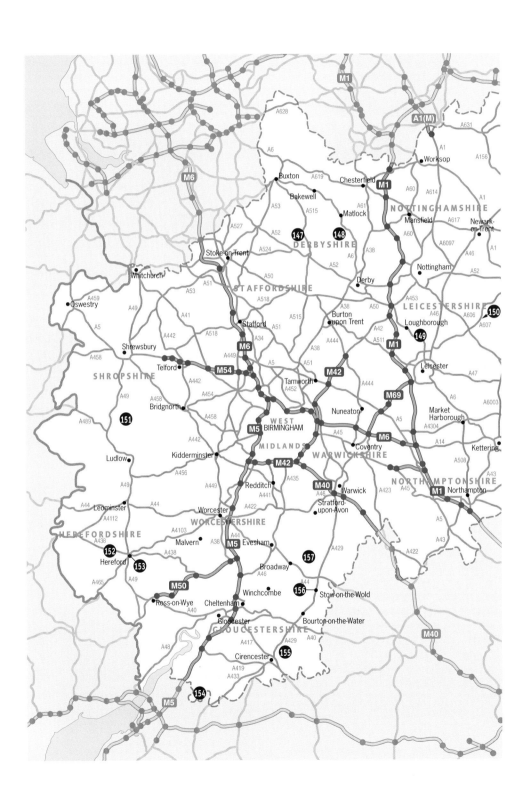

147 Dove Cottage Fishing Lodge ★ ★ ★ ★ ★

Lode Mill, Alstonefield, Ashbourne, Derbyshire **Web:** www.dovecottages.co.uk
Contact: Ms Hignett, Foxleaze Court, Preston, Cirencester, Gloucestershire GL7 5PS
Tel: (01285) 655875 or 07974 718067 **Fax:** (01285) 655885 **E-mail:** info@dovecottages.co.uk

Situated in a beautiful and idyllic part of Wolfscote Dale, enjoying stunning views along the River Dove. Recently refurbished throughout, relax in a comfortable and highly maintained family home. Fires laid daily, welcome grocery basket and even hand cream! We have everything to make your stay relaxing and easy, from electric blankets to tumble drier. Large gardens (one enclosed), toys, videos and ride-ons. There is something for everyone; fantastic fishing, walks and scenery. Excellent local culture, heritage and hospitality. Dogs welcome. Two seasonal rods on River Dove included.

Low season per week: £275.00–£480.00
High season per week: £760.00–£990.00

1 cottage: sleeping 5/6 people

148 Hog Cottage ★ ★ ★ ★

Gorsey Bank, Wirksworth, Matlock, Derbyshire **Web:** www.bluelagoon.co.uk
Contact: Mrs Fern, Blue Lagoon, 46 London Road, Alderley Edge, Cheshire SK9 7DZ
Tel: (01625) 583107 **Fax:** (01625) 890001 **E-mail:** anna@bluelagoon.co.uk

A south-facing stone cottage offering pure luxury. Carefully renovated to retain the original features, this beautiful cottage is set high in the hills, overlooking the historic market town of Wirksworth in Derbyshire – Hog Cottage has an idyllic settng. The cottage offers a cosy lounge, a relaxing snug, which leads into a luxuriously appointed kitchen. Just off the kitchen is a good size dining room that leads out onto the secure patio area. There are two double bedrooms and a luxuriously appointed bathroom with bath and separate power shower.

Low season per week: £230.00–£300.00
High season per week: £390.00–£430.00
Short breaks: from £150.00 (except during school holidays)

1 cottage: sleeping 4 people
Cards accepted: Mastercard, Visa, Switch/ Delta, Amex

149 Kingfisher Cottage ★ ★ ★ ★

Barrow upon Soar, Loughborough, Leicestershire **Web:** www.AnEnglishCottage.com
Contact: Mr D Petty, 634 Pine Street, Philadelphia, PA 19106, USA
Tel: (1) 215 925-4648 **Fax:** (1) 215 925-2126 **E-mail:** nikkidavid@aol.com

Kingfisher Cottage was built as a mill worker's dwelling at 19th-century's end. Situated roadside in a quiet corner of Barrow upon Soar in Leicestershire, it backs on to the Grand Union Canal, separated from the waterside by a sizeable, mainly lawned garden. The location is convenient for shops, pubs, eating establishments, public transportation and the railway station – all only minutes' walk away. Recently extensively remodelled to accommodate up to six, the cottage has much to offer the most discerning visitor.

Low season per week: £400.00–£500.00
High season per week: £600.00–£600.00
Short breaks: from £190.00–£275.00

1 cottage: sleeping 4/6 people

150 28 Melton Road

★★★★

Waltham on the Wolds, Melton Mowbray, Leicestershire
Contact: Mrs Watchorn, Chester House, 26 Melton Road, Waltham on the Wolds, Melton Mowbray, Leicestershire LE14 4AJ
Tel: (01664) 464255 **Fax:** (01664) 464130 **E-mail:** awatchorn1314@yahoo.com

Delightful stone cottage within the Vale of Belvoir overlooking open countryside. Close to village amenities and local pub with good cuisine. Footpaths and bridleways close by, with coarse fishing available within the village. Large breakfast kitchen recently refurbished to high specifications. Cosy sitting room, with open fireplace, and separate dining room to seat 6–8 people (bedroom 3). Spacious family bathroom on first floor. Sleeps up to 6 people. Private garden and off-road parking adjacent to cottage.

Low season per week: £175.00–£275.00
High season per week: £275.00–£400.00
Short breaks: details available on request

1 cottage: sleeping 6 people

DW

Brewers of Burton-upon-Trent

The smell of hops and malt pervades the town of Burton-upon-Trent, the centre of British brewing. No fewer than three major breweries are here: Carlsberg Tetley, Marston's and Bass. The historic reason for their presence is the mineral-rich water drawn from local sources and found to be especially suitable for brewing beer; the old wells with romantic sounding names – Nile and Cairo, The Hay, Andressey – are still tapped. Today, however, the water has to be completely purified before being used in lager (more popular than beer these days) and, if needed for beer-making, the all-important minerals, calcium and magnesium salts, now have to be added afresh!

The history of the industry dates back to medieval times when ales were brewed here by the monks of Burton Abbey. Despite the dissolution of the monastery in the 16th century, brewing continued in Burton, and was well-established when William Bass set up his brewery in the 18th century. When the Trade Marks Act was introduced in 1875 Bass, with its famous red triangle, was the first company to register; it is said that a loyal company

employee spent an uncomfortable night outside the registrar's office in order to be first in the queue. The Bass family gave the town some of its finest buildings including the Town Hall, St Paul's Institute and St Paul's Church. Michael Arthur Bass, who became Lord Burton in 1886, also paid for the development of Kind Edward's Place and the building of the Ferry Bridge.

The Bass Museum throws light on the company's historic role in the brewing history of Burton-upon-Trent. Exhibits include items from its transport fleet, such as its famous Daimler (shaped like a beer bottle) and its four splendid shire horses (the company once used more than 90 shire horses to deliver its beer). The museum also offers tours of the modern brewery where the complicated stages in the brewing process – malting, milling, mashing, boiling, cooling, fermenting and canning – can be observed firsthand. Here, too, visitors can familiarise themselves with the arcane terminology of brewing. Intriguing words such as barm, grist, mash, shive, sparging, trub and wort are all part of the brewer's vocabulary.

Marston's, too, offers tours of its traditional Victorian brewery for groups of between 10 and 50.

151 Eaton Manor Rural Escapes

★ ★ ★ ★

Eaton Manor, Eaton-under-Heywood, Church Stretton, Shropshire **Web:** eatonmanor.co.uk
Contact: Eaton Manor Rural Escapes, Eaton Manor, Eaton-under-Heywood, Church Stretton, Shropshire SY6 7DH
Tel: (01694) 724814 **Fax:** (01694) 722048 **E-mail:** ruralescapes@eatonmanor.co.uk

Rural luxury in our 17th-century manor house on our 500-acre estate in an unspoilt valley between the Wenlock Edge and the Shropshire Hills. Facilities include an indoor pool (April–October), sauna, four-poster beds, Aga, beams, inglenook fireplace and more… an acre of private stream side gardens, three-course dinner and daily maid service available, and livery for your horse. We welcome non-smokers, children and well-behaved dogs. Short breaks available. Convenient location for Ludlow, Shrewsbury and Ironbridge. Call for our latest brochure or be tempted by our website.

Low season per week: £595.00–£685.00
High season per week: £760.00–£1490.00
Short breaks: from £416.00–£450.00

1 house: sleeping 9 + 3 people

DW

Cruck-framed Houses

The Midlands are particularly rich in timber-framed or, to use the popular term, half-timbered buildings – 'half-timbered' being a reference to the early medieval period when the timbers were formed by cutting logs in half. These buildings are classified as either box-frame construction or cruck construction. By far the more common type was box-frame, where jointed horizontal and vertical timbers formed a wall and either the panels were infilled or the whole wall was covered with some sort of cladding. In the cruck construction, the structure was supported by pairs of inclined, slightly curved timbers that normally met at the ridge of the roof and were tied by a collar or tie-beam, making an A shape. These timbers, called crucks or blades, were spaced at regular intervals along the building to take the weight of the roof and often of the walls too. Wherever possible crucks were cut from the trunk of one tree split along its length to get a symmetrical arch. Alternatively, they were taken from trees with a natural curve in the trunk and blades matched as closely as possible.

There were various forms of cruck construction, the most important being full cruck, base or truncated cruck, raised cruck and jointed cruck. Full crucks extend from ground level to the apex.

Base or truncated begin on the ground but stop below the apex and are joined by a tie-beam or collar that supports the roof. Raised crucks start a few feet off the ground in a solid wall, and in jointed cruck construction the curving blade is jointed to a vertical post that begins on the ground.

Many crucks have been incorporated into larger buildings, hidden behind a cladding of stone or brick or plastered over, but where they are visible as the gable end they are an attractive and striking feature. Cruck-framing is particularly prevalent in the Midlands, the North and West (and is more or less entirely absent in East Anglia and the South-East, where box-framing predominates), and it is in Hereford & Worcester that the greatest concentration of cruck buildings is to be found. There are some fine examples in Weobley, unsurpassed for its black-and-white buildings. Explore its streets and you cannot fail to admire the skills of the 15th-, 16th- and 17th-century craftsmen. Other towns in the county worth visiting for their half-timbering are Eardisley, Eardisland, Pembridge and Dilwyn. Some excellent examples of cruck-framed buildings have been reconstructed at the Avoncroft Museum of Historic Buildings in Bromsgrove.

152 Canon Bridge House ★★★★

Canon Bridge, Madley, Hereford **Web:** www.cottageguide.co.uk/canonbridge
Contact: Mrs Anscomb, Canon Bridge House, Canon Bridge, Madley, Hereford HR2 9JF
Tel: (01981) 251104 **Fax:** (01981) 251412 **E-mail:** timothy.anscomb4@virgin.net

The Garden Wing (on right of photograph) is part of a fine Georgian house on the banks of the River Wye in the beautiful, quiet, unspoilt Herefordshire countryside. The extremely spacious elegant accommodation comprises two bedrooms, bathroom, shower room, large farmhouse kitchen with Aga (winter only), sitting room with open fire, bright airy dining room and glorious views over the surrounding countryside. A welcome hamper including home-made bread and marmalade, complimentary toiletries and flowers greet all visitors. Short breaks.

Low season per week: £250.00–£285.00
High season per week: £295.00–£350.00
Short breaks: from £140.00–£210.00

1 house: sleeping 4 people

153 Castle Cliffe East ★★★★

East House, Quay Street, Hereford
Contact: Mr Hubbard or Mr P Wilson,Castle Cliffe West, Quay Street, Hereford, Herefordshire HR1 2NH
Tel: (01432) 272096 or 07786 605123 **E-mail:** mail@castlecliffe.net

Originally a medieval castle watergate, Castle Cliffe has one of the most perfect settings in Hereford. Surrounded by historic parkland and with a south facing riverside garden, it is both wonderfully tranquil and incredibly convenient – the town centre is a two minute walk. Castle Cliffe East has been beautifully restored with period furniture, open fires, a four-poster bed, a gorgeous bathroom complete with 13th-century arch and absolutely no chintz! Castle Cliffe is the perfect place to unwind and shake off those 21st-century blues.

Low season per week: £350.00–£550.00
High season per week: £650.00–£850.00
Short breaks: from £175.00–£325.00 (low season only)

1 house: sleeping 6 people
Cards accepted: on-line booking by credit card is available at www.cottagesdirect.com

154 La Vacherie and The Gunroom ★★★★

The Old Farmhouse, Alderley, Wotton-under-Edge, Gloucestershire **Web:** www.sophiecharles.co.uk
Contact: Sarah Shearer, The Old Farmhouse, Alderley, Wotton-under-Edge, Gloucestershire GL12 7QT
Tel: (01453) 843454 or 07930 367621 **E-mail:** sophiecharlesuk@aol.com

Stunning properties commanding spectacular views over this Area of Outstanding Natural Beauty. The Gunroom is a 1-bedroom converted annexe of the main 18th-century traditional Cotswold stone farmhouse, whilst La Vacherie is a spectacular conversion of two integrated 18th-century and 17th-century barns, retaining original flagstone floors, beams, walls and loads of character features. The heated outdoor pool lends itself well to idle away the summer days. The woodburner is perfect for the cosy winter evenings. Both properties are equipped and furnished to the highest standards.

Low season per week: £250.00–£400.00
High season per week: £400.00–£700.00
Short breaks: from £190.00–£490.00 (low season only)

2 cottages: sleeping 3–7 people

155 Glebe Farm Holiday Lets ★ ★ ★ ★

Glebe Farm, Barnsley Road, Cirencester, Gloucestershire **Web:** www.glebefarmcottages.co.uk
Contact: Mrs P Handover, Glebe Farm, Barnsley Road, Cirencester, Gloucestershire GL7 5DY
Tel: (01285) 659226 **Fax:** (01285) 642622 **E-mail:** enquiries@glebefarmcottages.co.uk

Located in rural surroundings, but only three miles from Cirencester, these fine cottages have been converted to a very high standard, keeping the character with exposed beams and stone. One hour from Stratford-upon-Avon, Bath and Oxford, the cottages make an ideal base for touring the Cotswolds. Perfect for a quiet break in the country. All cottages are fully equipped with all mod cons, with gardens, patios and barbecues. Pets welcome.

Low season per week: £150.00–£275.00
High season per week: £230.00–£490.00
Short breaks: from £100.00–£210.00

5 cottages: sleeping 2–6 people

156 Holly Cottage ★ ★ ★ ★ ★

Stow-on-the-Wold, Cheltenham, Gloucestershire **Web:** www.broadoakcottages.fsnet.co.uk
Contact: Mrs M Wilson, The Counting House, Stow-on-the-Wold, Cheltenham, Gloucestershire GL54 1AL
Tel: (01451) 830794 **Fax:** (01451) 830794 **E-mail:** mary@broadoakcottages.fsnet.co.uk

Holly Cottage is a cosy, period cottage within a few minutes walk of the market square, shops and restaurants. The living room has a beamed ceiling and is furnished with comfortable sofa, chairs, antique pine dresser and dining set. The modern kitchen has a microwave, oven, ceramic hob with extractor, fridge, freezer, washer-dryer machine and dishwasher. The bathroom has a pressure shower over the bath and an airing cupboard. Upstairs are double and twin bedrooms with pretty casement windows with window seats. There is a long south-facing patio overlooking open parkland beyond a long garden.

Low season per week: £275.00–£300.00
High season per week: £300.00–£500.00
Short breaks: from £175.00–£195.00

4 cottages: sleeping 4 people

157 Fox Cottage ★ ★ ★ ★

Stapenhill Farmhouse, Paxford, Chipping Campden, Gloucestershire **Web:** www.campdencottages.co.uk
Contact: Campden Cottages, Folly Cottage, Paxford, Chipping Campden, Gloucestershire GL55 6XG
Tel: (01386) 593315 **Fax:** (01386) 593057 **E-mail:** info@campdencottages.co.uk

Attractive, romantic hideaway in peaceful Cotswold countryside on non-working farm. Two and a half miles from Chipping Campden and its lovely High Street, with its honey coloured stone buildings dating from 14th–18th centuries. Spacious, sunny, ground floor barn conversion. Exposed beams/rafters/log fire. Suitable for limited mobility (one step). Large bedroom with king-size bed. Cot/highchair on request. Additional sleeping up ladder to loft platform – two single full-size beds, suitable for teenage/adults. Ideally situated for visiting Stratford, Hidcote Gardens, Warwick, Blenheim and Oxford.

Low season per week: £285.00–£360.00
High season per week: £365.00–£465.00

1 cottage: sleeping 2–4 people + cot
Cards accepted: Mastercard, Visa, Switch/Delta

158 Orchard Cottage

★★★★

Denton Village, Stilton, Peterborough **Web:** www.higgo.com/orchard
Contact: Mrs J Higgo, 22 Stocks Hill, Manton, Oakham, Leicestershire LE15 8SY
Tel: (01572) 737420 **E-mail:** orchard@higgo.com

This is a rare example of a sympathetically converted 18th-century cottage. In a half-acre garden with mature trees and croquet lawn, the cottage has fine farmland views. An ideal hideaway within easy reach of London, it is perfect for weekend breaks. There are three double bedrooms (one with en-suite shower). Much of the furniture is antique – even the large bathroom has Victorian fittings. There is a large open fireplace in the sitting room. A well-appointed kitchen/diner of character leads into the conservatory.

Low season per week: £450.00–£600.00
High season per week: £600.00–£900.00
Short breaks: from £350.00–£675.00

1 cottage: sleeping 6+1 people

Painswick Rococo Garden

Painswick Rococo Garden enjoys its superb Cotswold position largely because Charles Hyett, an asthmatic, believed that its elevation would benefit his respiratory complaint. It seems, however, that his faith was misplaced, for he died in 1738, just three years after the completion of Painswick House (which he had poignantly named 'Buenos Aires', or 'Good Airs').

On inheriting the house his son, Benjamin, decided that a garden in the height of contemporary fashion was needed and, rather than landscaping the grounds in front of the mansion, he elected to create a 'rococo' garden on the slopes of the sheltered combe at the back. Rococo was a decorative style of the early 18th-century characterised by elaborate ornamentation and asymmetrical motifs. In a horticultural context it meant a departure from the formal gardens of the late 17th-century, with an inclusion of natural landscape features, asymmetrical views and voluptuous shapes based on swirls and flourishes. Quite who designed the garden is unclear, but a painting of 1748 by local artist Thomas Robins reveals it in remarkable clarity – so much so that some claim the painting fulfilled the function of a proposed design rather than a reproduction of the complete garden. In recent times, the survival of this painting has also ensured the survival of the garden.

Until 1955 a team of five gardeners maintained the six-acre garden, a small lawnmower their only mechanical aid. Ten years later, the then owner, unable to sustain sufficient gardeners for its upkeep

planted a wood on the site. In 1984, with the combe a tangle of brambles and old man's beard, bulldozers began to undo the ravages of 19 years neglect. Since then many elements of the magnificent garden have been restored and, thanks entirely to Robins' painting, they match exactly what was here 250 years ago. Particularly attractive and important garden structures include the Red House, the Gothic Alcove, the Pigeon House (from where Robins created his detailed record), the Plunge Pool and the Eagle House (an ornate and partially subterranean building).

The garden has been replanted with trees, shrubs and plants in keeping with the original 18th-century scheme. A fine example grows in the Melon Ground (an enclosed area where melons were cultivated under cold frames): the cornus controversa 'variegata', or wedding-cake tree. Unlike most gardens, Painswick is particularly good in February, when a thick carpet of snowdrops swathe the slopes.

159 The School House   ★ ★ ★ ★

High Street, Horningsea, Cambridge
Contact: Mr & Mrs Mann, The School House, High Street, Horningsea, Cambridge CB5 9JG
Tel: (01223) 440077 **Fax:** (01223) 441414 **E-mail:** schoolhse1@aol.com

A wonderful Victorian school house situated in an unspoilt village 3.5 miles from Cambridge city centre which accomodates 6–8 people. Decorated and furnished to a high specification, the house comprises of a sitting room, dining room, fully fitted kitchen, garden room and first-floor bedroom with en-suite shower room. Upstairs has two further bedrooms and a main bathroom. Small garden to the rear of the property. Two lovely village pubs/restaurants. Local riverside and country walks.

Low season per week: £350.00–£750.00
High season per week: £450.00–£750.00
Short breaks: from £250.00–£500.00

1 house: sleeping 6–8 people
Open: all year except Christmas/New Year
Cards accepted: Mastercard, Visa, Switch/Delta, Amex, Diners, Eurocard

QUALITY ASSURED
VISITOR ATTRACTION

Visitor Attraction Quality Assurance

VisitBritain operates a Visitor Attraction Quality Assurance Standard. Participating attractions are visited annually by trained, impartial assessors who look at all aspects of the visit, from initial telephone enquiries to departure, customer service to catering, as well as all facilities and activities. Only those attractions which have been assessed by VisitBritain and meet the standard receive the quality marque, your sign of a 'Quality Assured Visitor Attraction'.

Look out for the quality marque and visit with confidence.

160 Victoria Court   ★ ★ ★ ★

Sheringham, Norfolk **Web:** www.camberleyguesthouse.co.uk
Contact: Mr G R Simmons, Camberley, 62 Cliff Road, Sheringham, Norfolk NR26 8BJ
Tel: (01263) 823101 or (01263) 821433 **E-mail:** graham@camberleyguesthouse.co.uk

Two superb, recently-constructed apartments on the first floor of this award-winning small development. Ideally situated by the sea in a quiet part of Sheringham, with immediate access to the beach and enjoying excellent coastal and sea views. Many fine amenities and attractions close by. Furnished and equipped to a very high standard. Parking for two cars for each apartment in the grounds.

Low season per week: £195.00–£345.00
High season per week: £370.00–£460.00
Short breaks: from £135.00

2 apartments: each sleeping 4 people

161 Windmill Lodges   ★ ★ ★ ★

Saxtead, Woodbridge, Suffolk **Web:** www.windmilllodges.co.uk
Contact: Mrs Coe, Red House Farm, Saxtead, Woodbridge, Suffolk IP13 9RD
Tel: (01728) 685338 **Fax:** (01728) 684850 **E-mail:** holidays@windmilllodges.co.uk

Luxury log cabins set around a peaceful fishing lake in the heart of beautiful rural Suffolk. Our lodges are individually furnished and equipped to a high standard. Each lodge features a private hot tub on the veranda. Coal-effect fireplaces and underfloor heating ensure cosy evenings in. Decked veranda with patio furniture and barbeque for dining al fresco in summer. Our guests have use of our heated indoor pool and fishing in our private lake.

Low season per week: £184.00–£265.00
High season per week: £403.00–£750.00
Short breaks: from £110.00–£314.00

4 chalets: sleeping 2–8 people
Cards accepted: Mastercard, Visa, Switch/Delta, Amex

162 Easton Farm Park   ★ ★ ★ ★

Pound Corner, Easton, Woodbridge, Suffolk **Web:** www.eastonfarmpark.co.uk
Contact: Fiona Kerr, Easton Farm Park, Easton, Woodbridge, Suffolk IP13 0EQ
Tel: (01728) 746475 **Fax:** (01728) 747861 **E-mail:** fionakerr@suffolkonline.net

Easton Farm Park's two premier cottages are located on an award-winning farm in the heart of Suffolk. Ideally situated for many local attractions, including Snape Maltings, Sutton Hoo and the Suffolk heritage coast, all cottages provide a relaxed and comfortable atmosphere after a day out. Hire a bike to explore one of the many bike routes surrounding the farm, take a walk along the river and meet some of our friendly farm animals. Easton Farm Park is ideal for a relaxing, rural family holiday.

Low season per week: £365.00–£560.00
High season per week: £640.00–£1200.00

2 cottages: sleeping 5–10 people
Cards accepted: Mastercard, Visa, Switch/Delta

163 The Country Club Apartments ★ ★ ★ ★

Thorpeness, Leiston, Suffolk **Web:** www.thorpeness.co.uk
Contact: Thorpeness Hotel, Golf & Country Club, Lakeside Avenue, Thorpeness, Suffolk IP16 4NH
Tel: (01728) 452176 **Fax:** (01728) 453868 **E-mail:** info@thorpeness.co.uk

Delightful seaside 2 and 3-bedroom family apartments and houses with views out to sea. Fully fitted kitchens with dishwasher and washing machine. Television in lounge. Linen, towels and electricity included. Some apartments allow pets and smoking. Tennis courts and 18-hole golf course. Cycling and wonderful walks make up a perfect holiday. Off-season short breaks also available.

Low season per week: £242.00–£727.00
High season per week: £276.00–£876.00
Short breaks: from £181.00

2 houses and 9 apartments: sleeping 4–7 people
Cards accepted: Mastercard, Visa, Switch/Delta, Eurocard

164 Cragside ★ ★ ★ ★

9 Hertford Place, Aldeburgh, Suffolk
Contact: Mrs L Valentine, Rookery Farm, Cratfield, Halesworth, Suffolk IP19 0QE
Tel: (01986) 798609 **Fax:** (01986) 798609 **E-mail:** j.r.valentine@btinternet.com

Characterful and deceptively spacious self-contained ground floor flat in large Victorian house on Crag Path, comfortably furnished. Recently completely refurbished. Central heating, inglenook fireplaces. 20 yards to sea. Really well equipped with dishwasher, microwave, fridge/freezer, washer/dryer, telephone/answerphone (incoming calls). Televisions in sitting room and bedroom. Comfortable beds with good quality duvets and electric blankets. Good lighting for reading in bed. Sleeps three in one twin and one single bedroom. Good easy parking. Regret no pets, no children, no smokers.

Low season per week: £200.00–£280.00
High season per week: £285.00–£375.00
Short breaks: from £100.00–£150.00

1 apartment: sleeping 3 people

England's West Country

Hawker's Morwenstow

Morwenstow, near Bude, was the home of Robert Stephen Hawker, a remarkable 19th-century parson and poet who left his whimsical mark upon the village. The vicarage chimneys are built to resemble the various churches with which he had been connected, while a capital on the village church displays the message 'This is the house of God' carved upside-down – for a celestial readership! High on the cliffs near by is a tiny driftwood hut, now owned by the National Trust, where, often in a fug of opium, he composed much of his poetry.

Lundy Island

Lundy is as remote an island as England has to offer and makes a magnificent day out from Ilfracombe and Bideford, both some 24 miles (38.5km) distant on the north Devon coast. The island, 3 miles (5km) long and never much more than half a mile (1km) wide, boasts some superb scenery, and there can be no better way of passing time here than strolling its gentle paths. The west coast is the highlight of the island: here Soay sheep and feral goats pick their way over stacks of granite tumbling hundreds of feet to the Atlantic while ravens wheel above. www.lundyisland.co.uk

An unrivalled coastline

The very pace of life seems to slow as you head west. The counties of Cornwall, Devon, Dorset, Somerset and Wiltshire somehow conduct their various businesses at a more civilised speed. Wiltshire alone is land-locked, so perhaps the sea's proximity has a relaxing effect. The magnificent coastline certainly draws people, but its huge length – the South-West Coastal Path,

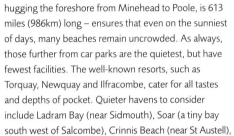

hugging the foreshore from Minehead to Poole, is 613 miles (986km) long – ensures that even on the sunniest of days, many beaches remain uncrowded. As always, those further from car parks are the quietest, but have fewest facilities. The well-known resorts, such as Torquay, Newquay and Ilfracombe, cater for all tastes and depths of pocket. Quieter havens to consider include Ladram Bay (near Sidmouth), Soar (a tiny bay south west of Salcombe), Crinnis Beach (near St Austell), Pendower Beach (east of St Mawes), Portheras (west of St Ives), Lee Bay (near Ilfracombe) and St Audrie's Bay (just east of Watchet). Five minutes with a detailed map, especially of the superb southern coasts of Devon and Cornwall, will reveal countless other coves, bays and beaches, often with perfect sand.

Where the catch is landed

And if the weather is too cold for the beach, why not explore a Cornish or Devonian fishing village? These, as much a West Country speciality as Exmoor ponies or clotted cream, are one of the region's most engaging attractions. Some, such as Clovelly, on the northern coast of Devon, are justifiably famous. Cascading in picturesque manner down the cliffs into the sea and with a main 'street' too steep and too narrow for cars, it nevertheless copes admirably with its visitors. Others – some popular, some little-known – to explore include Port Isaac (on the North Cornish coast and also without cars), Helford, Looe (both East and West), Gorran Haven, Gunwalloe, Porthcurno (all on the southern coast of Cornwall) and Beer (on Devon's southern shores).

Perfect bases for exploration

As the sumptuous fishing villages are mainly in the extreme south-west, so the historic towns and cities tend to be further east in Somerset, Dorset and Wiltshire. Here you can choose from the incomparable cities of Salisbury, Bath and Wells, each with a magnificent range of secular and ecclesiastical architecture. Sherborne, too, has a glorious abbey and many fine buildings dating from the 16th and 17th centuries, as well as two castles, one in ruins, the other home to a range of art treasures. Shaftesbury is the setting for one of England's best-loved views – the steep, cobbled Gold Hill was famously used for a bread commercial – but has other intriguing nooks and crannies.

Marlborough's broad High Street is lined with substantial 18th-century houses, yet is only a mile from Savernake, England's largest privately-owned forest, criss-crossed with footpaths. Ilchester dates from Roman times, but the town prospered in the medieval and Georgian periods; the houses round the green reveal the town's latter lineage. Looking further west, Salcombe, wonderfully situated on the Kingsbridge Estuary and enjoying the mildest of climates, became a resort in the 19th century. It has a gentle charm all its own, and is near Totnes, an appealing market town that has whole-heartedly embraced alternative culture. Just over the Tamar into Cornwall lies Launceston, a town of old-world character with two 16th-century bridges and a ruined medieval castle. Surrounded by unspoilt countryside, all make ideal bases for a long weekend's meandering.

Pasties, scrumpy and Yarg

An important part of a weekend away is to indulge in local specialities. The West Country has its fair share, with few visitors able to resist the cream tea. Clotted cream, the essential ingredient, is widely available throughout the region. Cornwall has its pasty, now eaten the length and breadth of the land, but nowhere as good, so they say, as in its home. Somerset's many orchards have long been given over to cider and the earthier, more potent scrumpy. Many farms still produce – and a couple of museums at Dowlish Wake and Bradford-on-Tone celebrate – the heady brews. The name of Cheddar is synonymous with cheese, but there are many more beside, from Cornish Yarg to Somerset Brie. And throughout, sold in market, shop, pub and restaurant, are fresh fish of the finest quality. The West Country is a piscivore's paradise!

Getting away from it all

Few places in the West Country have an urban feel. Bristol and Plymouth are cities redolent of their maritime history yet remaining close to their rural hinterlands. Elsewhere, the predominant mood is of the country, and visitors are spoilt for choice when it comes to walking territory. The three moors – Bodmin, Exmoor and Dartmoor – are all wild enough to have challenging routes suitable for the experienced hiker only, but on their gentler fringes are endless, easier options

that reveal some of England's most sublime countryside. The national parks of Dartmoor and Exmoor have many suggestions for walks; outside these, areas particularly rewarding for exploration on foot include the Mendips in north Somerset, the Lizard in south west Cornwall, the Marlborough Downs in north east Wiltshire and the Quantock Hills just east of Exmoor. Thanks to the South-West Coastal Path, walking the coast is straightforward, though often strenuous. Other long-distance paths in the region include the Exe

The Tate

At the end of the Second World War St Ives became home to an influential clan of artists. Following the death of the sculptress Barbara Hepworth in 1975, her studio was given to the Tate Gallery in London and is now open as a museum. The Tate slowly acquired other works by St Ives artists, but was unable to display them until the opening of the magnificent and airy former gasworks as a gallery in 1993. Overlooking Porthmeor beach, few arts venues can boast a closet specially designed for visitors to leave their surfboards...
www.tate.org.uk/stives

Wookey Hole

Since the 15th century visitors have come to peer into the dark caverns and subterranean passages of Wookey Hole, near Wells. Today, dramatic electric lighting illuminates fantastic rock-formations and the glassy surface of an underground lake. There are a number of other attractions on offer too: paper-making demonstrations on the site of a 19th-century paper-mill; a collection of fairground art; a re-creation of Madame Tussaud's touring 'Cabinet of Curiosities'; and an exhibition of amusements from penny pier arcades.
www.wookey.co.uk

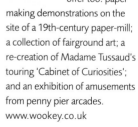

Brunel's Bristol

The great engineer Isambard Kingdom Brunel was only 23 when he won a competition to design a bridge across the Avon Gorge at Bristol. This was the start of a long association with the city, one which produced its most famous landmarks. Brunel, chief engineer for the Great Western Railway, designed its splendid neo-Tudor station, Temple Meads, now a Grade I listed building. His great steam-ships SS *Great Western*, and SS *Great Britain* were built in Bristol: the latter, in the city docks, is now a museum. www.ss-great-britain.com

Chesil Beach

One of the stranger natural phenomena of the South Coast, Chesil Beach is a 16-mile (26km) strip of shingle running from the Dorset village of Abbotsbury to the Isle of Portland. Fashioned entirely by the sea to a height of some 30–40ft (9–12m), the bank forms a thin barrier between the Fleet, the largest lagoon in Britain, and the sea. Barely disturbed by mankind, the Fleet supports as many as 150 species of seaweed, as well as abundant fish and water-fowl. www.coastlink.org/chesil

Valley Way (a 45 mile (72km) level route following the River Exe from Exmoor to its estuary); the West Devon Way, a shorter path that runs along Dartmoor's western edge from Plymouth to Okehampton; the Two Moors Way, a magnificent and demanding path extending over 100 miles (160km) and linking Dartmoor and Exmoor; the Liberty Trail, following the route taken by the Monmouth Rebellion through south Somerset and west Dorset; and the Saints Way, a 37 mile (60km) coast to coast route across Cornwall from Padstow to Fowey. Public transport links with many of these longer paths, allowing them to be tackled in sections; most also have shorter, circular routes using part of their length. For the walker keen to get away from motor traffic, there is an alternative suggestion. The island of Lundy has a pub, church and shop, and just one small road within 12 miles (19km). But it does have spectacular cliff-top paths.

A celebration of words and music

Held annually in late May and early June, the Salisbury Festival presents both classical and jazz concerts, poetry and exhibitions, folk, circus and children's events. Further west, the Roman city of Bath hosts a festival of literature (February) and of music (May). The latter kicks off with opening-night celebrations featuring fireworks, and celebrates contemporary European jazz, early and classical music. On a smaller scale and at roughly the same time of year, Chard, in southern Somerset, promotes music in a variety of styles composed by women. Held over six weeks or so in July and August, the Dartington Festival gives a series of concerts devoted to opera, dance and classical music in the medieval Dartington Hall and gardens. It is aimed as much at those who wish to partake as to listen. Also in July is the Exeter Festival, when the broad-ranging programme may include classical music in the Gothic cathedral, opera and fireworks, lectures, comedy, jazz, theatre and fringe events.

Houses of substance

The region's historic houses range from the large-scale – such as Longleat and Wilton House, both in Wiltshire – to the more compact Coleridge Cottage at Nether Stowey, where the eponymous poet found inspiration for *The Rime of the Ancient Mariner*. Little has changed in the two centuries since Coleridge moved in. Other remarkable – and visitable – residences of the region include Great Chalfield Manor (near Melksham), a 15th-century house of mellow stone with a fine great hall, and Forde Abbey, a former monastery near Chard now also known for its gardens. By contrast, Bristol and Bath each preserve a magnificent 18th-century townhouse: Bristol's is appropriately called The Georgian House, while Bath's proudly proclaims its address – No. 1 Royal Crescent. The latter was once the home of the Duke of York who famously marched his men up and down hills. Devon, meanwhile, invites you to a couple of castles a little out of the ordinary. Castle Drogo, perched above the River Teign near Drewsteignton is the work of Edwin Lutyens, and was not completed until the 1930s. Of more authentic age for a castle is Bickleigh, though it is in reality more fortified manor house than full-blooded medieval castle. One of its attractions is a display of gadgets used by Second World War spies. It is best to turn up at Pencarrow, a Georgian family home near Bodmin, in late spring or early summer when no fewer than 692 separate species of rhododendron welcome visitors, whether of a botanical bent or not. Trerice, a few miles south east of Newquay, is a glorious Elizabethan house with unusual curved and scrolled gables. It is home to a remarkable collection of lawnmowers.

In search of St Hyacinth

Cornwall offers the church-hunter rich pickings. There are superb buildings – such as Launcells Church, inland from Bude, little altered since its completion in the 15th century. There are incomparable settings: the churches at St Anthony-in-Meneage on the Helford River and at St Just-in-Roseland are two of the best. And there are the wondrous names. Churches in Cornwall are dedicated to St Petroc, St Hyacinth, St Nonna, St Germans and St Winnow. Other consecrated buildings to seek out in the West Country include St Brannock's in Braunton and St Andrew's in Cullompton (both Devon), St Andrew's in Banwell (Somerset) and St Mary's in Lydiard Tregoze (near Swindon).

Some useful web addresses

Perry's Cider Mills, Dowlish Wake	www.southsomerset.gov.uk/commune/perry.htm
Sheppy's Farmhouse Cider, Bradford-on-Tone	www.sheppyscider.com
Dartmoor National Park	www.dartmoor-npa.gov.uk
Exmoor National Park	www.exmoor-nationalpark.gov.uk
Salisbury Festival	www.salisburyfestival.co.uk
Bath Literature Festival	www.bathlitfest.org.uk
Bath International Music Festival	www.bathmusicfest.org.uk
Chard Festival of Women in Music	chardfestival.org.uk
Dartington International Summer School	www.dartingtonsummerschool.org.uk
Exeter Festival	www.exeter.gov.uk/festival
Longleat, Warminster	www.longleat.co.uk
Wilton House, Wilton	www.wiltonhouse.co.uk
Coleridge Cottage, Nether Stowey	www.nationaltrust.org.uk
Great Chalfield Manor, Melksham	www.nationaltrust.org.uk
Forde Abbey, Chard	www.fordeabbey.co.uk
The Georgian House, Bristol	www.bristol-city.gov.uk/mus/georg.html
No. 1 Royal Crescent, Bath	www.bath-preservation-trust.org.uk/museums/no1
Castle Drogo, Drewsteignton	www.nationaltrust.org.uk
Pencarrow, Bodmin	www.pencarrow.co.uk
Trerice, Newquay	www.nationaltrust.org.uk

Swindon, the Railway Town

In the hundred years between 1830 and 1930, Swindon's population increased from 1,740 to 65,000. The reason was the arrival of the Great Western Railway (GWR) and the setting up of its manufacturing works in the town. The company built a 'railway village' to house its growing workforce: no. 34 Faringdon Road is now a museum furnished as it might have been in the late 19th century. The company's hostel for male workers is now the GWR museum, displaying locomotives and railway memorabilia. www.steam-museum.org.uk

Dartmoor Longhouses

A defining feature of the longhouse is that humans and livestock lived under a single roof. This arrangement, common on the continent, is very rare in England, and only occurs where it was vital to keep livestock warm and near at hand in harsh winter conditions. Around a hundred longhouses remain on Dartmoor: low, rectangular buildings, built between 1150 and 1700 from huge blocks of granite, often partly recessed into the hillside to maximise shelter.

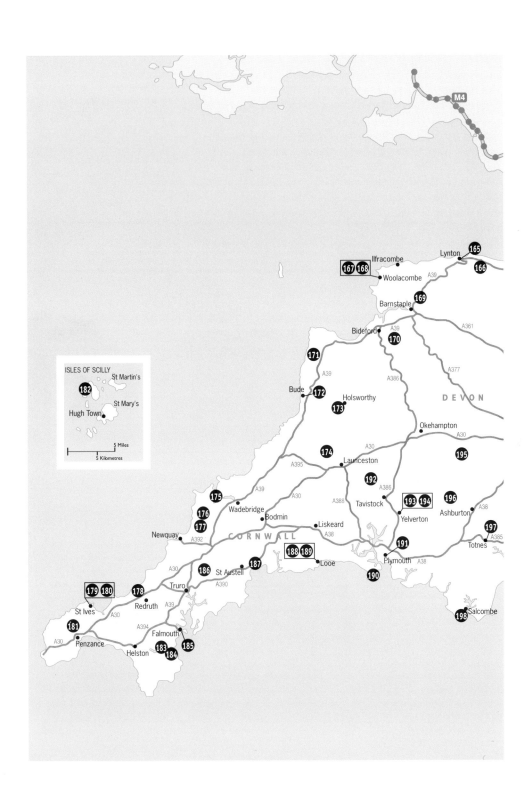

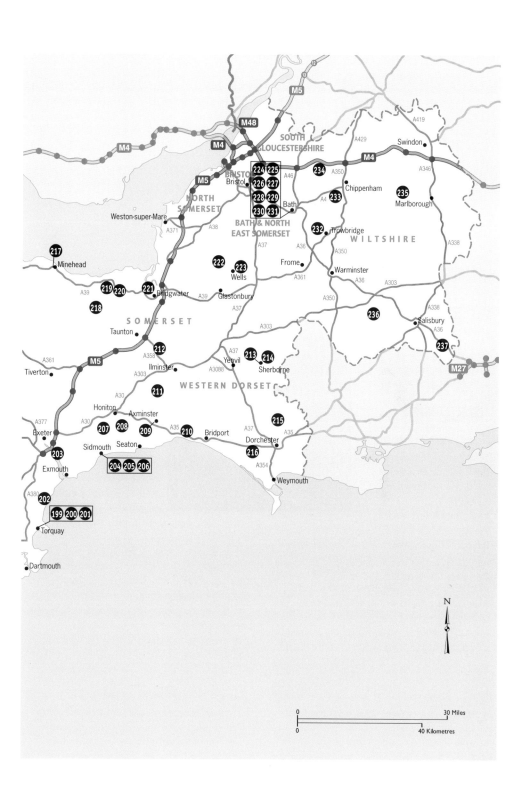

165 Sinai House

Lynway, Lynton, Devon EX35 6AY **Tel:** (01598) 753227 **Fax:** (01598) 752633
Web: www.sinaihouse.co.uk **E-mail:** enquiries@sinaihouse.co.uk

A delightful Victorian house, full of warmth and character set in half an acre of terraced gardens but only five minutes walk from the village centre, where hospitality and guest care are our main priority. Magnificent scenic and coastal views from all the bedrooms. The bedrooms are tastefully decorated and full of personal touches, a private residence lounge, there is a golf theme bar and a large dining room. The house has its own private car park and large patio.

Bed & Breakfast per night: single room from £23.00–£25.00; double room from £46.00–£54.00

Bedrooms: 1 single, 5 double, 2 twin
Bathrooms: 6 en-suite, 2 private
Parking: 8 spaces
Open: mid February–mid November
Cards accepted: Mastercard, Visa, Switch/Delta

Exmoor

Exmoor's coastline is stupendous, a series of high, 'hogsback' cliffs, dropping precipitously from 1,300ft to a rocky shoreline. Where rivers have carved a path to the sea, the great cliffs are intersected by valleys: peaceful Heddon's Mouth, accessible only on foot, the narrow defile of the Lyn where the river tumbles noisily over its stony bed, and the great wide sweep of Porlock Bay. The dramatic Valley of the Rocks, near Lynmouth, was another such riverbed until the Lyn took another course and left the extraordinary geological formations high and dry 500ft above sea level. From Foreland Point to Porlock, the steep coastal slopes are softened by a mantle of oak woodlands – and on a spring day there are few more delightful sights than the blue sea glinting through a mist of unfurling young leaves.

The South-West Coastal Path, of course, offers the perfect means of exploring Exmoor's northern fringe. Inland, two other long-distance paths, the Tarka Trail and the Two Moors Way, lead through some of the region's wild and exquisite scenery. In all, there is a network of some 600 miles (1,000km) of rights-of-way criss-crossing the landscape to create rewarding walks of all lengths and terrains. And of these, some 288 miles (464km) are bridleways offering endless scope for horse-rider and mountain-biker.

Exmoor's interior is a vast, high tableland, sloping imperceptibly from its high cliffs to the gentle farmland of mid-Devon. The higher ground is covered in heather or bracken, grazed by sheep or rugged Exmoor ponies. South of Lynmouth, the Chains – a boggy hump of moorland – is as remote a spot as any in the South. Exmoor's highest point is Dunkery Beacon (1,704ft, 519m), a rounded shoulder of land commanding a superb panorama, encompassing, on a clear day, the distant Black Mountains to the north, and the jagged tors of Dartmoor to the south. Less apparent from the wide, bald heights are the deep wooded combes which form unexpected clefts in the flat 'table' above. Entering them is to reach a different world, for the contrast between the windswept heaths and the luxuriant woodland, all cushioned with moss, loud with birdsong and dappled with light and shade, could hardly be greater. Follow the streams into the wider valleys and the landscape changes again as cosier farmland encroaches into the wilderness, replacing brown moor and dark forest with a higgledy-piggledy patchwork of bright green.

166 Brendon House Hotel

◆◆◆◆

Brendon, Lynton, Devon EX35 6PS **Tel:** (01598) 741206
Web: www.brendonvalley.co.uk/brendon_house.htm **E-mail:** brendonhouse4u@aol.com

Brendon House is a licensed former 18th-century farmhouse, nestling in the delightful Lyn Valley and offering the highest standards of friendly service and comfort. Fully equipped en-suite bedrooms, comfortable residents' lounge and spacious gardens set in stunning Exmoor scenery and only a couple of miles from the dramatic North Devon coast. Diners can choose from our extensive menu of delicious fine country fare, seafood dishes and local game complemented by locally produced vegetables, often from our garden. Vegetarian dishes are also available.

Bed & Breakfast per night: single occupancy from £33.00–£38.00; double room from £48.00– £56.00
Dinner, Bed & Breakfast per person, per night: £40.00–£44.00
Lunch available: light lunches 1100–1500

Evening meal: 1900
Bedrooms: 3 double, 1 twin, 1 family, 1 suite
Bathrooms: 4 en-suite, 1 private
Parking: 5 spaces

All this has been subtly shaped and embellished by human hand. Bronze Age burial mounds and standing stones are often found on the high ground: Five Barrows near Sherracombe, for example, or the famous Caractacus Stone near Winsford. Of the many Iron-Age hill forts, Cow Castle, below Simonsbath, commands an impressive position above the river Barle. But the clapperbridge at Tarr Steps, long thought to be a prehistoric monument, is probably medieval.

From Norman times, Exmoor was a royal hunting ground, ensuring habitats – and their wildlife – have long been preserved. Indeed, red deer are still common, and Exmoor is the only place in England where stags are hunted on horseback, much as they were 900 years ago with hounds. Conceding Exmoor's uselessness as a tree-growing area, the Crown in 1818 sold the land to John Knight, who, followed by his son Frederic, settled at Simonsbath House (now a hotel) and began an ambitious programme of land improvement. In the family's most enduring legacy, Frederic Knight promoted a sturdy windbreak for cattle by planting beech hedges on wide earth banks. Today rows of vast, wind-sculpted trees still cling to the hillsides, their knotted roots binding the banks below.

Ironically, the Knights were engaged in taming the landscape just when tourists began to arrive in ever greater numbers, driven by an appreciation of the area's romantic wildness. Many visitors came to explore 'Doone Country', a fictional area based on Richard Blackmore's novel Lorna Doone (1869) and centred on the remote Badgworthy Valley where the band of outlaws, the Doones, supposedly had their hideout. Many local landmarks quickly acquired spurious

Doonish titles, such as Lorna's Cott and Lorna Doone Farm, which endure today. As the tourists arrived, the twin villages of Lynton, perched on its huge cliff, and Lynmouth, down by the sea, became genteel seaside resorts, linked, in 1890, by a hair-raising cliff railway.

Today, the towns and villages of Exmoor have much to offer the visitor, their whitewashed cottages and mellow churches focal points in the intricate patchwork of this lovely landscape. Dunster's great castle dominates the town, but also here are a beautiful wool market, 15th-century nunnery and splendid priory church, complete with 13th-century dovecote. Dulverton, in the south, is a charming, busy market town, set in glorious countryside, while nearby Bury attracts photographers with its rustic packhorse bridge, pretty ford, and Norman castle. Many picture-postcard settlements cluster in Porlock Vale: Allerford, Bossington, Horner, Luccombe and the model village of Selworthy on the Holnicote Estate. Intriguing churches include remote Stoke Pero, clinging to the hillside miles from anywhere; the parish church at Oare, famous as the scene of Lorna Doone's shooting; and the tiny church at Culbone, at 12ft x 35ft, said to be the smallest complete parish church in the country.

Exmoor became a National Park in 1954 and is administered by the National Park Authority which works closely with local people, landowners, farmers and other organisations, offering wide-ranging advice and support. As custodians of Exmoor, the Authority is committed to maintaining the delicate balance between conservation and recreation. There are National Park Visitor Centres at Combe Martin, Lynmouth, County Gate, Dunster and Dulverton.

167 Watersmeet Hotel
★★★ Silver Award

Mortehoe, Woolacombe, Devon EX34 7EB **Tel:** (01271) 870333 **Fax:** (01271) 870890
Web: www:watersmeethotel.co.uk **E-mail:** info@watersmeethotel.co.uk

Set on the National Trust Atlantic coastline with panoramic views of Hartland Point and Lundy Island, the three acres of garden enclose a lawn tennis court, an open air swimming pool and steps to the beach below. A superb indoor pool and spa is popular with everybody. Watersmeet offers the comfort and peace of a country house, and all the bedrooms, lounges and the octagonal restaurant overlook the sea. The Watersmeet offers a wine list to complement its national award-winning cuisine and service.

Bed & Breakfast per night: single room from £75.00–£125.00; double room from £150.00–£250.00
Lunch available: 1200–1345
Evening meal: 1900 (last orders 2030)

Bedrooms: 1 single, 19 double/twin, 2 family
Bathrooms: 23 en-suite
Parking: 50 spaces
Cards accepted: Mastercard, Visa, Switch/Delta, Amex, Barclaycard

168 Woolacombe Bay Hotel
★★★ Silver Award

Woolacombe, Devon EX34 7BN **Tel:** (01271) 870388 **Fax:** (01271) 870613
Web: www.woolacombe-bay-hotel.co.uk **E-mail:** woolacombe.bayhotel@btinternet.com

Safeway England in Excellence Awards 2003 – South West Tourism Regional Finalist. Set in six acres of quiet gardens gently leading to three miles of EC Blue Flag golden sands. Built in the halcyon days of the mid-1800s, the hotel has a relaxed style of comfort and good living. Guests can enjoy free unlimited use of superb sporting facilities, or just relax with a good book in spacious lounges overlooking the Atlantic. The 'Hothouse' for fitness and the 'Haven' for massage, beauty treatments and in-house hairdresser. Superb cooking of traditional and French dishes. Golf, shooting, fishing, horse-riding, ten-pin bowling and boating available.

Bed & Breakfast per night: single occupancy from £45.00–£90.00; double room from £90.00–£180.00
Dinner, Bed & Breakfast per person, per night: from £65.00–£150.00
Evening meal: 1900 (last orders 2100)

Bedrooms: 24 double, 8 twin, 17 family, 15 suites **Bathrooms:** 64 en-suite
Parking: 100 spaces
Open: February –2nd January
Cards accepted: Mastercard, Visa, Switch/Delta, Amex, Diners

169 The Spinney
◆◆◆◆ Silver Award

Shirwell, Barnstaple, Devon EX31 4JR **Tel:** (01271) 850282
Web: www.thespinneyshirwell.co.uk **E-mail:** thespinny@shirwell.fsnet.co.uk

Set in over an acre of grounds, with views towards Exmoor. A former rectory with spacious accommodation. Delicious meals are cooked by the chef/proprietor, served during the summer months in our restored Victorian conservatory under the ancient vine. Residential licence. The Spinney is non-smoking. An ideal centre for sandy beaches, gardens of Marwood Hill and Rosemoor, the National Trust house of Arlington Court or Exmoor National Park.

Bed & Breakfast per night: single room from £20.50–£23.50; double room from £41.00–£47.00
Dinner, Bed & Breakfast per person, per night: £33.50–£36.50
Evening meal: 1900 (last bookings 1700)

Bedrooms: 1 single, 1 double, 1 twin, 2 family
Bathrooms: 3 en-suite, 1 private, 1 shared
Parking: 6 spaces

170 Bulworthy Cottage ◆◆◆◆

Stony Cross, Bideford, Devon EX39 4PY **Tel:** (01271) 858441
E-mail: bulworthy@aol.com

Once three 18th-century miners' cottages, Bulworthy has been sympathetically renovated to modern standards whilst retaining many original features. Our twin and double guest rooms both offer en-suite accommodation, with central heating and colour television. Standing in quiet countryside, Bulworthy is within easy reach of the moors, Tarka Trail, South West Coastal Path, Rosemoor and numerous National Trust properties. Golf may be pre-booked at local courses. We offer a choice of breakfasts and evening meals, with a wine list chosen to complement the local food.

Bed & Breakfast per night: single occupancy from £24.00–£28.00; double room from £48.00– £56.00
Dinner, Bed & Breakfast per person, per night: £36.00–£43.00
Evening meal: 1830 (last orders 2030)

Bedrooms: 1 double, 1 twin
Bathrooms: 2 en-suite
Parking: 6 spaces
Cards accepted: Mastercard, Visa, Switch/Delta, JCB

171 Golden Park ◆◆◆◆◆ Gold Award

Hartland, Bideford, Devon EX39 6EP **Tel:** (01237) 441254
Web: www.goldenpark.co.uk **E-mail:** lynda@goldenpark.co.uk

17th-century farmhouse situated at the end of a private drive. All rooms are spacious, comfortable and tastefully decorated with lovely views of the old walled garden or the coast. This country house with its friendly atmosphere has an oak-beamed drawing room, dining room and garden room for guest use. Golden Park would make an ideal base for a relaxing and tranquil break in an area designated as an Area of Outstanding Natural Beauty.

Bed & Breakfast per night: single occupancy from £34.00–£50.00; double room from £46.00– £60.00

Bedrooms: 3 double, 1 twin, 3 suites
Bathrooms: 3 en-suite
Parking: 5 spaces

172 The Falcon Hotel ★★★ Silver Award

Breakwater Road, Bude, Cornwall EX23 8SD **Tel:** (01288) 352005 **Fax:** (01288) 356359
Web: www.falconhotel.com **E-mail:** reception@falconhotel.com

Overlooking the famous Bude Canal, with beautiful walled gardens and yet only a short stroll from the beaches and shops, the Falcon has one of the finest settings in North Cornwall. Established in 1798, it still retains an old-world charm and atmosphere. The bedrooms are furnished to a very high standard, and have televisions with Teletext and Sky. Excellent local reputation for the quality of the food, both in the Coachman's bar and Tennyson's restaurant.

Bed & Breakfast per night: single room from £48.00–£51.00; double room from £96.00–£102.00
Dinner, Bed & Breakfast per person, per night: £61.00–£64.00
Evening meal: 1900 (last orders 2100)

Bedrooms: 7 single, 15 double, 7 family
Bathrooms: 29 en-suite
Parking: 40 spaces
Cards accepted: Mastercard, Visa, Switch/Delta, Amex, Diners, Barclaycard

173 Leworthy Farmhouse Bed & Breakfast ◆◆◆◆ Silver Award

Leworthy Farmhouse, Lower Leworthy, Pyworthy, Holsworthy, Devon EX22 6SJ **Tel:** (01409) 259469
Web: www.s-h-systems.co.uk/hotels/leworthy.html

A charming Georgian farmhouse nestling in an unspoilt backwater. Delightful en-suite guest rooms with chintzy curtains, crisp bedlinen, fluffy towels, tea trays with pretty bone china, chocolate and biscuits, antiques and objet d'art, books and glossy magazines, fresh flowers and warm hospitality. Scrumptious full English breakfasts, or choose organic porridge, fresh fruit salad, kippers, prunes, yogurt or muesli. Elegant dining room and peaceful lounge. Lovely spacious gardens. Country lanes surround us. Spectacular coastline nearby. A welcoming haven of peace.

Bed & Breakfast per night: single occupancy from £32.00–£40.00; double room from £50.00–£55.00

Bedrooms: 4 double, 2 twin, 1 family
Bathrooms: 6 en-suite, 1 private
Parking: 10 spaces

174 West Barton ◆◆◆◆

North Petherwin, Launceston, Cornwall PL15 8LR **Tel:** (01566) 785710
Web: www.westbarton.co.uk **E-mail:** enquiries@westbarton.co.uk

A splendid Grade II listed stone dwelling, originally the west wing of a large medieval farmhouse. Situated in the shadows of the parish church, guests can relax in a friendly countryside atmosphere. Bedrooms are very comfortably furnished with en-suite facilities. Within easy reach of North Cornwall's superb rugged coastline, beaches and the moors, there are many other places of interest to visit, including Tintagel, the Eden Project, Lanhydrock and Padstow. Guest parking is provided. Evening meals are available from the local inn approximately 1.75 miles away.

Bed & Breakfast per night: single occupancy from £35.00–£39.00; double room from £50.00–£60.00

Bedrooms: 2 double, 1 twin (only 2 rooms available at any one time)
Bathrooms: 3 en-suite
Parking: 3 spaces **Open:** March–November
Cards accepted: Mastercard, Visa, Switch/Delta, JCB

175 Symply Padstow ◆◆◆◆ Silver Award

32 Dennis Road, Padstow, Cornwall PL28 8DE **Tel:** (01841) 532814 **Fax:** (01841) 533480
Web: www.symply-padstow.co.uk **E-mail:** buttfish@btinternet.com

An elegant Edwardian house with stunning estuary views. Quiet, yet only a stone's throw from the bustling quayside with its world-famous restaurant and exciting shops. Spacious, comfortable interior with three very attractive en-suite bedrooms, with all those little extras to make your stay that little bit special. Padstow is an ideal base for exploring all the delights of Cornwall, including the Eden Project and the coastal footpath, and we guarantee you a warm welcome and a relaxing stay.

Bed & Breakfast per night: double room from £60.00–£80.00

Bedrooms: 3 double, 1 twin
Bathrooms: 3 en-suite
Cards accepted: Mastercard, Visa, Switch/Delta

176 The Old Rectory

♦♦♦♦♦ Gold Award

St Ervan, Wadebridge, Cornwall PL27 7TA **Tel:** (01841) 540255 **Fax:** (01841) 540255
Web: www.stervanmanor.co.uk **E-mail:** mail@stervanmanor.freeserve.co.uk

Elegant Grade II listed Victorian rectory set in beautiful grounds of four acres. Fantastic peaceful setting yet only four miles from Padstow, three miles from North Cornwall beaches and thirty minutes from Eden Project. The individual bedrooms are luxurious. Four bedrooms are en-suite, including feature master double bedroom, four-poster and twin rooms. A fifth bedroom has a private bathroom. Guests have use of a splendid drawing room next to which is the superb breakfast room. See also our self-catering accommodation on page 144.

Bed & Breakfast per night: double room from £80.00–£160.00

Bedrooms: 4 double, 1 twin
Bathrooms: 4 en-suite, 1 private
Parking: 10 spaces
Cards accepted: Mastercard, Visa, Switch/Delta

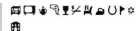

The Camel Trail

Increasingly our disused railway-lines are finding a new and popular lease of life as traffic-free paths for cyclists and walkers. The Camel Trail is one of a growing network of old railway lines which the charity SUSTRANS has helped to redesign as 'greenways' for the use of cyclists, walkers and horse-riders. For all of its 17-mile (27km) route it clings, more or less, to the banks of the River Camel. Between Padstow and Wadebridge it runs for 5½ miles (9km) along the trackbed of the former London and South Western Railway line and then from Wadebridge it follows part of the old Bodmin and Wadebridge Railway to Boscarne Junction on the western outskirts of Bodmin (5½ miles - 9km) and then, turning north, to Poley's Bridge (6 miles - 9.5km). The Bodmin and Wadebridge was Cornwall's first locomotive-hauled railway and, opening in 1834, one of the earliest in Britain.

From Padstow the trail hugs the southern edge of the estuary, crossing Little Petherick Creek on a magnificent triple-span girder bridge. Built in 1898, this is a rare survivor, most girder bridges having been demolished for scrap. The stretch alongside the estuary offers wonderful views and a rich diversity of birdlife – flocks of oystercatchers and curlews swirl above the water all year round, golden plover and lapwing in the winter. East of Old Town Cove are relics of Penquean slate quarry. In Wadebridge the trail passes through the remains of the station and then a mile or so east of the town crosses over Pendavey bridge on to the north bank of the river and along a steep, wooded stretch that offers good views across the Camel. The platform at Grogley halt still stands beside the track and, shortly before Boscarne, Nanstallon halt is now a tea garden.

North of Bodmin the trail follows the river's eastern bank through quiet woodland between Dunmere and the hamlet of Hellandbridge. From here there follows a particularly pretty stretch, with plentiful woodland flowers and birds, before the trail ends in a car park at Poley's Bridge, near the buildings of the Wenfordbridge clayworks that were the raison d'être of what was always a mineral line. This section of the Bodmin and Wadebridge was used solely for the carrying of china clay right up to its closure in 1983 and, ironically, there are already plans to reopen it to china clay traffic. This would mean the loss of this fine stretch of the Camel Trail, but would remove 3,000 lorries from local roads each year. Bikes can be hired in Padstow, Wadebridge and Bodmin.

177 The Falcon Inn   ◆◆◆◆

St Mawgan, Newquay, Cornwall TR8 4EP **Tel:** (01637) 860225 **Fax:** (01637) 860884
Web: www.falconinn.net **E-mail:** enquiries@falconinn.net

A beautiful 16th-century inn, situated in a quiet village within a conservation area, only one mile from the coast, six miles from Padstow and 20 minutes from the Eden Project. Rooms are individually furnished to a high standard. We offer a varied menu, both lunchtimes and evenings, with local produce and fresh fish featured. A varied wine list, award-winning gardens and log fires in winter make The Falcon an ideal base for business or pleasure. Plus new awards for dining, gardens and signature dish – first prize winners!

Bed & Breakfast per night: single room £26.00; double room from £54.00–£75.00
Lunch available: 1200–1400
Evening meal: 1830 (last orders 2100)

Bedrooms: 1 single, 2 double, 1 twin
Bathrooms: 2 en-suite, 1 shared
Parking: 25 spaces
Cards accepted: Mastercard, Visa, Switch/Delta, Diners, Eurocard, JCB

178 Aviary Court Hotel   ◆◆◆◆

Marys Well, Illogan, Redruth, Cornwall TR16 4QZ **Tel:** (01209) 842256 **Fax:** (01209) 843744
Web: www.aviarycourthotel.co.uk **E-mail:** info@aviarycourthotel.co.uk

A charming 300-year-old Cornish country house set in two acres of secluded well-kept gardens with tennis court. An ideal touring location – the coast is five minutes away and St Ives Tate, Heligan Gardens, the Eden Project and St Michael's Mount are all within easy reach. Six well-equipped bedrooms with en-suite, tea/coffee making facilities, biscuits, mineral water, fresh fruit, telephone and a view of the gardens. The resident family proprietors ensure personal service, offering well-cooked varied food that uses as much Cornish produce as possible.

Bed & Breakfast per night: single occupancy from £47.50–£47.50; double room from £68.50– £71.50
Dinner, Bed & Breakfast per person, per night: £49.75–£51.25
Evening meal: 1900

Bedrooms: 4 double, 2 twin, 1 family
Bathrooms: 6 en-suite
Parking: 15 spaces
Cards accepted: Mastercard, Visa

179 Chy An Gwedhen   ◆◆◆◆

St Ives Road , Treloyhan, St Ives, Cornwall TR26 2JN **Tel:** (01736) 798684 **Fax:** (01736) 798684
Web: www.chyangwedhen.com **E-mail:** info@chyangwedhen.com

Delightful bed and breakfast adjoining the coastal footpath, 1 mile walk into beautiful St. Ives with its picturesque, safe sandy beaches, quaint cobbled streets and artists' quarter, Tate Gallery etc. Perfectly located as a base for exploring Cornwall. All rooms are en-suite and equipped for guests' every need. Chy An Gwedhen is totally non-smoking. Excellent choice of full English breakfasts, continental and locally oak-smoked fish. We have an on-site car park and patio garden. Enjoy a warm welcome in a relaxed, friendly atmosphere. Guests return again and again.

Bed & Breakfast per night: single occupancy from £30.00–£50.00; double room from £56.00–£68.00

Bedrooms: 4 double, 1 twin
Bathrooms: 5 en-suite, 1 shared
Parking: 7 spaces
Cards accepted: Mastercard, Visa, Switch/Delta, Eurocard, JCB

180 Blue Hayes Private Hotel

◆◆◆◆◆ Gold Award

Trelyon Avenue, St Ives, Cornwall TR26 2AD **Tel:** (01736) 797129 **Fax:** (01736) 799098
Web: www.bluehayes.co.uk **E-mail:** bluehayes@btconnect.com

A country house by the sea, within its own grounds and car park, overlooking St Ives Bay and harbour. Recently extended and completely refurnished to provide a higher standard and elegant relaxation. Five luxury rooms: Master Suite with balcony overlooking Bay and harbour, and four-poster bed; Godrevy Suite and Bay Suite, both with sea views; Garden Suite with direct access to garden; Trelyon Suite with roof garden and balcony overlooking woodlands and with sea views. Private licensed bar with terrace overlooking Bay and harbour.

Bed & Breakfast per night: single room from £85.00–£115.00; double room from £110.00–£170.00
Evening meal: 1900 (last orders 2030)

Bedrooms: 1 single, 5 double
Bathrooms: 6 en-suite
Open: February–November
Parking: 8 spaces
Cards accepted: Mastercard, Visa, Switch/Delta, Amex, JCB

The Leach Pottery

A large artists' colony had been established in St Ives for several decades when in 1920 Bernard Leach returned to England from Japan and set up a pottery here with his lifelong Japanese friend, Shoji Hamada. Leach was born in Hong Kong, of English parents, in 1887 and lived in the Far East as a child. He returned to Japan in 1909 to study pottery, one of the first Westerners to learn the techniques of Oriental pottery. Leach and Hamada chose a site three-quarters of a mile up the hill from the town centre, by the Stennack stream. They wanted to produce 'genuine handicrafts of quality rather than machine craft in quantity', the aim being to combine the traditions of craftsmanship that were still alive in the East with pre-Industrial Revolution English handcrafted pottery. Leach was ideally suited to this, a man able to bridge the spirit of the West and the East, and he was quickly established as the leader of the studio pottery movement. He proved too to be an inspirational teacher, passing on not only practical skills but his philosophy of what it meant to be an artist potter, and always attracted visitors and students from all over the world, the first being Michael Cardew, who later built Wenfordbridge pottery, near Bodmin. In 1923 Hamada went back to Japan, but remained in close touch with Leach. Bernard's son David joined the pottery in 1930, aged 19, and worked as his father's right-hand man for 25 years before starting up on his own in Bovey Tracey, Devon. David's brother, Michael, also worked in St Ives between 1950 and 1955, when he moved to Yelland, North Devon. His son John maintains the family tradition at Mulchelney Pottery in Somerset.

In 1956 Bernard married an American potter, Janet Darnell, and she took over the management of the pottery, showroom and students, while continuing to pot in her own right. Bernard was therefore freed up for more writing and travel, only giving up potting when his sight began to fail in the mid-1970s. After his death in 1979, Janet Leach kept the pottery going, a mecca for collectors and admirers of the art. There is a big collection of Leach and Hamada pots, and work for sale by Trevor Corser, Amanda Brier and Joanna Wason, who work there.

181 Laidback Trailblazers ◆◆◆◆

The Old Barn, Newmill, Penzance, Cornwall TR20 8XA **Tel:** (01736) 367742 **Fax:** (01092) 033725
Web: www.laidback-trails.co.uk **E-mail:** info@laidback-trails.co.uk

A converted barn set in a peaceful hamlet, this beautiful character residence enjoys delightful open views towards Mounts Bay over a picturesque rural landscape. Serviced accommodation, spacious yet cosy, with bedrooms individually furnished with modern facilities. Excellent Cornish food whether eating at the Old Barn, award-winning restaurants or the local pub. Tailor-made holidays including guided and self-led walking, horse riding and fishing. Days out can include visiting the Tate Gallery, St. Ives, Cornish gardens (Eden Project, Tresco and others), St Michael's Mount and many spectacular Cornish coves (Lamorna/Mousehole/Porthcurno).

Bed & Breakfast per night: single occupancy from £30.00–£40.00; double room from £50.00–£60.00
Dinner, Bed & Breakfast per person, per night: £75.00–£80.00 (only available for walking or special holidays)

Bedrooms: 2 double, 1 twin
Bathrooms: 1 en-suite, 1 private, 1 shared
Parking: 4 spaces

182 Hell Bay ★★★ Silver Award

Bryher, Isles of Scilly TR23 0PR **Tel:** (01720) 422947 **Fax:** (01720)423004
Web: www.hellbay.co.uk **E-mail:** contactus@hellbay.co.uk

Bryher's only hotel and England's last, boasts a spectacular natural location that blends with the contemporary style of the hotel to produce a unique venue. All suite accommodation is beautifully appointed and most have direct sea views. The award-winning food and informal service, combined with light and airy public rooms that feature original local art, complete the experience. Facilities include heated pool, gym, sauna, spa bath, games room, children's play area and 9-hole, par 3 golf. Stylish escapism on the edge of England.

Dinner, Bed & Breakfast per person, per night: £90.00–£200.00
Evening meal: 1900 (last orders 2100)

Bedrooms: 4 family, 19 suites
Bathrooms: 23 en-suite
Open: March–November
Cards accepted: Mastercard, Visa, Switch/Delta

183 Budock Vean - The Hotel on the River ★★★★ Silver Award

Helford Passage, Mawnan Smith, Falmouth, Cornwall TR11 5LG
Web: www.budockvean.co.uk **E-mail:** relax@budockvean.co.uk

This family run 4-star hotel, voted Cornwall Tourist Board Hotel of the Year 2002 is nestled in 65 acres of gardens and parkland on the banks of the Helford River. Our award-winning restaurant uses the finest local produce with fresh seafood the speciality. The hotel has it's own golf course, private foreshore with Sunseeker motor boat, large indoor pool, snooker room, all weather tennis courts and natural health spa. This is an ideal place from which to explore Britain's most dramatic coastline and visit the Great Gardens of Cornwall. Awarded South West Tourism Large Hotel of the Year 2003.

Bed & Breakfast per night: single room from £54.00–£97.00; double room from £108.00–£194.00
Dinner, Bed & Breakfast per person, per night: £66.00–£109.00
Lunch available: bar snacks 1230–1430, Sunday lunch 1230–1400

Evening meal: 1930 (last orders 2100)
Bedrooms: 7 single, 24 double, 23 twin, 2 family, 1 suite **Bathrooms:** 57 en-suite
Parking: 60 spaces
Cards accepted: Mastercard, Visa, Switch/Delta, Diners

184 Tregildry Hotel   ★★ Silver Award

Gillan, Manaccan, Helston, Cornwall TR12 6HG **Tel:** (01326) 231378 **Fax:** (01326) 231561
Web: www.tregildryhotel.co.uk **E-mail:** trgildry@globalnet.co.uk

An elegant small hotel with stunning sea views. Tucked away in an undiscovered corner of the Lizard Peninsula, this is for those seeking relaxed and stylish comfort in 'away from it all' surroundings. Large, light lounges with panoramic sea views have comfy sofas, fresh flowers and the latest books and magazines. The glamourous restaurant has won awards for cuisine and the pretty sea-view bedrooms are attractively decorated with colourful fabrics. Near coastal path walks and an ideal peaceful base for exploring Cornwall.

Dinner, Bed & Breakfast per person, per night: £75.00–£95.00
Evening meal: 1900 (last orders 2030)

Bedrooms: 1 single, 6 double, 3 twin
Bathrooms: 10 en-suite
Parking: 15 spaces
Open: March–October
Cards accepted: Mastercard, Visa, Switch/Delta

185 Dolvean Hotel   ◆◆◆◆◆ Gold Award

50 Melvill Road, Falmouth, Cornwall TR11 4DQ **Tel:** (01326) 313658 **Fax:** (01326) 313995
Web: www.dolvean.co.uk **E-mail:** reservations@dolvean.co.uk

Historic Falmouth, with it's beautiful natural harbour and splendid Tudor castle, is one of Cornwall's finest locations for exploring the far south west. Experience the elegance and comfort of our Victorian home, where carefully chosen antiques, fine china and fascinating books create an ambience where you can relax and feel at home. Each bedroom has it's own character, with pretty pictures and lots of ribbons and lace – creating an atmosphere that makes every stay a special occasion.

Bed & Breakfast per night: single room from £30.00–£45.00; double room from £60.00–£90.00

Bedrooms: 3 single, 7double, 1 twin
Bathrooms: 11 en-suite
Parking: 11 spaces
Open: all year except Christmas
Cards accepted: Mastercard, Visa, Switch/Delta, Amex, Eurocard, JCB

186 Bissick Old Mill   ◆◆◆◆◆ Silver Award

Ladock, Truro, Cornwall TR2 4PG **Tel:** (01726) 882557 **Fax:** (01726) 884057
E-mail: sonia.v@bissickoldmill.ndo.co.uk

Bissick Old Mill is known to be 300 years old and continued as a flour mill until the mid-1960s. Its conversion has been sympathetically conceived to provide modern conveniences whilst maintaining its former character, including slate floors, natural stone walls and beamed ceilings. Our aim is to provide you with the perfect environment in which to relax and enjoy the beauty of Cornwall, all areas of which are readily accessible from our central location. Close to the Eden Project.

Bed & Breakfast per night: double room from £65.00–£80.00
Evening meal: 1900 (last bookings 1000)

Bedrooms: 1 double, 1 twin, 2 suites
Bathrooms: 4 en-suite
Open: February–November
Parking: 6 spaces
Cards accepted: Mastercard, Visa, Switch/Delta, JCB, Maestro, Solo

187 Wisteria Lodge Country House

◆◆◆◆ Silver Award

Boscundle, Tregrehan, St Austell, Cornwall PL25 3RJ **Tel:** (01726) 810800
Web: www.wisterialodgehotel.co.uk **E-mail:** info@wisterialodgehotel.co.uk

Your very special place to stay, just one mile from the Eden Project. Wisteria Lodge offers a truly unique experience. Timeless elegance, gourmet cooking and beautiful, luxurious bedrooms and suites with the highest levels of personal service. The Lost Gardens of Heligan are a five-minute drive away and there are a number of delightful beaches within a 15-minute walk. Two spacious en-suite bedrooms, two executive suites with luxury lounge areas and jacuzzi baths, complimentary cream tea on arrival and all rooms have a mini bar, satellite television and video.

Bed & Breakfast per night: single occupancy from £90.00–£100.00; double room from £100.00–£140.00
Dinner, Bed & Breakfast per person, per night: £75.00–£90.00 (min 2 nights)
Evening meal: 1830 (last orders 2030)

Bedrooms: 1 double, 2 double/twin, 2 suites
Bathrooms: 4 en-suite
Parking: 5 spaces
Cards accepted: Mastercard, Visa, Switch/ Delta, Solo, Electron

---

188 Bucklawren Farm

◆◆◆◆ Silver Award

St Martin-by-Looe, Looe, Cornwall PL13 1NZ **Tel:** (01503) 240738 **Fax:** (01503) 240481
Web: www.bucklawren.com **E-mail:** bucklawren@btopenworld.com

Enjoy a warm welcome at Bucklawren, an elegant farmhouse set in the Cornish countryside, only one mile from the beach and the South-West Coastal Path. The bedrooms are en-suite and individually decorated, with all the comforts you would expect. Enjoy a traditional farmhouse breakfast of local produce. The on-site Granary Restaurant offers an excellent menu of high quality, freshly prepared food, using local produce.

Bed & Breakfast per night: single occupancy from £30.00–£37.50; double room from £50.00– £55.00

Bedrooms: 2 double, 2 twin, 2 family
Bathrooms: 6 en-suite
Open: March–November
Cards accepted: Mastercard, Visa, Switch/ Delta

---

189 Fieldhead Hotel

★★ Silver Award

Portuan Road, Hannafore, West Looe, Looe, Cornwall PL13 2DR **Tel:** (01503) 262689 **Fax:** (01503) 264114
Web: www.fieldheadhotel.co.uk **E-mail:** enquiries@fieldheadhotel.co.uk

Built in 1896, the hotel occupies a commanding site on West Looe, providing remarkable views across Looe Bay to Rame Head, Eddystone Lighthouse and the intriguing Looe Island. Set in one acre of landscaped tropical gardens with heated outdoor pool, the Fieldhead has 15 individually styled en-suite bedrooms, most with sea views, including four superior and two with balconies. Mainly fresh produce and locally caught seafood are served in the stylish restaurant. On-site private car park. Just 30 minutes from the exciting Eden Project – tickets available.

Bed & Breakfast per night: single room from £35.00–£50.00; double room from £60.00– £100.00
Dinner, Bed & Breakfast per person, per night: £50.00–£75.00
Evening meal: 1830 (last orders 2030)

Bedrooms: 1 single, 8 double, 4 twin, 2 family
Bathrooms: 15 en-suite
Parking: 15 spaces
Cards accepted: Mastercard, Visa, Switch/ Delta

190 Penmillard Farm

♦♦♦♦ Silver Award

Rame, Cawsand, Torpoint, Cornwall PL10 1LG **Tel:** (01752) 822215 **Fax:** (01752) 822454
Web: www.penmillard.co.uk **E-mail:** stay@penmillard.co.uk

We have the location, the facilities and the will to make it a memorable stay! Penmillard is situated in one of the most wonderfully unspoilt areas you could hope to find, but rarely do. The coastal footpath, which leads you to the old fishing villages of Kingsand and Cawsand, surrounds the farm. The Wiltons have welcomed guests into Penmillard for the past three generations. The house has been tastefully modernised with three double bedrooms, all with generous en-suite facilities, refreshment tray and television. Facilities available for horse riders/owners.

Bed & Breakfast per night: double room from £55.00–£65.00

Bedrooms: 2 double, 1 twin
Bathrooms: 3 en-suite
Parking: 3 spaces
Cards accepted: Mastercard, Visa, Switch/Delta

191 Bowling Green Hotel

♦♦♦♦♦ Silver Award

9-10 Osborne Place, Lockyer Street, Plymouth, Devon PL1 2PU **Tel:** (01752) 209090 **Fax:** (01752) 209092
Web: www.bowlinggreenhotel.com **E-mail:** info@bowlinggreenhotel.com

Situated in the historic naval city of Plymouth opposite the world famous 'Drake's Bowling Green', this elegant Georgian hotel has superbly appointed bedrooms offering all the modern facilities the traveller requires. With a full breakfast menu and friendly and efficient family staff, you can be sure of a memorable visit to Plymouth. The Bowling Green Hotel is centrally situated for the Barbican, Theatre Royal, leisure/conference centre and ferry port, with Dartmoor only a few miles away.

Bed & Breakfast per night: single room from £40.00–£48.00; double room from £56.00–£56.00

Bedrooms: 1 single, 8 double, 2 triple, 1 family
Bathrooms: 12 en-suite
Parking: 4 spaces
Cards accepted: Mastercard, Visa, Switch/Delta, Amex, Diners, Eurocard, Solo

192 Tor Cottage

♦♦♦♦♦ Gold Award

Chillaton, Lifton, Devon PL16 0JE **Tel:** (01822) 860248 **Fax:** (01822) 860126
Web: www.torcottage.co.uk **E-mail:** info@torcottage.co.uk

Enjoy the ambience of this special place. Twice national winner of the English Tourist Board's 'England for Excellence' Award and holder of a Gold Award. 2003 'Guest Accommodation of the Year' Award for All England. Tor Cottage has a warm and relaxed atmosphere and nestles in its own private valley. Streamside setting, lovely gardens and 18 acres of wildlife hillsides. Peace, tranquillity and complete privacy in beautiful en-suite bedsitting rooms, each with a log fire and private garden/terrace. Superb traditional and vegetarian breakfasts. Heated pool (summer). Early booking advisable. 45 minute easy drive from the new Eden Project. Special winter breaks available.

Bed & Breakfast per night: single occupancy £89.00; double room £130.00

Bedrooms: 4 double/twin
Bathrooms: 4 en-suite
Parking: 5 spaces
Open: mid January–mid December
Cards accepted: Mastercard, Visa, Switch/Delta

193 Brook House

◆◆◆◆◆ Silver Award

Horrabridge, Yelverton, Devon PL20 7QT **Tel:** (01822) 859225 **Fax:** (01822) 859225
Web: www.brook-house.com **E-mail:** info@brook-house.com

Peaceful Victorian home on the edge of Dartmoor set in five acres of gardens with stunning views across the Walkham Valley, offers a warm friendly welcome and delicious cooked breakfasts using high quality local produce. All bedrooms are individually furnished to an extremely high standard and all have en-suite facilities, colour television, tea/coffee making facilities, refrigerator, CD alarm clock radio. Brook House is ideal for exploring the moor as well as Tavistock, Plymouth and other attractions in West Devon and Cornwall.

Bed & Breakfast per night: single occupancy from £35.00–£53.00; double room from £50.00–£76.00

Bedrooms: 2 double, 1 twin
Bathrooms: 3 en-suite
Parking: 4 spaces
Cards accepted: Mastercard, Visa, Switch/Delta

Clapperbridges

Near Ashway in Exmoor, the River Barle flows wide and shallow over its brown stony bed. On either side, the road ends abruptly in a somewhat intimidating ford, but walkers may remain dry-shod, crossing the Barle via a magnificent walkway of vast stone slabs, known as Tarr Steps.

Tarr Steps is a type of ancient bridge known as a clapperbridge, and at 177ft (54m) in length is the longest and most elaborate of its type in England. The term 'clapperbridge' is used for any bridge constructed from large, flat slabs of stone forming a level pathway over a river or stream; the word probably developed from the Anglo Saxon *cleaca* meaning 'stepping stones'. Indeed a number of clapperbridges may well have begun as simple stepping-stones, which later formed the piers upon which linking slabs of stone were balanced. While some clapperbridges consist simply of a single slab thrown across the stream, multi-span bridges have typically between two and five spans (Tarr Steps with its magnificent 17 spans, is actually something of an anomaly).

No-one knows exactly when Tarr Steps was built, and, although for many years considered a pre-historic monument, it is now thought to be of much more recent construction. Most clapperbridges were built in the 14th century on packhorse routes, but a few appeared as late as the 18th and 19th centuries. They were simple and functional, and when routes changed or more superior structures superseded

them, they were very often allowed to disappear. Today, only about 40 remain in England.

Clapperbridges are found in parts of the country where the local rock yields large slabs of strong stone. There are consequently two main concentrations: one in North and West Yorkshire, the other in Devon and Cornwall. The greatest number are in Dartmoor, which boasts a wide range of variations. Postbridge, a lonely village in the heart of the Moor, has one of the finest of its type (shown above). It consists of three vast slabs of granite, some 17ft (5m) by 7ft (2m) in size, supported by four piers of granite blocks. Also on Dartmoor are Teignhead's bridge, built in 1790, and one over the Cowsic River at Two Bridges, built in 1837. At Wallabrook is a single-span clapperbridge, while the bridge at Yar Tor Down, Hexworthy, has three spans. Runnage bridge, near Postbridge, is a late example fitted with parapets.

194 The Old Orchard

◆◆◆◆ Silver Award

Harrowbeer Lane, Yelverton, Devon PL20 6DZ   **Tel:** (01822) 854310 **Fax:** (01822) 854310
Web: www.baross.demon.co.uk/theoldorchard **E-mail:** babs@baross.demon.co.uk

The Old Orchard is a small, select bed and breakfast – a real home-from-home. For the perfect stay in beautiful surroundings we offer comfortable accommodation in a quiet, yet accessible area close to village facilities. We offer satisfying breakfasts in elegant surroundings. Vegetarian options. Local organic produce. Breakfast when you choose. We provide a guest lounge with television and video. Everyone welcome – couples, business people, children, walkers and dogs. Washing, drying and ironing facilities available. Posh bed and breakfast on Dartmoor – open all year.

Bed & Breakfast per night: single occupancy from £30.00–£45.00; double room from £50.00–£60.00

Bedrooms: 1 double, 1 twin
Bathrooms: 1 en-suite, 1 private
Parking: 3 spaces

195 Easton Court

◆◆◆◆

Easton Cross, Chagford, Dartmoor, Devon TQ13 8JL   **Tel:** (01647) 433469 **Fax:** (01647) 433654
Web: www.easton.co.uk **E-mail:** stay@easton.co.uk

'Brideshead Revisited' was written by Evelyn Waugh in this lovely thatched Tudor house, sitting in four acres of gardens and paddocks within the Dartmoor National Park. Today, in a dedicated creeper-clad wing, built in Edwardian times, the en-suite guest accommodation offers the comfort of a hotel and magnificent views in a peaceful setting – an ideal base for the discerning traveller exploring the West Country. Easton Court is also available for groups of up to ten people on a self-catering basis, with optional daily maid service.

Bed & Breakfast per night: single occupancy from £50.00–£65.00; double room from £60.00–£75.00

Bedrooms: 3 double, 2 twin
Bathrooms: 5 en-suite
Parking: 5 spaces
Cards accepted: Mastercard, Visa, Switch/Delta

196 The Forest Inn

◆◆◆◆

Hexworthy, Yelverton, Devon PL20 6SD **Tel:** (01364) 631211 **Fax:** (01364) 631515
Web: www.theforestinn.co.uk **E-mail:** info@theforestinn.co.uk

The Forest Inn is situated in the middle of Dartmoor and offers an atmosphere from a more relaxed era. There is an excellent restaurant plus an extensive range of bar meals, together with a selection of Devon beers and cider. Quench your thirst after the efforts of the day with a drink at the bar or relax on the chesterfields in the lounge, complete with log fire for winter evenings. Muddy paws and boots welcome!!

Bed & Breakfast per night: single room from £31.00–£40.00; double room from £52.00–£70.00
Lunch available: 1200–1400
Evening meal: 1900 (last orders 2100)

Bedrooms: 2 single, 4 double, 2 twin, 2 family
Bathrooms: 8 en-suite, 2 private
Parking: 25 spaces
Cards accepted: Mastercard, Visa, Switch/Delta, Amex

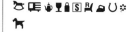

197 The Old Forge at Totnes

◆◆◆◆ Silver Award

Seymour Place, Totnes, Devon TQ9 5AY **Tel:** (01803) 862174 **Fax:** (01803) 865385
Web: www.oldforgetotnes.com **E-mail:** enq@oldforgetotnes.com

A warm welcome is assured at this delightful 600 year-old stone building. The coach arch leads through to a secluded walled garden. Enjoy the whirlpool spa. Relax in the conservatory lounge. Extensive breakfast menu. Wheelwright's Cottage is a two-bedroom suite. The Old Courtroom has a private roof terrace. Visit the ancient blacksmith's prison cell. Quiet, yet close to the town centre and riverside walks. An ideal base for the coast and Dartmoor. Only 1hour 30 minutes from the Eden Project. Car parking.

Bed & Breakfast per night: single occupancy from £44.00–£52.00; double room from £54.00–£74.00

Bedrooms: 6 double, 2 twin, 1 family, 1 suite
Bathrooms: 9 en-suite, 1 private
Parking: 8 spaces
Cards accepted: Mastercard, Visa, Switch/Delta, Amex, Diners, Eurocard

198 Tides Reach Hotel

★★★ Silver Award

South Sands, Salcombe, Devon TQ8 8LJ **Tel:** (01548) 843466 **Fax:** (01548) 843954
Web: www.tidesreach.com **E-mail:** enquire@tidesreach.com

Located on a tree-fringed sandy cove in an Area of Outstanding Natural Beauty where country meets the sea, with a glorious view across the Salcombe Estuary, you can relax in style in this beautifully furnished and decorated hotel. Pamper yourself in the superb leisure complex, extensively equipped and with a sunny tropical atmosphere. Award-winning creative cuisine (AA 1 Rosettes) served with courtesy and care in our garden-room restaurant.

Bed & Breakfast per night: single room from £66.00–£105.00; double room from £128.00–£260.00
Dinner, Bed & Breakfast per person, per night: £75.00–£145.00
Evening meal: 1900 (last orders 2100)

Bedrooms: 2 single, 18 double, 10 twin, 5 suites **Bathrooms:** 35 en-suite
Parking: 100 spaces
Open: February–November
Cards accepted: Mastercard, Visa, Switch/Delta, Amex, Diners, JCB

199 Rawlyn House Hotel

★★ Silver Award

Rawlyn Road, Chelston, Torquay TQ2 6PL **Tel:** (01803) 605208
Web: www.rawlynhousehotel.co.uk **E-mail:** shirley@rawlynhousehotel.co.uk

One of Torbay's most exceptional hotels – 'where comfort and quality matter'. A glorious Victorian villa, still maintaining many original features, has all the requirements of a modern-day hotel. Totally non-smoking, and set in tranquil and secluded grounds with heated swimming pool. Chef/proprietor Tony produces traditional food with home-made soups, sweets and pastries, whilst also catering for special diets, including coeliac, diabetic, vegetarian etc. Rawlyn House Hotel offers quality traditional bedrooms and luxury rooms for that extra treat. Ample parking, flexible bookings and over-60s discount.

Bed & Breakfast per night: single room from £33.00–£37.00; double room from £66.00–£74.00
Dinner, Bed & Breakfast per person, per night: £41.00–£48.00 (min 2 nights)
Evening meal: 1830 (last orders 1900)

Bedrooms: 2 single, 6 double, 3 twin, 1 family
Bathrooms: 11 en-suite, 1 private
Parking: 14 spaces
Open: April–October
Cards accepted: Mastercard, Visa, Switch/Delta

200 Kings Hotel

◆◆◆◆

44 Bampfylde Road, Torquay, TQ2 5AY **Tel:** (01803) 293108 **Fax:** (01803) 201499
Web: www.kingshoteltorquay.co.uk **E-mail:** kingshotel@bigfoot.com

A delightful licensed Victorian hotel situated in a peaceful yet convenient position minutes from Abbey Sands and the Riviera Centre. The eight bedrooms are en-suite, comfortable and well equipped, including colour television and tea/coffee making facilities. The Kings Hotel offers a relaxed, comfortable, friendly atmosphere where guests are made to feel welcome. There is a small bar, a bright and cheerful dining room and a non-smoking sitting room and outside there is a garden and patio area where guests can relax and enjoy the sunshine.

Bed & Breakfast per night: single room from £22.00–£30.00; double room from £44.00–£60.00
Evening meal: last orders 2100

Bedrooms: 1 single, 4 double, 1 twin, 2 family
Bathrooms: 8 en-suite
Parking: 4 spaces
Cards accepted: Mastercard, Visa, Switch/Delta, Amex

201 Osborne Hotel & Langtry's Restaurant

★★★★ Silver Award

Hesketh Crescent, Meadfoot Beach, Torquay, Devon TQ1 2LL **Tel:** (01803) 213311 **Fax:** (01803) 296788
Web: www.osborne-torquay.co.uk **E-mail:** enq@osborne-torquay.co.uk

This 29-bedroomed hotel, centrepiece of an elegant Regency crescent, overlooks the seclusion of Meadfoot Beach. The hotel offers the friendly ambience of a country home complemented by superior standards of comfort, five acres of gardens, indoor/outdoor pools, tennis court, gym, sauna, solarium, snooker room and putting green. Langtry's guide-acclaimed restaurant offers superlative food every evening and is one of the foremost restaurants on the English Riviera. The all-day Brasserie serves an international selection of food and drinks.

Bed & Breakfast per night: single room from £57.00–£78.00; double room from £104.00–£173.00
Dinner, Bed & Breakfast per person, per night: £74.00–£107.00
Evening meal: 1900 (last orders 2130)

Bedrooms: 1 single, 21 double, 2 family, 5 suites
Bathrooms: 29 en-suite
Parking: 120 spaces
Cards accepted: Mastercard, Visa, Switch/Delta, Amex

202 Britannia House B&B

◆◆◆◆◆ Silver Award

26 Teign Street, Teignmouth, Devon TQ14 8EG **Tel:** (01626) 770051 **Fax:** (01626) 776302
Web: www.britanniahouse.org **E-mail:** gillettbritannia@aol.com

A 17th-century Grade II listed house situated in a conservation area of Old Teignmouth. Recent refurbishment has resulted in a luxurious home-from-home for discerning travellers. The two double and one twin/double rooms have an en-suite shower room, television, fan, hairdryer and many other amenities. Showers are high pressure and thermostatically controlled. There is a guest sitting room (where smoking is permitted) which has an air purifier, music centre, books, magazines and payphone. The full English breakfast uses mainly fresh local produce.

Bed & Breakfast per night: double room from £55.00–£70.00

Bedrooms: 2 double, 1 twin
Bathrooms: 3 en-suite
Cards accepted: Mastercard, Visa, Switch/Delta, Amex

203 The Galley Restaurant with Cabins   ◆◆◆◆◆ Silver Award

41 Fore Street, Topsham, Exeter EX3 0HU **Tel:** (01392) 876078 **Fax:** (01392) 876078
Web: www.galleyrestaurant.co.uk **E-mail:** fish@galleyrestaurant.co.uk

An award-winning fish restaurant with nautical cabins, offering suites, double or twin rooms with panoramic river views or olde worlde 17th-century features with exposed beams, slate flooring and open log fire, minibars, hot and cold beverages, private bath or shower room, cable television, telephones with internet connection. Non-smoking and with private parking. 'Ideal for the business, romantic or city break user.'

Bed & Breakfast per night: single occupancy from £49.95–£62.50; double room from £99.90–£125.00
Evening meal: 1900 (last orders 2130)

Bedrooms: 3 double, 1 twin
Bathrooms: 1 en-suite, 3 private
Parking: 4 spaces
Open: all year except Christmas/New Year
Cards accepted: Mastercard, Visa, Switch/Delta, Amex, Diners

The South-West Coastal Path

'Poole 500 miles' reads the signpost pointing west along the Somerset coast at Minehead. In this daunting manner begins the South-West Coastal Path, a walk around England's 'toe' taking in some of the most magnificent coastal scenery in the land. The walk starts dramatically as it enters the Exmoor national park, hugging steep, wooded slopes that drop precipitously down to the sea, with stupendous views of the Welsh coast. Further on, the section of Devon coastline from Westward Ho! (the only British placename to include an exclamation mark) to the Cornish border is equally lovely as it passes the huddled village of Clovelly and the heights of Hartland Point with fine views of Lundy Island.

The Cornish Coast, both north and south, displays a stunning array of rocky promontories and soaring cliffs, interspersed with superb sandy beaches and fishing villages nestling in tiny coves. In general, the south coast, here and further on, is harder to negotiate than the north because of the many estuaries cutting into the lower-lying terrain, often requiring long detours inland.

The path re-enters Devon and, almost immediately, Plymouth, the largest city on its route. After rounding the wild promontories of Bolt Head and Prawle Point, it meanders through the gentler landscape of the 'Devon Riviera' and the seaside resorts of Paignton, Torquay, Teignmouth, and Dawlish. In Dorset, chalk cliffs run from Lyme Regis to Lulworth, interrupted by the long finger of shingle, Chesil Bank. The walk ends on a scenic high point as it negotiates the limestone heights of the Isle of Purbeck, an island in name only, for it remains firmly attached to the mainland.

As well as offering stunning scenery, the walk is rich in historical interest, from prehistoric hillforts in Dorset to Palmerston forts in Plymouth, or the abandoned village of Tyneham (Dorset) taken over by the army in 1943. In Cornwall, defunct engine houses and empty pilchard 'palaces' are relics of a rich industrial past.

The naturalist, as well as the historian, will find much of interest. The protruding coastline provides a landfall for migrating birds, while sub-tropical species of plants flourish in the mild climes of the south west. The Lizard, in particular, supports a unique flora, while army ranges at Lulworth, untouched by modern farming practices, have preserved a rare botanical habitat.

There are several guides to the South-West Coastal Path available, some suggesting shorter, circular walks and offering advice on accommodation, local attractions and other practical information.

204 The Salty Monk

◆◆◆◆◆ Gold Award

Church Street, Sidford, Sidmouth, Devon EX10 9QP **Tel:** (01395) 513174 **Fax:** (01395) 577232
Web: www.saltymonk.co.uk **E-mail:** enquirys@saltymonk.co.uk

A haven of luxury where you will be made to feel very special. Nestling next to the Regency town of Sidmouth, this 16th-century character restaurant is ideally located for exploring Dartmoor and the heritage coastline. Five individually decorated and superbly appointed bedrooms, some with spa baths, and a suite with king-size waterbed. The award-winning, elegant restaurant overlooks the beautiful gardens. Imaginative, fresh food using Devon's finest ingredients is prepared on the premises by the resident chef/proprietors.

Bed & Breakfast per night: single occupancy from £55.00–£85.00; double room from £85.00–£110.00
Dinner, Bed & Breakfast per person, per night: £66.00–£96.00
Lunch available: 1200–1345 (reservation only)

Evening meal: 1900 (last orders 2100)
Bedrooms: 2 double, 2 twin, 1 suite
Bathrooms: 5 en-suite
Parking: 20 spaces
Cards accepted: Mastercard, Visa, Switch/ Delta, Eurocard, JCB

205 Royal York and Faulkner Hotel

★★ Silver Award

Esplanade, Sidmouth, Devon EX10 8AZ **Tel:** Freephone 0800 220714 or (01395) 513043 **Fax:** (01395) 577472
Web: www.royalyorkhotel.net **E-mail:** stay@royalyorkhotel.net

In a superb position at the centre of Sidmouth's elegant esplanade and adjacent to the picturesque town centre. Family-run hotel with a long-standing reputation for hospitality and service, combining beautifully appointed public areas with excellent modern facilities and amenities. Our restaurant, which retains the traditional high standards of silver service, offers excellent cuisine, ranging from classic to modern. De luxe rooms lead to the balcony overlooking the sea and esplanade. Excellent range of in-house leisure facilities, plus complimentary swimming at Sidmouth's indoor pool, which is just 200 yards from the hotel.

Bed & Breakfast per night: single room from £31.50–£56.50; double room from £63.00–£113.00
Dinner, Bed & Breakfast per person, per night: £41.50–£66.50 (min 2 nights)
Lunch available: 1130–1600 (ex Sunday)

Evening meal: 1900 (last orders 2030)
Bedrooms: 22 single, 9 double, 29 twin, 8 family **Bathrooms:** 66 en-suite, 2 private
Parking: 21 spaces
Cards accepted: Mastercard, Visa, Switch/ Delta

206 Hotel Riviera

★★★★ Gold Award

The Esplanade, Sidmouth, Devon EX10 8AY **Tel:** (01395) 515201 **Fax:** (01395) 577775
Web: www.hotelriviera.co.uk **E-mail:** enquiries@hotelriviera.co.uk

Splendidly positioned at the centre of Sidmouth's esplanade, overlooking Lyme Bay. With its mild climate and the beach just on the doorstep, the setting echoes the south of France and is the choice for the discerning visitor. Behind the hotel's fine Regency façade lies an alluring blend of old-fashioned service and present-day comforts. Glorious sea views can be enjoyed from the recently redesigned en-suite bedrooms, which are fully appointed and have many thoughtful extras. In the elegant bay-view dining room guests are offered a fine choice of dishes from extensive menus, prepared by French and Swiss-trained chefs, with local seafood being a particular speciality.

Bed & Breakfast per night: single room from £89.00–£120.00; double room from £158.00–£220.00
Dinner, Bed & Breakfast per person, per night: £90.00–£132.00
Lunch available: 1230–1400

Evening meal: 1900 (last orders 2100)
Bedrooms: 7 single, 11 double, 7 twin, 2 suites
Bathrooms: 27 en-suite
Parking: 26 spaces
Cards accepted: Mastercard, Visa, Switch/ Delta, Amex, Diners

207 Combe House Hotel & Restaurant

★★★ Silver Award

Gittisham, Honiton, Nr Exeter, Devon EX14 3AD **Tel:** (01404) 540400 **Fax:** (01404) 46004
Web: www.thishotel.com **E-mail:** stay@thishotel.com

A Grade I Elizabethan manor set in 3,500 acres of Devon estate, where Arabian horses and pheasants roam freely. Stroll down Combe's mile-long drive to Gittisham – Prince Charles's 'ideal English village' – with thatched cottages, a Norman church and village green. Inside are squashy sofas and flamboyant flowers, and roaring log fires beckon. 15 romantic bedrooms exude style and relaxed informality. The candlelit restaurant serves memorable, contemporary British cuisine. Nearby are the Jurassic World Heritage coastline, the cathedral city of Exeter, and Honiton – famous for its lace and antiques. Room for Romance - UK Hotel of the Year 2003 - runner up.

Bed & Breakfast per night: single room from £99.00–£165.00; double room from £138.00–£146.00
Dinner, Bed & Breakfast per person, per night: £96.00–£154.00 (min 2 nights at weekends)
Lunch available: 1200–1430

Evening meal: 1900 (last orders 2130)
Bedrooms: 13 double/twin, 2 suites
Bathrooms: 15 en-suite
Parking: 50 spaces
Cards accepted: Mastercard, Visa, Switch/Delta

---

208 Smallicombe Farm

◆◆◆◆ Silver Award

Northleigh, Colyton, Devon EX24 6BU **Tel:** (01404) 831310 **Fax:** (01404) 831431
Web: www.smallicombe.com **E-mail:** maggie_todd@yahoo.com

Relax in a really special place, an idyllic rural setting abounding with wildlife yet close to the coast. All rooms en-suite overlooking our unspoilt valley landscape that changes throughout the year. The ground floor 'garden suite' of sitting room, bedroom and bathroom is wheelchair accessible. Scrumptious farmhouse breakfasts including prize-winning Smallicombe sausages from our rare breed pigs. Sit by a welcoming inglenook fire after walking the East Devon Way or the nearby coastal footpath along the Jurassic coast, England's only natural World Heritage site. Accessible Mobility 3

Bed & Breakfast per night: single occupancy from £35.00–£40.00; double room from £50.00–£60.00
Evening meal: by arrangement

Bedrooms: 1 double, 1 twin, 1 double/family
Bathrooms: 3 en-suite
Parking: 10 spaces
Cards accepted: Mastercard, Visa, Switch/Delta

---

209 Kerrington House Hotel

◆◆◆◆◆ Gold Award

Musbury Road, Axminster, Devon EX13 5JR **Tel:** (01297) 35333 and 35345 **Fax:** (01297) 35333 and 35345
Web: www.kerringtonhouse.com **E-mail:** james.reaney@kerringtonhouse.com

On the Devon/Dorset borders, close to Lyme Regis and the heritage coast, a fine period house, lovingly restored and furnished with comfort and style. Sumptuous bedrooms with lots of little luxuries, stunning drawing room overlooking the delightful landscaped gardens. Elegant dining room in which to enjoy fine wines and good food, freshly cooked with flair using local produce. Conveniently located on the edge of town and ideal for exploring this beautiful region.

Bed & Breakfast per night: single occupancy from £70.00–£75.00; double room from £100.00–£110.00
Dinner, Bed & Breakfast per person, per night: £75.00–£85.00
Evening meal: 1900 (last orders 2030)

Bedrooms: 4 double, 1 twin
Bathrooms: 5 en-suite
Parking: 5 spaces
Cards accepted: Mastercard, Visa, Switch/Delta

210 Wisteria Cottage ◆◆◆◆

Taylors Lane, Morcombelake, Bridport, Dorset DT6 6ED **Tel:** (01297) 489019
Web: www.dorsetcottage.org.uk **E-mail:** dave@dorsetcottage.org.uk

Enjoy panoramic views from our comfortable ensuite rooms. In a tranquil location within a designated Area of Outstanding Natural Beauty, Wisteria Cottage offers the ideal place to unwind amongst wonderful scenery. The World Heritage Jurassic Coast, Lyme Regis and Bridport are within easy reach. Specatacular walking country, right from our doorstep. Breakfasts are prepared using local produce wherever possible and we also offer vegetarian and dairy free options. There are two inns serving evening meals within close proximity. Low season breaks are also available.

Bed & Breakfast per night: single occupancy from £30.00; double room from £50.00

Bedrooms: 1 double, 1 twin
Bathrooms: 2 en-suite
Parking: 2 spaces
Open: all year except Christmas

211 Bellplot House Hotel ◆◆◆◆◆

High Street, Chard, Somerset TA20 1QB **Tel:** (01460) 62600
Web: www.bellplothouse.co.uk **E-mail:** info@bellplothouse.co.uk

Grade II listed Georgian townhouse with traditional-style drawing room and restaurant. Seven luxury bedrooms with every modern facility. Relax and enjoy yourself with friendly service whilst relishing the delights of drinking from fine Brierley cut glass crystal and large, sociable wine glasses. Enjoy Dennis's fine, high quality food and wines at affordable prices. Many excellent historic houses and gardens nearby and within easy driving distance of Lyme Bay. An ideal halfway stopover from Midlands/London to the Eden Project.

Bed & Breakfast per night: single room £76.00; double room £84.50
Evening meal: 1900 (last orders 2100)

Bedrooms: 1 single, 5 double, 1 family
Bathrooms: 7 en-suite
Parking: 12 spaces
Cards accepted: Mastercard, Visa, Switch/Delta, JCB

212 Farthings Hotel and Restaurant   ★★ Silver Award

Hatch Beauchamp, Taunton, Somerset TA3 6SG **Tel:** (01823) 480664 **Fax:** (01823) 481118
Web: www.farthingshotel.com **E-mail:** farthing1@aol.com

Enjoy a glass of wine on the two acres of lawn surrounding this elegant Georgian country house hotel, whilst dinner is prepared by owner Stephen Murphy, who has been a chef for 25 years. Emphasis is on good quality, English food and local produce. A short drive will take you to the cathedral cities of Wells, Bath, Exeter and Taunton. The Somerset/Dorset coast, Exmoor, Cheddar Gorge and the undulating Mendip hills are also convenient. Also suitable for business, incorporating well-equipped meeting facilities, good communications and friendly and efficient staff.

Bed & Breakfast per night: single occupancy from £75.00–£90.00; double room from £105.00– £130.00
Dinner, Bed & Breakfast per person, per night: £75.00–£85.00 (min 2 nights)
Evening meal: 1900 (last orders 2030)

Bedrooms: 5 double, 3 twin, 1 family, 1 suite
Bathrooms: 10 en-suite
Parking: 20 spaces
Cards accepted: Mastercard, Visa, Switch/Delta, Amex, Eurocard

213 Cumberland House ◆◆◆◆

Green Hill, Sherborne, Dorset DT9 4EP **Tel:** (01935) 817554 **Fax:** (01935) 817398
E-mail: cumberlandbandb@aol.com

Cumberland House is a delightful cottage with parking space in the centre of Sherborne. The shops, Abbey and railway station are all within a short walking distance. The cottage has two double bedrooms, one en-suite and one with private shower. Come and enjoy a roaring log fire in winter and during summer relax in our pretty walled garden. Dinner is offered on request and special diets are catered for. Please bring your own wine. You will be welcomed by Sammie, a well-behaved labrador.

Bed & Breakfast per night: double room from £58.00–£69.00
Dinner, Bed & Breakfast per person, per night: £50.00–£65.00
Evening meal: 1930

Bedrooms: 2 double
Bathrooms: 1 en-suite, 1 private
Parking: 2 spaces

214 The Old Vicarage ◆◆◆◆◆

Sherborne Road, Milborne Port, Sherborne, Dorset DT9 5AT **Tel:** (01963) 251117 **Fax:** (01963) 251515
Web: www.milborneport.freeserve.co.uk **E-mail:** theoldvicarage@milborneport.freeserve.co.uk

A Victorian Gothic listed building set in three acres of beautiful grounds affording glorious views of open country. The property is privately owned and run by two ex-London restaurateurs. Every room has a different character and the spacious lounge is furnished with antiques. Dinner of the highest standard is served on Friday and Saturday. On other nights pubs within five minutes' walk serve good food. Situated on the edge of a charming village and two miles from the historic town of Sherborne with its magnificent Abbey and two castles. Within easy reach are stately homes and gardens. The most attractive Dorset coast is only 30 miles away.

Bed & Breakfast per night: single occupancy from £47.00–£71.00; double room from £61.00– £107.00
Dinner, Bed & Breakfast per person, per night: £51.00–£70.00 (min 2 nights at weekends)
Evening meal: 1900 (last orders 2100)

Bedrooms: 2 double, 1 twin, 3 family
Bathrooms: 6 en-suite
Parking: 10 spaces
Open: February–December
Cards accepted: Mastercard, Visa, Switch/Delta, Amex, JCB

215 The Poachers Inn ◆◆◆◆

Piddletrenthide, Dorchester, Dorset DT2 7QX **Tel:** (01300) 348358 **Fax:** (01300) 348153
Web: www.thepoachersinn.co.uk **E-mail:** thepoachersinn@piddletrenthide.fsbusiness.co.uk

A country inn, set in the heart of the lovely Piddle Valley, eight miles from Dorchester and within easy reach of all Dorset's attractions. All rooms are en-suite and have a colour television, tea/coffee making facilities and telephone. Outdoor swimming pool from May to September. Half-board guests choose from the à la carte menu at no extra cost. Short breaks: three nights for the price of two (half board), October to April. Please send for a brochure.

Bed & Breakfast per night: double room £60.00
Dinner, Bed & Breakfast per person, per night: £45.00–£50.00
Lunch available: all day
Evening meal: all day

Bedrooms: 14 double, 3 twin, 1 family
Bathrooms: 18 en-suite
Parking: 40 spaces
Cards accepted: Mastercard, Visa, Switch/Delta

216 The Old Rectory

◆◆◆◆ Silver Award

Winterbourne Steepleton, Dorchester, Dorset DT2 9LG **Tel:** (01305) 889468 **Fax:** (01305) 889737
Web: www.trees.eurobell.co.uk **E-mail:** trees@eurobell.co.uk

Genuine 1850 Victorian rectory situated in a quiet hamlet, surrounded by breathtaking countryside. Close to historic Dorchester and Weymouth's sandy beaches. We specialise in providing a quiet comfortable night's sleep followed by a copious English, vegetarian or continental breakfast with fresh organic produce, home-made jams, yoghurt and bread. Enjoy our superbly appointed guest drawing room, croquet, putting green and badminton lawns. Local pub within walking distance and excellent restaurants within a short drive.

Bed & Breakfast per night: single room £50.00; double room from £55.00–£110.00

Bedrooms: 3 double/twin
Bathrooms: 2 en-suite, 1 private
Parking: 6 spaces
Open: all year except Christmas/New Year

217 Channel House Hotel

★★ Gold Award

Church Path, Off Northfield Road, Minehead, Somerset TA24 5QG **Tel:** (01643) 703229 **Fax:** (01643) 708925
Web: www.channelhouse.co.uk **E-mail:** channel.house@virgin.net

An elegant Edwardian country house perfectly located for exploring the beauty of Exmoor and situated on the lower slopes of Exmoor's picturesque North Hill where it nestles in two acres of award-winning gardens. The high standards of cuisine and accommodation will best suit those seeking superior quality and comfort. If you would like to experience smiling service in the tranquil elegance of this lovely hotel, we will be delighted to send you our brochure and sample menu. A non smoking hotel.

Bed & Breakfast per night: single occupancy from £62.00–£75.00; double room from £94.00– £120.00
Dinner, Bed & Breakfast per person, per night: £62.00–£75.00
Evening meal: 1900 (last orders 2030)

Bedrooms: 3 double, 5 twin
Bathrooms: 8 en-suite
Parking: 10 spaces
Open: March–November & Christmas
Cards accepted: Mastercard, Visa, Switch/ Delta, Eurocard, JCB

218 Northam Mill

◆◆◆◆ Silver Award

Water Lane, Stogumber, Taunton, Somerset TA4 3TT **Tel:** (01984) 656916 or (01984) 656146 **Fax:** (01984) 656144
Web: www.northam-mill.co.uk **E-mail:** bmsspicer@aol.com

Hidden for 300 years! This converted corn mill and trout stream (bordering five acres and beautiful gardens) is set in an area of outstanding natural beauty, one mile from Exmoor National Park at the foot of the Brendons and at the neck of the Quantock Hills. The sounds of the waterfall and abundance of wildlife are interrupted only by the whistle of the occasional steam train. All food, including bread, is home made and served in a beamed dining room/library. Licensed with a fine cellar. A three course dinner menu changes daily. Superior en-suite bedrooms, a separate garden suite, and a self-contained apartment. House party weekends are a speciality and include archery, fishing and clay shooting with the exclusive use of Northam Mill.

Bed & Breakfast per night: single room from £30.00–£50.00; double room from £55.00– £80.00
Dinner, Bed & Breakfast per person, per night: £55.00–£75.00
Lunch available: 1200–1400 (house parties only)

Evening meal: 1930 (last orders 2000)
Bedrooms: 1 single, 2 double, 2 twin, 1 suite
Bathrooms: 4 en-suite, 2 private
Parking: 12 spaces
Cards accepted: Mastercard, Visa, Switch/ Delta, Eurocard

219 Combe House Hotel

★★ Silver Award

Holford, Bridgwater, Somerset TA5 1RZ **Tel:** (01278) 741382 **Fax:** (01278) 741322
Web: www.combehouse.co.uk **E-mail:** enquiries@combehouse.co.uk

In the heart of the Quantock Hills (renowned as an area of outstanding natural beauty) lies this 17th-century house of great character. Once a tannery, this cottage-style hotel offers absolute peace and quiet in beautiful surroundings. Inside the beamed building, with its charming collection of pictures, pottery and period furniture, the visitor will find the relaxed atmosphere and friendly service ideal to enjoy Combe House, its restaurant, the Quantocks and the many attractions in the area.

Bed & Breakfast per night: single room from £37.00–£45.00; double room from £76.00–£101.00
Dinner, Bed & Breakfast per person, per night: £65.00–£75.00
Lunch available: 1200–1400
Evening meal: 1930 (last orders 2030)

Bedrooms: 4 single, 5 double, 7 twin
Bathrooms: 16 en-suite
Parking: 20 spaces
Cards accepted: Mastercard, Visa, Switch/Delta, Amex

220 Castle of Comfort Country House Hotel & Restaurant ◆◆◆◆◆ Silver Award

Dodington, Nether Stowey, Bridgwater, Somerset TA5 1LE **Tel:** (01278) 741264 or (07050) 642002 **Fax:** (01278) 741144
Web: www.castle-of-comfort.co.uk **E-mail:** reception@castle-of-comfort.co.uk

The Castle of Comfort is believed to date from the 16th century. Once described as 'a stone inn at the foot of the Quantock Hills where it is rumoured that pirates off the English coast used to dispose of their loot', it is now a small country house hotel set in four acres of grounds. Luxurious accommodation of the highest standard for families, business people and honeymoon couples. À la carte dinner (1900-2030) and lunches (1200-1400), Monday–Saturday, reservations only.

Bed & Breakfast per night: single room from £38.00–£85.00; double room from £96.00–£130.00
Dinner, Bed & Breakfast per person, per night: £56.00–£93.00
Lunch available: 1200–1400

Evening meal: 1900 (last orders 2000)
Bedrooms: 2 single, 3 double, 1 family
Bathrooms: 6 en-suite
Parking: 10 spaces
Cards accepted: Mastercard, Visa, Switch/Delta, Eurocard, JCB

221 Model Farm

◆◆◆◆

Perry Green, Wembdon, Bridgwater, Somerset TA5 2BA **Tel:** (01278) 433999
Web: www.modelfarm.com **E-mail:** info@modelfarm.com

Richard and Carol Wright invite you to share the peaceful setting of their licensed Victorian country house. Set in five acres of garden and surrounded by fields, Model Farm is an ideal location in which to unwind. Relax in spacious en-suite bedrooms – all with tea/coffee making facilities, or enjoy a pre-dinner drink in the lounge by an open fire. Dine by candlelight, with your hosts, around an oak refectory table beside a roaring log fire.

Bed & Breakfast per night: single occupancy from £40.00–£45.00; double room from £60.00–£70.00
Dinner, Bed & Breakfast per person, per night: £42.00–£65.00
Evening meal: by arrangement

Bedrooms: 1 double, 1 twin, 1 family
Bathrooms: 3 en-suite
Parking: 6 spaces
Cards accepted: Mastercard, Visa, Switch/Delta, JCB

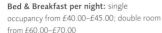

222 The Old Stores

Westbury-sub-Mendip, Wells, Somerset BA5 1HA **Tel:** (01749) 870817 or 07721 514306 **Fax:** (01749) 870980
E-mail: moglin980@aol.com

This charming cottage, once the village stores, is set in the heart of the village, midway between the scenic attractions of Wells and Cheddar Gorge. It is ideally situated for exploring this area of outstanding scenic beauty. All guest rooms are equipped with television, facilities for making hot drinks and have en-suite or private facilities. There is also a guest sitting room with television and books and maps of the local area.

Bed & Breakfast per night: single occupancy from £23.00–£24.00; double room from £46.00–£48.00

Bedrooms: 2 double, 1 twin
Bathrooms: 2 en-suite, 1 private
Parking: 3 spaces
Cards accepted: Mastercard, Visa, Switch/Delta, Eurocard, JCB

223 Beryl

Beryl, Wells, Somerset BA5 3JP **Tel:** (01749) 678738 **Fax:** (01749) 670508
Web: www.beryl-wells.co.uk **E-mail:** stay@beryl.co.uk

'Beryl' – a precious gem in a perfect setting. Small 19th-century Gothic mansion, set in peaceful gardens, one mile from the centre of Wells. Well placed for touring the area. Offers comfortable, well-equipped bedrooms and relaxed use of the beautifully furnished reception rooms. Dinner is served with elegant style using fresh produce from the vegetable garden and local supplies. Children and pets are welcome. Outdoor heated pool, June–September. Chair lift to first floor bedrooms.

Bed & Breakfast per night: single occupancy from £55.00–£75.00; double room from £70.00–£110.00
Dinner, Bed & Breakfast per person, per night: £77.50–£97.50
Evening meal: 1930

Bedrooms: 5 double, 3 twin
Bathrooms: 8 en-suite
Parking: 16 spaces
Cards accepted: Mastercard, Visa, Switch/Delta

224 Carfax Hotel

13–15 Great Pulteney Street, Bath BA2 4BS
Web: www.carfaxhotel.co.uk **E-mail:** reservations@carfaxhotel.co.uk

A trio of Georgian townhouses overlooking Henrietta Park with a view to the surrounding hills. A mere stroll to the Pump Room, Roman Baths, Kennet and Avon Canal and the river. Well-appointed superior rooms restored to their original glory – all en-suite with television/radio, some Sky channels, direct-dial telephones, lift to all floors, car park for 11 cars, plus garage (fee payable). Senior citizen and group rates on application. Special off-peak breaks. Accessible Mobility 1

Bed & Breakfast per night: single room from £56.00–£72.00; double room from £80.00–£110.50
Dinner, Bed & Breakfast per person, per night: £47.75–£83.50
Evening meal: 1800 (last orders 1930)

Bedrooms: 6 single, 17 double, 6 twin, 2 family, 1 suite
Bathrooms: 31 en-suite
Parking: 11 spaces
Cards accepted: Mastercard, Visa, Switch/Delta, Amex

225 Ravenscroft

♦♦♦♦ Silver Award

Sydney Road, Bath BA2 6NT **Tel:** (01225) 469267 **Fax:** (01225) 448722
E-mail: ravenscroft@tiscali.co.uk

This is an early Victorian Italianate villa is situated within Sydney Gardens, an historic park. The garden backs onto the Kennet and Avon canal. Although the house is in a semirural seting, it is only a level walk of less than half a mile into the city centre. Giving easy access to entertainments, restaurants etc. without having to use your car which is securely parked in the grounds of the house. A full quality breakfast is provided and there is a no smoking rule.

Bed & Breakfast per night: single occupancy from £55.00–£70.00; double room from £55.00–£70.00

Bedrooms: 2 double
Bathrooms: 2 private
Parking: 4 spaces
Open: all year except Christmas/New Year

Claverton American Museum

The city of Bath, so quintessentially English, attracts American tourists like a magnet, so it is perhaps appropriate that just outside the city is a museum which offers a good measure of

cultural exchange. Claverton Manor, a large 19th-century neo-classical mansion set in beautiful grounds overlooking the peaceful Avon valley, is now the American Museum in Britain and is devoted entirely to the cultural history of the United States.

The museum has been based at Claverton since 1961 and was the brainchild of two Americans, Dallas Pratt and John Judkyn, whose desire it was to encourage greater mutual understanding between Britain and America. The bulk of the museum's collection takes the form of furnished rooms brought, often in their entirety, from houses in the United States, and representing different aspects of American society. Other galleries are devoted to specific crafts (pewter, silver, glass, textiles) or themes (North American Indians, maritime history, westward expansion).

The museum is something of a revelation in the sheer range and variety of cultural influences on display; it vividly demonstrates the enormous mixture of ethnic

and social influences which were combined in the melting pot of American society, and the contrasts are immense. One room, for example, contains the austere furniture of the Shakers, a puritanical religious sect which settled in New England in the late 18th century. Utility and simplicity were the hallmarks of their plain, but beautiful, hand-made wooden furniture. Roughly contemporary, but a world apart, is the New Orleans bedroom. Its factory-made, dark mahogany furniture is heavily adorned with curly, baroque flourishes while curtains and carpets riot with elaborate patterns.

Displays on American Indians and Spanish colonists compete for space with less well-known ethnic groups. The Pennsylvania Dutch, for example (actually 17th-century refugees from Germany and Switzerland) brought a colourful decorative tradition manifested in vividly painted furniture and kitchenware.

The large number of different styles and traditions demanding representation has meant that the exhibits have spilled out into the manor's immediate surroundings. While one part of the grounds is planted as a colonial herb garden, another is a replica of George Washington's garden at Mount Vernon. An 18th-century Dutch summerhouse is furnished as a 19th-century American milliner's shop, and a stable block is devoted to American naive folk art.

226 The Ayrlington

◆◆◆◆◆ Gold Award

24/25 Pulteney Road, Bath BA2 4EZ **Tel:** (01225) 425495 **Fax:** (01225) 469029
Web: www.ayrlington.com **E-mail:** mail@ayrlington.com

A handsome Victorian house set in a splendid award-winning walled garden with exceptional views of the Abbey. Bath's centre and historic sites are just a five minute level stroll away. The elegant interior is a graceful blend of English and Asian antiques artwork and fine fabrics. All bedrooms have an individual theme and are beautifully furnished, some with four-poster beds and spa baths. The hotel has oriental style gardens overlooking the Abbey, a residents bar, secure private parking and is entirely non-smoking.

Bed & Breakfast per night: single occupancy from £85.00–£100.00; double room from £99.00–£160.00

Bedrooms: 11 double, 1 twin, 2 family
Bathrooms: 14 en-suite
Parking: 14 spaces
Cards accepted: Mastercard, Visa, Switch/Delta, Amex

227 Grove Lodge

◆◆◆◆

11 Lambridge, Bath BA1 6BJ **Tel:** (01225) 310860 **Fax:** (01225) 429630
Web: www.grovelodgebath.co.uk **E-mail:** stay@grovelodgebath.co.uk

Grove Lodge is a Grade II listed Georgian villa (1788) in an enclosed green landscape setting, yet convenient for the city centre. Owned by an architect, Grove Lodge has been refurbished to provide Georgian elegance with modern comfort. The en-suite bedrooms have high ceilings, majestic marble fireplaces and large sash windows with fine views. Furnishings are an eclectic mix of antique and modern styles with neutral colour schemes. The contemporary white bathrooms are generous in size. This is a friendly, informal family home.

Bed & Breakfast per night: single occupancy from £38.00–£46.00; double room from £56.00–£72.00

Bedrooms: 4 double/twin, 1 triple
Bathrooms: 4 en-suite, 1 private
Open: all year except Christmas/New Year
Cards accepted: Mastercard, Visa, Switch/Delta

228 Walton Villa

◆◆◆◆

3 Newbridge Hill, Bath BA1 3PW **Tel:** (01225) 482792 **Fax:** (01225) 313093
Web: www.walton.izest.com **E-mail:** walton.villa@virgin.net

You will receive a warm and friendly welcome to our immaculate, non-smoking family-run bed and breakfast. Our en-suite bedrooms are delightfully decorated and furnished for your comfort, with colour television, hairdryer and complimentary hospitality tray. Our generous and delicious full English or vegetarian breakfasts are cooked to order and served in our elegant dining room. Situated one mile west of the city centre, we are convenient for exploring Roman and Georgian Bath and an ideal base for visiting Wells, Glastonbury, Stonehenge etc. Off-street parking available.

Bed & Breakfast per night: single room from £25.00–£40.00; double room from £50.00–£55.00

Bedrooms: 1 single, 3 double/twin
Bathrooms: 4 en-suite
Parking: 5 spaces
Cards accepted: Mastercard, Visa, Switch/Delta, Barclaycard

229 The Hollies

Hatfield Road, Bath BA2 2BD **Tel:** (01225) 313366 **Fax:** (01225) 313366
Web: www.visitus.co.uk/bath/hotel.hollies.html **E-mail:** davcartwright@lineone.net

The Hollies was built in 1850 in a meadow beside the old Fosse Way, built by the Romans 2000 years ago. The house, with its handsome facade, has three individually designed rooms overlooking the pretty, scented garden. Enjoy a full English breakfast in the dining room or, if you prefer, a Continental breakfast in your bedroom. Parking is available in the drive. So that our guests may relax we regret that we do not take dogs or children. Smoking is allowed in the garden.

Bed & Breakfast per night: single occupancy from £55.00–£65.00; double room from £65.00–£75.00

Bedrooms: 2 double, 1 twin
Bathrooms: 2 en-suite, 1 private
Parking: 3 spaces
Open: February–December
Cards accepted: Mastercard, Visa, Switch/ Delta, JCB

230 Athole Guest House
◆◆◆◆◆ Gold Award

33 Upper Oldfield Park, Bath BA2 3JX **Tel:** (01225) 334307 **Fax:** (01225) 320001
Web: www.atholehouse.co.uk **E-mail:** info@atholehouse.co.uk

No chintz or dusty four-posters at Athole House. Instead, a large Victorian home restored to give bright, inviting, quiet bedrooms, sleek furniture, sparkling bathrooms and hotel facilities (mini-bar, laptop connection, satellite television, safe). Easy walking distance to the town centre. The hospitality is old-style, with award-winning breakfasts (full English, home-made bread, fruit salad, speciality muesli etc). Relax in our gardens, or let us help you explore the area. Secure parking behind remote-control gates or in garage. Free transfer to and from the railway/bus station is included.

Bed & Breakfast per night: single room from £48.00–£58.00; double room from £68.00–£78.00

Bedrooms: 3 single, 3 double, 3 twin, 1 family
Bathrooms: 10 en-suite
Parking: 6 spaces
Cards accepted: Mastercard, Visa, Switch/ Delta, Amex, Eurocard, JCB

231 Monkshill
◆◆◆◆◆ Gold Award

Shaft Road, Monkton Combe, Bath BA2 7HL **Tel:** (01225) 833028 **Fax:** (01225) 833028
Web: www.monkshill.com **E-mail:** monks.hill@virgin.net

Five minutes from the centre of Bath lies this secluded and very comfortable country residence, surrounded by its own peaceful gardens and enjoying far-reaching views over one of the most spectacularly beautiful parts of the Avon Valley. You can be assured of a warm welcome at Monkshill, where the emphasis is on luxurious comfort and complete relaxation. The drawing room, with its fine antiques, Steinway grand and open log fire, is for the exclusive use of the guests and the spacious bedrooms enjoy fine views over the gardens and valley below. Monkshill is situated within a designated Area of Outstanding Natural Beauty.

t: single).00; double room

Bedrooms: 2 double, 1 twin, 1 family
Bathrooms: 2 en-suite, 1 private
Parking: 6 spaces
Cards accepted: Mastercard, Visa, Switch/ Delta, Amex, Eurocard, JCB, Electron, Maestro, Solo

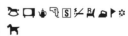

K cover

;s referenced by number to the maps on pages 108–109

232 Widbrook Grange Hotel

Widbrook, Bradford-on-Avon, Wiltshire BA15 1UH **Tel:** (01225) 864750 **Fax:** (01225) 862890
Web: www.widbrookgrange.com **E-mail:** stay@widbrookgrange.com

The home of resident owners Jane and Peter Wragg, this elegant 250 year-old Georgian country house hotel and restaurant is just 17 minutes from the historic city of Bath, peacefully positioned in 11 acres near the Kennet and Avon Canal amidst rolling countryside on the edge of the medieval town of Bradford-on-Avon. In the courtyard are some of the 20 bedrooms, a heated indoor swimming pool and a conference suite. Its Medlar Tree Restaurant serves award-winning British regional cuisine, and comfortable drawing rooms and a log fire on cold winter nights all add to the informal, intimate and relaxing atmosphere.

Bed & Breakfast per night: single room from £60.00–£105.00; double room from £80.00–£125.00
Dinner, Bed & Breakfast per person, per night: £80.00–£130.00
Evening meal: 1900 (last orders 2030)

Bedrooms: 1 single, 12 double, 4 twin, 3 family
Bathrooms: 19 en-suite, 1 private
Parking: ample
Cards accepted: Mastercard, Visa, Switch/Delta, Amex, Diners, Eurocard, JCB

West Country Cheeses

The West Country is ideal cattle-rearing country: its climate is mild and damp, its grass lush, and much of its landscape too hilly and higgledy-piggledy to make good arable farmland. At one time almost every small region had its own variety of cheese, and though many have disappeared, the region has preserved some of its most popular old varieties and has developed many new ones, too.

Somerset is the home of the acknowledged 'king of cheeses', the great and versatile Cheddar. Sixty percent of all cheese produced in creameries throughout England and Wales is Cheddar. First recorded in the early 16th century, it got its name because visitors to the famous Cheddar Gorge bought the flavoursome hard cheese there. Today visitors to the Cheddar Rural Village may watch cheesemaking displays, while not far away, Chewton Cheese Dairy, near Wells continues to make Cheddar to traditional methods.

Cheddar's nearest rival, also a full-flavoured hard cheese, is Double Gloucester, originally made from the rich milk of the Gloucester black cattle. A 'single' variety, known as the 'haymaking cheese' was made from early-season milk, and was matured quickly, resulting

in a light colour. The larger 'double' Gloucesters were allowed to mature longer and were consequently darker. Both are made at Old Ley Court near Birdwood, Gloucestershire, where cheese-making demonstrations can be seen on certain days.

At one time, Dorset Blue Vinney, a hard blue-veined cheese, was made on numerous farms throughout Dorset. Though it went out of production in the 1980s, it is again produced near Sherborne (not open to the public, but the cheese is readily available in local shops). Cornish Yarg, by contrast, is a recent innovation, a crumbly white cheese with a black covering of nettle leaves, first produced in the 1980s by the Gray family – Yarg is Gray backwards – at Lynher Dairies near Liskeard (open Monday–Saturday).

Another new development is the creation in the West Country of French-type soft cheeses, with Somerset Brie and Somerset Camembert now widely available. The range of West Country cheeses is wide, and although little can beat a slice of tasty traditional farmhouse Cheddar, look out for some more unusual varieties: Brendon Blue, Vulscombe, Cloisters, Tala, Wedmore, Little Rydings, Hazlewood, Devon Oke, Blackdown, Capricorn and the irresistible Stinking Bishop.

Heatherly Cottage

...dbrook Lane, Gastard, Corsham, Wiltshire SN13 9PE **Tel:** (01249) 701402 **Fax:** (01249) 701412
Web: www.smoothhound.co.uk/hotels/heather3.html **E-mail:** ladbrook1@aol.com

A 17th-century cottage in a quiet lane with two acres and views across open countryside. There is ample off-road parking and guests have a separate wing of the house with their own entrance and staircase. All rooms are en-suite (the larger double has a king-size bed) and all are equipped with colour television, clock/radio, tea/coffee tray and hairdryer. Close to Bath, Lacock, Castle Combe, Avebury, Stonehenge and National Trust properties. Restaurants nearby for good food.

Bed & Breakfast per night: single occupancy from £32.00–£34.00; double room from £50.00–£55.00

Bedrooms: 2 double, 1 twin, 1 family
Bathrooms: 3 en-suite
Open: mid January–mid December
Parking: 8 spaces

234 Fosse Farmhouse

♦♦♦♦

Nettleton Shrub, Nettleton, Chippenham, Wiltshire SN14 7NJ **Tel:** (01249) 782286 **Fax:** (01249) 783066
Web: www.fossefarmhouse.8m.com **E-mail:** caroncooper@compuserve.com

Located in an Area of Outstanding Natural Beauty, beside the Roman Fosse Way. The farmhouse dates from 1750 and has been fully restored by the present owner to provide three stunning en-suite guest bedrooms. The set menu dinner is prepared daily using the best local ingredients. Delicious afternoon teas are also a speciality here. Enjoy walking across the valley to the picturesque village of Castle Combe, or take a short drive into Bath and visit the superb new spa complex.

Bed & Breakfast per night: single occupancy from £55.00–£70.00; double room from £85.00–£125.00
Dinner, Bed & Breakfast per person, per night: £70.00–£90.00
Evening meal: 1900 (last orders 2100)

Bedrooms: 1 double, 1 twin, 1 family
Bathrooms: 3 en-suite
Parking: 8 spaces
Cards accepted: Mastercard, Visa, Switch/Delta, JCB

235 Manor Farm

♦♦♦♦

Avebury, Marlborough, Wiltshire SN8 1RF **Tel:** (01672) 539294 **Fax:** (01672) 539294

Our exclusive guests enjoy our 18th-century Grade II listed farmhouse, depicted on Stukley's map of 1724, situated within the Avebury Stone Circle. Rooms are large and comfortable with exceptional views of the World Heritage site which is within an Area of Outstanding Natural Beauty. We offer a full and varied breakfast menu and pubs are within 100 yards and 1 mile. Visit the National Trust manor house, museum and local ancient sites, and antique hunt in Marlborough, Hungerford and Bath. We look forward to welcoming you to our home.

Bed & Breakfast per night: single occupancy from £40.00–£45.00; double room from £60.00–£70.00

Bedrooms: 1 double, 1 twin
Bathrooms: 1 guest
Parking: 5 spaces
Open: all year except Christmas/New Year

236 Marshwood Farm B&B   ◆◆◆◆

Dinton, Salisbury SP3 5ET **Tel:** (01722) 716334

A beautiful farmhouse, dating from the 17th century, on a working farm, overlooking fields and woodlands. Situated a short walk from the village of Dinton. An ideal location for cycling, walking and exploring the Wiltshire countryside, Salisbury, Stonehenge, Bath, the New Forest and many other places of interest. Guests are welcome to relax in our garden and use the tennis court. There are a variety of pubs locally for lunches and evening meals. See also our self-catering accommodation on page 151.

Bed & Breakfast per night: single occupancy from £30.00–£50.00; double room from £50.00–£60.00

Bedrooms: 1 double/family, 1 twin/family
Bathrooms: 2 en-suite
Parking: ample

237 Newton Farm House   ◆◆◆◆◆ Silver Award

Southampton Road, Whiteparish, Salisbury, Wiltshire SP5 2QL **Tel:** (01794) 884416 **Fax:** (01794) 884416
Web: www.newtonfarmhouse.co.uk **E-mail:** enquiries@newtonfarmhouse.co.uk

Historic listed 16th-century farmhouse, originally part of the Trafalgar Estate. Near the New Forest and convenient for Salisbury, Stonehenge, Romsey, Winchester, Portsmouth and Bath. Delightful en-suite bedrooms (five with genuine four-poster beds). Beamed dining room with flagstones, inglenook and bread oven plus Nelson memorabilia. Superb breakfasts include home-made breads and preserves, fresh fruit and free-range eggs. Extensive grounds with swimming pool. Dinner by arrangement using garden produce. AA Premier selected.

Bed & Breakfast per night: double room from £55.00–£75.00
Dinner, Bed & Breakfast per person, per night: £52.50–£62.50
Evening meal: 1900 (by arrangement)

Bedrooms: 3 double, 2 twin, 3 family
Bathrooms: 8 en-suite
Parking: 10 spaces

At-a-glance symbols are explained on the flap inside the back cover

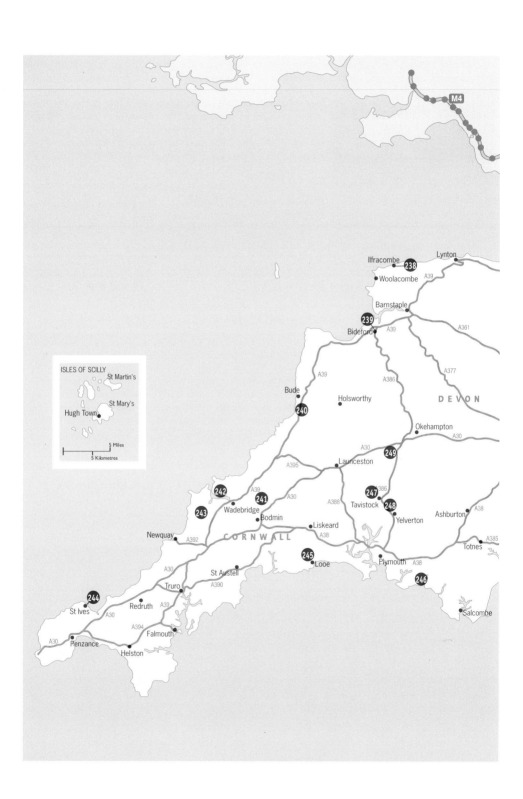

ISLES OF SCILLY
St Martin's
St Mary's
Hugh Town
5 Miles
5 Kilometres

M4

Lynton
Ilfracombe 238
Woolacombe
A39
Barnstaple
239
Bideford
A39
A361

A39
A386
A377
Bude
Holsworthy   D E V O N
240
Okehampton
A30
A30
249
A395   Launceston
242
A39   A30   A388   247 386
241   Tavistock 248
243   Wadebridge   Yelverton   Ashburton A38
Bodmin
Liskeard   A385
Newquay   A392   C O R N W A L L   A38   Totnes
245
A30   Looe   Plymouth A38
St Austell   246
Truro   A390
244   Redruth A39
St Ives   A30   Salcombe
A394
A30   Falmouth
Penzance
Helston

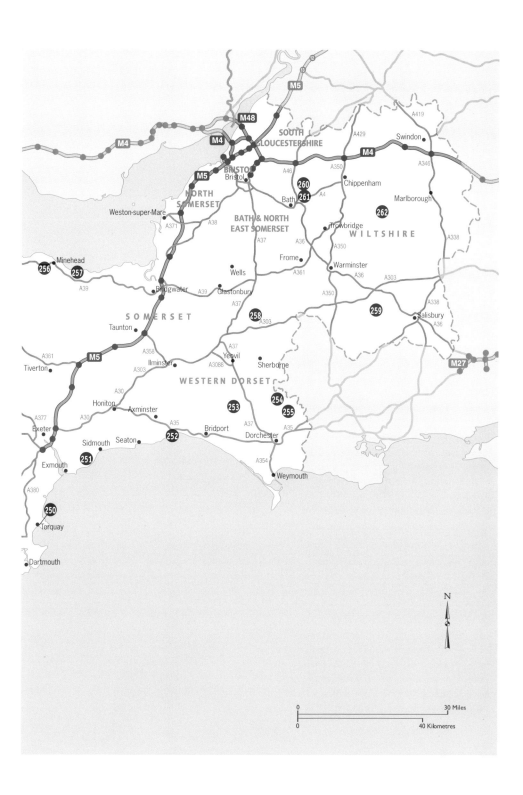

238 The Admirals House ★ ★ ★ ★

Ilfracombe, Devon   **Web:** www.theadmiralshouse.co.uk
Contact: The Ilfracombe Carlton Hotel, Runnacleave Road, Ilfracombe, Devon EX34 8AR
Tel: (01271) 864666 **Fax:** (01271) 864666 **E-mail:** enquiries@theadmiralshouse.co.uk

Stunning views of the harbour from these well-fitted characterful apartments in a Georgian manor house on the quayside. Luxury bathrooms with vibrant decor. A superb situation, close to seafood restaurants, local pubs and coastal walks etc. Open all year.

Low season per week: £200.00–£380.00
High season per week: £320.00–£650.00
Short breaks: from £120.00–£340.00

5 apartments: sleeping 4 people
Cards accepted: Mastercard, Visa, Switch/Delta

The Tarka Trail

The writer Henry Williamson (1895–1977) was born and bred in London, but in 1921 he decided to leave the city, mounted his motorcycle and headed south-west. His eventual destination was the Devonshire village of Georgeham, near Barnstaple, where he rented a small cottage and stayed for many years. Here he was given an orphaned otter cub which he reared and cared for. It gave him the inspiration for his famous book, *Tarka the Otter*, in which he displayed not only his fascination for these shy and beautiful creatures, but also his deep knowledge and love of the wildlife and landscapes of this most beautiful part of Devon.

An area roughly corresponding to that featured in the book is now being promoted as Tarka Country, a region which extends along Devon's north coast from Bideford to Lynton and southwards to the northern fringes of Dartmoor. As part of a major eco-tourism initiative, the Tarka Country Tourism Association has set up a long-distance route – the Tarka Trail – designed to encourage the visitor to explore the countryside without the use of the car. Describing an irregular figure of eight, the trail loops between Exmoor and Dartmoor, with Barnstaple at its centre, covering 180 miles (290km) of varied and often stunning scenery.

It is of course possible to walk the entire length of the Tarka Trail (except the section between Eggesford and Barnstaple which is a train journey), but shorter walks and

cycle routes with starting points on or near the trail have also been devised. Some are circular, some involve a return by bus. Full details of all the different options are available from the Tarka Country Tourism Association (www.tarka-country.co.uk).

The Tarka Trail passes many places mentioned in Williamson's famous book. Tarka's fictional birthplace, for example, is on the Torridge, just upstream from Bideford, while remote Cranmere Pool on Dartmoor was visited by Tarka after the death of his mate, Greymuzzle. But don't expect to see any otters on your travels. Due to river pollution and loss of habitat, otters are one of Europe's most endangered mammals. The best place to see them is at the Tamar Otter Sanctuary, near Launceston, Cornwall (about 25 miles - 40km - from Barnstaple) where otters are bred and re-introduced to the wild in a bid to save them from extinction.

239 Bowood Farm   ★ ★ ★ ★

Abbotsham, Bideford, Devon **Web:** www.toadhallcottages.com
Contact: Toad Hall Cottages, Elliot House, Church Street, Kingsbridge, Devon TQ7 1BY
Tel: 08700 777345 **Fax:** (01548) 853086 **E-mail:** thc@toadhallcottages.com

Bowood Farm has three cottages on the courtyard: two barn conversions and a 17th-century cottage. Each has pine furniture, fitted carpets throughout, fully equipped kitchens and a small enclosed garden which looks onto 9 acres of fields. Two miles from Westward Ho! and the quayside town of Bideford which boasts a Royal golf course, tennis and indoor swimming. Rosemoore RHS is only ten miles. Horseshoe Barn sleeps 8 + cot and highchair; Corn House sleeps 5/6 + cot and highchair (there are security doors between these cottages: when open sleeps 14 adults and 2 babies – ideal for re-unions); Bowood Cottage sleeps 6 + cot and highchair. Ample parking for cars, bicycles and boats.

Low season per week: £190.00–£275.00
High season per week: £475.00–£695.00
Short breaks: from £160.00–£275.00

3 cottages: sleeping 20 people
Cards accepted: Mastercard, Visa, Switch/Delta

---

240 Kennacott Court   ★ ★ ★ ★ ★

Widemouth Bay, Bude, Cornwall **Web:** www.kennacottcourt.co.uk
Contact: Mr & Mrs R Davis, Kennacott Court, Widemouth Bay, Bude, Cornwall EX23 0ND
Tel: (01288) 362000 **Fax:** (01288) 361434 **E-mail:** maureen@kennacottcourt.co.uk

Set in the midst of 75 acres with magnificent views overlooking the sea at Widemouth Bay, Bude, Kennacott Court is an outstanding collection of holiday cottages with unrivalled leisure and recreational facilities. Every cottage is extremely comfortable, beautifully furnished and comprehensively equipped. We have a leisure centre with large indoor pool, indoor badminton, skittles, snooker, sauna, mini gym and games room. In the grounds we have two all-weather tennis courts, golf course, nature walk and lots more. Open all year for an unforgetable holiday.

Low season per week: £230.00–£700.00
High season per week: £490.00–£2000.00
Short breaks: from £135.00–£440.00

19 houses, cottages and bungalows: sleeping 2–12 people
Cards accepted: Switch/Delta

---

241 Colesent Cottages   ★ ★ ★ ★

St Tudy, Wadebridge, Cornwall **Web:** www.colesent.co.uk
Contact: Colesent Cottages, St Tudy, Wadebridge, Cornwall PL30 4QX
Tel: (01208) 850112 **Fax:** (01208) 850112 **E-mail:** unwind@colesent.co.uk

These are two converted barn luxury self-catering cottages near Wadebridge. Found along a leafy drive, with wonderful views beside the lazy twisting Camel River with its 'trail' for walking and cycling. Cornwall Tourism Awards 2002 - self-catering establishment of the year - 'highly commended'. The famous sandy Rock beach is nearby, amongst many others. As well as the expanse of Bodmin Moor and Cornwall's many other hidden treasures to explore.

Low season per week: £370.00–£475.00
High season per week: £570.00–£925.00
Short breaks: from £65.00 per night

2 cottages: sleeping 2–7 people
Cards accepted: Mastercard, Visa, Switch/Delta

242 Cant Cove   ★ ★ ★ ★ ★

Cant Farm, Rock, Wadebridge, Cornwall **Web:** www.cantcove.co.uk
Contact: Mr Sleeman, The Cottage, Cant Farm, Rock, Wadebridge, Cornwall PL27 6RL
Tel: (01208) 862841 **Fax:** (01208) 862142 **E-mail:** info@cantcove.co.uk

Secluded hamlet of spacious stone cottages set in an idyllic location overlooking the Camel Estuary. The six houses accomodate from five to eight and are well furnished and equipped to a high standard. Each property has a private terrace and garden area. Open log fires for those chillier winter evenings. Set in 70 acres of private land enjoying uninterrupted views. There are wildlife walks, complimentary tennis and golf. Excellent beaches, golf, sailing, riding, historic houses all within easy reach.

Low season per week: £350.00–£595.00
High season per week: £1260.00–£1995.00
Short breaks: from £227.50–£570.00

6 cottages: sleeping 5–8 people
Cards accepted: Mastercard, Visa, Switch/Delta

243 St Ervan Manor and Country Cottages   ★ ★ ★ ★

St Ervan, Wadebridge, Cornwall **Web:** www.stervanmanor.co.uk
Contact: St Ervan Manor and Country Cottages, The Old Rectory, St Ervan, Wadebridge, Cornwall PL27 7TA
Tel: (01841) 540255 **Fax:** (01841) 540255 **E-mail:** mail@stervanmanor.freeserve.co.uk

The Spinney House is a newly renovated property now offering luxury four-bedroom accommodation. Spacious, yet cosy and warm in winter, with full central heating and double glazing. Fully-fitted kitchen, separate utility room, lounge/diner plus cloakroom. One en-suite bedroom, three others, plus full bathroom. The Spinney sleeps up to 8. Close to Padstow, beaches and the Eden Project. See also our serviced accommodation on page 115.

Low season per week: £600.00–£750.00
High season per week: £800.00–£1600.00
Short breaks: from £360.00–£750.00

1 house: sleeping up to 8 people
Cards accepted: Mastercard, Visa, Switch/Delta

244 Rotorua Apartments   ★ ★ ★ ★

Carbis Bay, St Ives, Cornwall **Web:** www.stivesapartments.com
Contact: Rotorua Apartments, Trencrom Lane, Carbis Bay, St Ives, Cornwall TR26 2TD
Tel: (01736) 795419 **Fax:** (01736) 795419 **E-mail:** rotorua@btconnect.com

Luxury apartments situated in a quiet wooded lane, within walking distance of Carbis Bay and other local beaches. Ideally situated for touring Cornwall. Large outdoor heated pool and garden areas. Each apartment has its own parking space. The apartments are very well equipped, including dishwasher, coffee maker, fridge/freezer, electric cooker and microwave. There is a colour television and video in the lounge and all bedrooms have colours televisions and hairdryers. Sorry, no pets.

Low season per week: £195.00–£350.00
High season per week: £425.00–£650.00

8 apartments: sleeping 6 people
Cards accepted: Mastercard, Visa, Switch/Delta, Amex

245 Treworgey Cottages

★ ★ ★ ★ ★

Duloe, Liskeard, Cornwall **Web:** www.cornishdreamcottages.co.uk
Contact: Mr & Mrs Wright, Treworgey Cottages, Duloe, Liskeard, Cornwall PL14 4PP
Tel: (01503) 262730 **Fax:** (01503) 263757 **E-mail:** treworgey@enterprise.net

Idyllic 18th-century country cottages for romantics, near the sea in the beautiful Looe river valley. Your own delightful private English cottage garden with roses around the door and breaktaking views to the river. Exclusively furnished with antiques. Crackling log fires, candlelit meals, dishwashers, videos etc. Four-poster beds and crisp white linen. Horse riding, indoor and outdoor play, tennis court and a beautiful heated swimming pool on-site. Golf, fishing, beaches, coastal walks all nearby. Looe 3 miles. These enchanting cottages are really warm and cosy in winter.

Low season per week: £246.00–£371.00
High season per week: £722.00–£1773.00
Short breaks: from £150.00–£280.00
(November–end March)

12 cottages: sleeping 2–8 people
Cards accepted: Mastercard, Visa, Switch/Delta

The Lizard

If it's Britain's most southerly point you're after, then come to the Lizard (Land's End is the westernmost point). This small Cornish peninsula has much to interest the visitor besides its location, being especially rich both geologically and botanically. Like almost every part of the county, the Lizard also has many historical connections and a glorious coastline.

Opinions vary as to how it got its name: some claim it means high palace, others that it derives from a Celtic word for outcast. Both explanations are plausible, for the Lizard is a level moorland plateau about 200ft (61m) above sea level, almost cut off from the rest of the county. Much of the peninsula is formed of serpentine stone, a soft, easily-worked material used in local churches (and on sale in the shops of Lizard village). A farmer reputedly chanced upon its ornamental qualities when he erected some large rocks in his field as rubbing posts for his cows. He soon noticed that the 'polished' areas showed patterns resembling snakeskin, and colours ranging from grey-green to pink. Once Queen Victoria had chosen it for Osborne House its popularity was assured. In the church of St Winwalloe at Landewednack it can be seen alternated with granite. This, the most southerly church in Britain, is where the last sermon was preached in Cornish (1678).

Kynance Cove, owned by the National Trust, is typical of the majestic coastline of the Lizard. Its rocky outcrops enjoy some unlikely names, including Man-o'-War Rock, the Devil's Postbox, the Devil's

Bellows and Asparagus Island (where the plant grows wild). There are some intriguing caves (the Parlour and the Drawing Room), but take care not to be stranded by the incoming tide.

The flora of the Lizard is a botanist's delight. Here can be found plants too tender to grow outdoors elsewhere in the country (such as tamarisks and the Hottentot fig) and others which are unique to this corner of England, such as Cornish Heath. These plants have to be able to withstand the frequent onslaught of sea gales, something which countless local vessels have not managed. More shipwrecks have occurred here than almost anywhere else in the country. Off the eastern coast of the peninsula are the Manacles, a group of ferocious rocks extending over a couple of square miles. In 1770 parishioners of the nearby church of St Arkerveranus (in the village of St Deverne) redesigned the steeple as a landmark to warn passing ships. They may have been successful, but there are still over 400 victims of shipwrecks buried in the churchyard.

246 The Flete Estate Holiday Cottages   ★ ★ ★ ★ – ★ ★ ★ ★ ★

Pamflete, Holbeton, Plymouth   **Web:** www.flete.co.uk
Contact: Josephine Webb
Tel: (01752) 830234 **Fax:** (01752) 830500 **E-mail:** cottages@flete.co.uk

The Flete Estate is undoubtedly the jewel in the crown of the beautiful South Hams. This private estate of 5,000 acres is designated an Area of Outstanding Natural Beauty and a Site of Special Scientific Interest, encompassing large broadleaf woodlands, rolling pastures, cliff paths and sandy beaches, secluded cottages, little hamlets and a tantalising network of private drives and pathways. Includes recently-restored beautiful mill cottage, three coastguards' cottages at water's edge, gamekeeper's cottage and large country house. Fishing, log fires, gardens and games room.

Low season per week: £440.00–£855.00
High season per week: £1120.00–£1700.00
Short breaks: from £352.00–£352.00

1 house and 6 cottages: sleeping 5–12 people

247 Downhouse Farm   ★ ★ ★ ★

Mill Hill Lane, Tavistock, Devon   **Web:** www.downhousefarm.co.uk
Contact: Ms Heaps, Downhouse Farm, Mill Hill Lane, Tavistock, Devon PL19 8NH
Tel: (01822) 614521 **Fax:** (01822) 613675 **E-mail:** downhousefarm@aol.com

Set in the grounds of an old farm just one mile from the town centre are four beautifully converted luxury cottages fully equipped to a high standard, inlcuding a log-burning stove for those chillier evenings. All cottages have wonderful views over the countryside. We have a tennis court, children's play area with equipment for all ages, a small outdoor pool, and stables should you wish to bring your horse with you. Well-behaved dogs are also welcome. Nearby there is golf, horse riding, fisheries and cycle hire.

Low season per week: £330.00–£500.00
High season per week: £550.00–£1000.00

4 cottages: sleeping 2–8 people

248 Edgemoor Cottage   ★ ★ ★ ★

Middlemoor, Tavistock, Devon
Contact: Mrs M S Fox, Edgemoor, Middlemoor, Tavistock, Devon PL19 9DY
Tel: (01822) 612259 **E-mail:** vicky@dartmoorcottages.info

An attractive, fully furnished and equipped country cottage in a peacful hamlet. Ideally situated to enjoy walking, cycling, golfing or riding over breathtakingly scenic Dartmoor. A perfect base to explore Dartmoor, Devon and Cornwall, with the north and south coasts and the Eden Project easily reachable for day excursions. Many historic attractions. The cottage has two en-suite bedrooms (one twin and one double, both with television), a kitchen/dining room and upstairs living room (with television and video) leading into a sun lounge/diner with patio overlooking fields.

Low season per week: £200.00–£300.00
High season per week: £300.00–£400.00
Short breaks: from £150.00–£200.00

1 cottage: sleeping 4 people

249 Little Bidlake Farm ★ ★ ★ ★

Bridestowe, Okehampton, Devon **Web:** www.dartmoor-holiday-cottages.co.uk
Contact: Mrs J Down, Little Bidlake Farm, Bridestowe, Okehampton, Devon EX20 4NS
Tel: (01837) 861233 **Fax:** (01837) 861233 **E-mail:** bidlakefrm@aol.com

Six luxury, fully equipped, barn conversions on the fringe of Dartmoor. Original beams, arched windows and underfloor heating. Most rooms en-suite with television. Perfect for touring Devon and Cornwall. Meals available. Local shop and pubs. Cycling, golf, fishing, riding, walking or water pursuits easily accessible. Pets and horses welcome. Sleeps 2, 4, 6 +12.

Low season per week: £275.00–£650.00
High season per week: £370.00–£925.00

6 cottages: sleeping 2–12 people
Cards accepted: Mastercard, Visa

---

250 Mirage and Oasis Apartments ★ ★ ★ ★ – ★ ★ ★ ★ ★

Hesketh Crescent, Meadfoot Sea Road, Torquay **Web:** www.torbayapartments.com
Contact: The Preferred Apartment Company, 21 Bishops Close, Torquay TQ1 2PL
Tel: (01803) 211116 or 07979 533963 **Fax:** (01803) 214023 **E-mail:** info@torbayapartments.com

Our luxurious sea-view apartments form part of Hesketh Crescent, an impressive and inspiring example of Grade II Regency architecture. This elegant and stylish building is set in the peaceful, leafy surroundings of Meadfoot, one of the most beautiful and unspoilt areas of Torquay. The apartments, which are beautifully furnished and comprehensively equipped, overlook Meadfoot Beach and enjoy uninterrupted panoramic views across the bay and beyond. From the perimeter of the grounds there are extensive woodland walks. Torquay has a lively and continental atmosphere in summer; it is warmed by subtropical winds from the Gulf Stream and enjoys a mild climate with an abundance of sunshine.

Low season per week: £315.00–£570.00
High season per week: £490.00–£790.00
Short breaks: from £110.00–£490.00

2 apartments: sleeping up to 6 people
Cards accepted: Mastercard, Visa, Switch/Delta

---

251 Christopher's Farmhouse ★ ★ ★ ★ ★

East Budleigh, Budleigh Salterton, Devon **Web:** www.thethatchedcottagecompany.com
Contact: The Thatched Cottage Company, 56 Fore Street, Otterton, Budleigh Salterton, Devon EX9 7HB
Tel: (01395) 567676 **Fax:** (01395) 567440 **E-mail:** info@thethatchedcottagecompany.com

A beautiful thatched 16th-century Devonshire longhouse, sleeping 8, set in two acres of gardens in the pretty village of East Budleigh, yet only a mile from the sea at Budleigh Salterton. There is an en-suite four-poster bedroom, two twin-bedded rooms and another two bathrooms. Also, in the original tannery, there is a dramatic en-suite bedroom, with vaulted ceiling and a brass bed, accessed by a spiral staircase from the large sitting room. Full central heating, television, video and dishwasher. There is a dining room to seat 10 people, two sitting rooms and a fully equipped kitchen in this spacious accommodation. Close to the beach, pubs, restaurants and tourist attractions. Sorry, no pets.

Low season per week: from £350.00
High season per week: max £1500.00
Short breaks: from £175.00

7 cottages: sleeping 2–8 people
Cards accepted: Mastercard, Visa, Switch/Delta

---

252 Sea Tree House

★★★★

Broad Street, Lyme Regis, Dorset **Web:** www.lymeregis.com/seatreehouse
Contact: Mr D Parker, Sea Tree House, 18 Broad Street, Lyme Regis, Dorset DT7 3QE
Tel: (01297) 442244 **Fax:** (01297) 442244 **E-mail:** seatree.house@ukonline.co.uk

Experience Georgian elegance with a touch of romance in the heart of Lyme Regis. These spacious, completely private, one-bedroom apartments have large bright sitting rooms. Each has south-facing bay windows with magnificent sea views. Ideal for couples wanting to celebrate an anniversary or special occasion in style. Your kitchen is fully equipped with extras such as washer-dryer and dishwasher. We are minutes' walk from the beach, shops, restaurants and heritage coastal walks.

Low season per week: £215.00–£365.00
High season per week: £415.00–£595.00
Short breaks: from £160.00–£250.00

2 apartments: sleeping 2/3 people

Cerne Abbas Giant

Even without its most famous landmark, Cerne Abbas in Dorset has many attractions. The town grew up around a Benedictine abbey founded in 987, and although only a few ancient remains of the abbey still stand, many of the prettiest houses date from the abbey's 500-year domination of the community. Later, the town flourished as a small market centre, but its decline in the 19th century meant that it never grew large or industrialised, and today it ranks as one of the prettiest villages in Dorset, complete with duckpond, village stocks, a holy well in the churchyard and a superb 14th-century tithe barn.

But what makes Cerne Abbas uniquely memorable is the enormous and extraordinary figure cut into the chalky hillside near by. Brandishing a knobbly club, the Cerne giant strides across the turf, arms outstretched, his naked form leaving little to the imagination. His origins and identity are obscure. Strangely, given that the abbey was a centre of literacy, there is no written record of the figure before 1754, but the current opinion is that the giant is most likely to be a representation of the Roman god Hercules, carved during the first few centuries AD.

Only two other similarly ancient hill-carvings exist in Britain – the White Horse of Uffington, Oxfordshire, and the Long Man of Wilmington, East Sussex. These were probably not the only ones; perhaps a whole panoply of colossal figures and beasts once marched across the English downland, only to be slowly smothered in vegetation and lost forever. The giant

has survived through regular and rigorous 'scourings', usually at seven-year intervals, a practice which was presumably, and rather surprisingly, condoned by the Benedictines despite the giant's obviously pagan nature and indecent nakedness. Today the National Trust is responsible for maintenance.

For obvious reasons the Cerne giant has always been regarded as something of a fertility symbol. It is thought that the village's annual spring revelries were held on a site near by, and to this day it is claimed that merely sitting on the giant's impressive 30ft (9m) member is a certain cure for infertility. This is not to be encouraged, however, because of the risk of eroding the carving's most prominent feature! Perhaps the best view of the Cerne giant is to be had from a viewpoint at the junction where Duck Street meets the A352 Sherborne–Dorchester road.

253 Stable Cottage ★★★★

Rampisham, Dorchester, Dorset
Contact: Mr & Mrs Read, School House, Rampisham, Dorchester DT2 0PR
Tel: (01935) 83555 **E-mail:** usatschoolhouse@aol.com

Converted from a stable, this luxury cottage is set in the grounds of a school built over 150 years ago. In deepest West Dorset it is surrounded by fields. Birds and wildlife abound. A peaceful location for two with a king-size bedroom with en-suite shower room. Fully-fitted maple kitchen, sitting/dining room. Villages nearby offering all facilities with post offices, pubs and restaurants. Numerous walks, close to World Heritage coastline and many historic sites.

Low season per week: £200.00
High season per week: £275.00
Short breaks: from £30.00–£50.00

1 cottage: sleeping 2 people
Open: mid January–mid December

254 Domineys Cottages ★★★★

Buckland Newton, Dorchester, Dorset **Web:** www.domineys.com
Contact: Domineys Cottages, Domineys Yard, Buckland Newton, Dorchester, Dorset DT2 7BS
Tel: (01300) 345295 or (01300) 345341 **Fax:** (01300) 345596 **E-mail:** cottages@domineys.com

Three delightful comfortable early 19th-century two bedroom cottages. Peacefully situated on village edge between Dorset Downs and Blackmore Vale in the Area of Outstanding Natural Beauty. Furnished and equipped to a high standard and immaculately maintained. Colour television, woodburner/coal fireplace, central heating, beautiful gardens, heated summer swimming pool. Babes in arms and children over 5 welcome. Tucked away off a no through road leading to farms and footpaths, Domineys is an ideal base for relaxing or exploring Wessex.

Low season per week: £190.00–£300.00
High season per week: £300.00–£460.00
Short breaks: from £100.00–£300.00 (off season only)

3 cottages: sleeping up to 4 people

255 Greygles ★★★★

Melcombe Bingham, Dorset **Web:** www.greygles.co.uk
Contact: Mr Sommerfeld, 22 Tiverton Road, Willesden, London NW10 3HL
Tel: 020 8969 4830 or 07979 860266 **Fax:** 020 8960 0069 **E-mail:** enquiry@greygles.co.uk

Enjoy rural peace in a spacious, well-equipped stone cottage with delightful views. A wonderful place to experience the English countryside at its best. Sleeping up to seven in four bedrooms (including a ground floor double and bathroom), with log fire and Aga cooker, antique refectory table, Wendy House in the garden and funky master bathroom, Greygles is ideal for family parties. This is Hardy country with lovely walking, plus coast, abbeys, gardens, old towns and even a tank museum within a half hour drive.

Low season per week: £375.00–£525.00
High season per week: £575.00–£775.00
Short breaks: from £175.00–£300.00

1 cottage: sleeping up to 7 people

256 Tethinstone Cottage   ★ ★ ★ ★

Tivington, Minehead, Somerset
Contact: Mr Challis, Tethinstone Cottage, Tivington, Minehead, Somerset TA24 8SX
Tel: (01643) 706757 **Fax:** (01643) 706757

Delightful, fully equipped and extremely comfortable thatched cottage overlooking Porlock Vale and Exmoor. Sleeps 5 people (one double, one twin and one single room) with all amenities within easy reach. Set in its own grounds of over 1 acre. Ideal for walking, riding and relaxing in superb countryside. Dogs and well-behaved children welcome! Prices include hot water, heating and electricity. Please phone for further details.

Low season per week: £275.00–£350.00
High season per week: £350.00–£500.00

1 cottage: sleeping 5 people

257 Huntingball Lodge   ★ ★ ★ ★

Blue Anchor, Minehead, Somerset **Web:** www.huntingball-lodge.co.uk
Contact: Mr & Mrs Hall, Huntingball Lodge, Blue Anchor, Minehead, Somerset TA24 6JP
Tel: (01984) 640076 **Fax:** (01984) 640076 **E-mail:** info@huntingball-lodge.co.uk

An elegant country house with the most spectacular far-reaching views over the Somerset coastline and Exmoor countryside from all apartments – the perfect quiet base to explore Exmoor. The house stands in beautiful gardens of 1.5 acres and comprises three luxurious and spacious self-catering apartments furnished and equipped to a very high standard. Each with its own private terrace or balcony. The beach is two minutes walk away and there are also two excellent pubs/restaurants, a farm shop/tea rooms and convenience store close by. Open all year with a guaranteed warm welcome from the resident owners.

Low season per week: £200.00–£225.00
High season per week: £260.00–£450.00
Short breaks: from £100.00–£225.00 (low season only)

3 apartments: sleeping 2/3 and 4/5 people

258 Ancient Barn, Old Stables & Weaver's Cottage   ★ ★ ★ ★

Lower Cockhill Farm, Castle Cary, Somerset **Web:** www.medievalbarn.co.uk
Contact: Mrs Peppin, Lower Cockhill Farm, Castle Cary, Somerset BA7 7NZ
Tel: (01963) 351288 **E-mail:** info@medievalbarn.co.uk

A medieval barn and an old stables: two listed buildings sensitively converted to provide high-quality, well-equipped holiday homes. Close to each other yet entirely separate: old beams and flagstone floors combined with all modern comforts. Set in lovely countryside next to a small farm – an ideal base for exploring this unspoilt, interesting part of Somerset: countryside, historic houses, gardens, abbeys, castles and much, much more. Also, a mile away in Castle Cary town, a pretty, listed 18th-century weaver's cottage with garden and an astonishing well.

Low season per week: from £200.00
High season per week: max £650.00
Short breaks: from £160.00–£335.00

3 cottages: sleeping 5 people + cot, 7 people + cot and 2 people + 2
Cards accepted: Mastercard, Visa, Switch/ Delta, JCB

259 The Cottage ★ ★ ★ ★

Marshwood Farm, Dinton, Salisbury, Wiltshire
Contact: Mrs F Lockyer, Marshwood Farmhouse, Dinton, Salisbury, Wiltshire SP3 5ET
Tel: (01722) 716334

The cottage is attached to Marshwood Farmhouse, dating from the 17th century. The property has been tastefully renovated, comprising a fully-fitted kitchen/dining room, lounge with sofa bed, bath/shower room, double bedroom, second bedroom with full size bunk beds. The historic town of Salisbury is approximately 10 miles. Other places of interest include Stonehenge, Amesbury, Longleat House and Safari Park, Stourhead. Ideal location for walking, cycling and touring. See also our serviced accommodation on page 139.

Low season per week: max £400.00
High season per week: max £400.00
Short breaks: max £250.00

1 cottage: sleeping 4 + 2 people

Arthurian Legends of the South West

No one knows if Arthur actually existed. What is certain is that when the Romans left Britain in the early 5th century AD, recorded history went with them, at least for several hundred years. So the shadowy figures from these 'Dark Ages' are inevitably reconstructions by later clerics or deductions by latter-day archaeologists.

In fact, historians think Arthur did exist, probably a 5th- or 6th-century British chieftain who fought the invading Anglo-Saxons. His base – Camelot? – may have been at South Cadbury, near Sherborne, since excavations have revealed that this Iron Age hillfort on the troubled frontline between Saxon and Briton, was reoccupied and refortified in the late 5th or early 6th century.

The complex web of Arthurian myth, however, claims earlier beginnings. One story has Joseph of Arimathea sailing to Cornwall, perhaps to trade in tin. With him on one trip to the West Country is the young Christ who walks on the Mendips at Priddy. Another version has Joseph hiding the Holy Grail, the cup Christ used at the Last Supper, on Glastonbury Tor, his staff, stuck firmly into the ground miraculously growing shoots and known as the Glastonbury Thorn. The quest for the Holy Grail – a metaphor for the search for spiritual perfection – preoccupies many of Arthur's knights in several myths.

The British king is said to have visited Glastonbury at least twice, once to rescue his wife Guinevere from the clutches of Melwas, and again when he went to Avalon (often equated with Glastonbury) to die. Glastonbury Tor indeed resembles the description of the Isle of Avalon, looming dramatically above the Somerset wetlands, which in Arthur's day were regularly inundated by the sea. In 1191 the monks of Glastonbury Abbey (shown here) found a tomb, apparently inscribed with the words 'Here lies the famous King Arthur in the Isle of Avalon'. Only the cynical would see this as a clever (and successful) ploy to attract pilgrims to an abbey recently devastated by fire.

Other West Country Arthurian sites can be found at Amesbury (where Guinevere became abbess after Arthur's death), Dozmary Pool on Bodmin Moor (where Excalibur was caught by a mysterious hand), Tintagel (Arthur's birthplace) and Badbury Rings in Dorset (one of a number of possible locations for the site of the Battle of Mount Badon, at which Arthur was mortally wounded).

260 Nailey Cottages   ★ ★ ★ ★

Nailey Farm, St. Catherines Valley, Bath   **Web:** www.naileyfarm.co.uk
Contact: Mrs B Gardner, Nailey Farm, St Catherines Valley, Bath BA1 8HD
Tel: (01225) 852989 **Fax:** (01225) 852989 **E-mail:** cottages@naileyfarm.co.uk

Three stylish retreats, surrounded by dramatic Cotswold panoramas in an Area of Outstanding Natural Beauty, on a 200-acre family run livestock farm. A recent and imaginative conversion offers highly desirable, well-appointed, spacious interiors which emulate the beauty and tranquillity of the location. Attention not only to detail and design, but also to comfort and the simple pleasures in life. Fabulous decked verandah, sunny terrraces, courtyard and garden. Abundant wildlife. Ideal walking. Approximately 15 minutes drive north of Bath city centre and convenient for the M4 and Bristol. Short break packages can often be arranged at short notice - please enquire.

Low season per week: £300.00–£550.00
High season per week: £500.00–£850.00
Short breaks: from £200.00–£550.00

3 cottages: 1 sleeping 7/8 people + cot, 2 sleeping 4/6 people + cot (interlinked up to 12)
Cards accepted: Mastercard, Visa, Switch/Delta, Amex, Eurocardm JCB

261 Avondale Riverside   ★ ★ ★ ★ – ★ ★ ★ ★ ★ ★

Avondale Coach House Units 1 & 2, London Road East, Bathford, Bath   **Web:** www.riversapart.co.uk
Contact: Mr & Mrs Pecchia, 104 Lower Northend, Batheaston, Bath BA1 7HA
Tel: (01225) 852226 or 07929 842504 **Fax:** (01225) 852226 **E-mail:** sheilapex@questmusic.co.uk

Part of a newly renovated coach house overlooking the river and wetland nature reserve. Good local facilities in the village of Batheaston. Ten minute drive to Bath centre. Private garden and barbecue area. Newly fitted kitchen, lounge with balcony overlooking the garden and river. Wide screen television and DVD. Two double bedrooms with en-suite facilities, two more bedrooms with shared bathroom with whirlpool bath. All bed linen/towels provided. Secure parking.

Low season per week: £345.00–£462.00
High season per week: £471.00–£648.00
Short breaks: from £25.00 per person (min 3 nights)

2 apartments: sleeping 2–8 people

262 The Gate House   ★ ★ ★ ★

Devizes, Wiltshire **Web:** www.visitdevizes.co.uk
Contact: Mrs L Stratton, The Gate House, Wick Lane, Devizes, Wiltshire SN10 5DW
Tel: (01380) 725283 **Fax:** (01380) 722382 **E-mail:** info@visitdevizes.co.uk

Recently a couple staying at No. 1 The Gatehouse said that it was the most spacious and pleasant accommodation they had ever stayed in. Situated only a 15-minute walk from Devizes centre, this is a quiet and peaceful ground floor holiday cottage. Surrounded by large, well looked after gardens next to the owner's own home. It has ample space for two with a well-equipped kitchen, comfortable living room and bathroom with separate shower cubicle. Bath and Salisbury are only 25 miles. Regrettably we cannot accept dogs or smokers.

Low season per week: from £175.00
High season per week: max £230.00
Short breaks: from £50.00

1 bungalow: sleeping 2 people

South and South East England

Ancient and modern

History pervades every pore of south eastern England. Despite the prosperity and modernity of these bustling counties, there lies a Roman villa, Saxon church, Tudor cottage, Georgian townhouse or Victorian railway station around almost every corner. Sometimes, the juxtaposition of old and modern is striking; at Folkestone, for example, visitors can choose to marvel at the engineering triumph of the Channel Tunnel or descend the steep cliffs to the Maritime Gardens in a lift built in 1885 and powered by water pressure. On other occasions, you will be hard-pushed to realise that you are now in the 21st century. Stroll through Chiddingstone, near Tonbridge (and not that far from the M25), and you leave the modern world behind. The houses are half-timbered, many dating from the Elizabethan and Jacobean periods, though the feel is of an idyllic, timeless age. Or hire a rowing boat at Odiham and explore the Basingstoke Canal. Trees shade the calm, quiet backwaters, the only sounds the gentle splash of oar and rustle of leaves.

The Bloomsbury Group in Sussex

Inside the 12th-century church at Berwick, near Eastbourne, a surprise awaits. Its walls are covered with astonishing modern murals, created in the 1940s by Duncan Grant, Vanessa Bell and her son, Quentin Bell. The three, who lived at nearby Charleston Farmhouse, were members of an eccentric affiliation of writers and

artists, the Bloomsbury Group. Charleston became a gathering place for the group and was vividly decorated in accordance with their artistic ideals. Virginia Woolf lived not far away, at Monk's House (NT), Rodmell. www.nationaltrust.org.uk

An Englishman's home...

The region specialises in gorgeous villages. Some, such as Chiddingstone, are celebrated, others less so. Into this latter category fall the following. Wherwell (near Andover) is a shrine to the thatcher's art that also enjoys a magnificent setting on the banks of the Test. Across the Solent on the Isle of Wight lies sleepy Shorwell, sheltering in a wooded valley beneath the closely grazed downs. In West Sussex, just three miles from Petworth – itself a delightful small town dominated by the majestic Petworth House – is Fittleworth, a straggling settlement that offers another group of picturesque stone or brick cottages at each twist of the woodland lanes. Flint is the prevailing material at Piddinghoe, just inland from Newhaven, where St John's Church has one of only three Norman round towers in Sussex. East Clandon, about four miles east of Guildford, is a compact community of brick-and-tile houses surrounding two of the staples of village life – the church and the inn. Milton Abbas is all tranquillity now, but two centuries ago Lord Dorchester provoked outrage from its residents when he razed it to the ground – in order to improve his view – and rebuilt it in a wooded valley a mile away. The replacement, six miles (10km) from Blandford Forum, is made up of regularly spaced, thatched cob cottages, allowing later generations to benefit from the landlord's ruthlessness. Pusey, down a 'no through road' east of Faringdon, is another appealing estate village, this one guarded by venerable beech and horse chestnut trees. Swanbourne, in the Vale of Aylesbury, has been attractively rebuilt since an 18th-century fire. Smithfield Close, however, survived the conflagration, and is a handsome group of whitewashed, 16th-century thatched cottages.

Castles of the Weald

The Weald is the wooded, fertile area of Kent and East Sussex lying between the North and South Downs. The region's historic prosperity and its proximity to London have ensured an array of impressive buildings, many of them castles. These include the fairy-tale Leeds Castle, near Maidstone, perched on two islands in the River Len, and, equally picturesque, ruined Scotney Castle (near Lamberhurst), the centrepiece of a stunning hillside garden. Hever, Knole, Penshurst (all Kent) and Bodiam (East Sussex) are other magnificent examples.

Choose a clear day...

All these villages make excellent centres to walk from, and most offer a pub for well-earned refreshment. If you believe all good walks should include some fine vistas, then try one of these four: Ditchling Beacon, a couple of miles north of Brighton, is arguably the best viewpoint in the South Downs. The stretch of the South Downs Way, leading west to the pair of windmills familiarly known as Jack and Jill, makes a rousing afternoon's hike. At the western end of the Way, and competing for the accolade of best viewpoint, is Butser Hill, highest point in the South Downs. The fort at Ditchling dates from the Iron Age; here Stone Age men and women flourished. The Queen Elizabeth Country Park – of which Butser hill is a part – provides leaflets for waymarked trails. Towards the northern end of the Chilterns – and at the end of the Ridgeway, a track used before the Romans arrived – is Ivinghoe Beacon; views extend to London, out over the Bedfordshire plain and south west to the Chilterns, home to glorious, underrated countryside. The final vantage point is beside the Cerne Abbas giant, that uncompromising symbol of male fertility etched on the Dorset Downs. And Dorset comprises the entire view: untaxing, unspoilt and ineffably beautiful.

Sir Stanley Spencer CBE RA

Baca Megibbon

Walk this way

Many of the long-distance paths in south eastern England follow the ridges of chalk downland, leading you past countless such viewpoints. With other rights-of-way criss-crossing these paths at regular intervals, it is a simple matter to devise shorter, circular walks. The 100 mile (160km) South Downs Way follows ancient tracks and old droveways in East and West Sussex and Hampshire. The North Downs Way, running 153 miles (246km) from Farnham to Canterbury, explores scenery of such splendour – sometimes wooded, sometimes grassland – it is hard to believe that for much of its length London lies less than 30 miles (48km) away. The Ridgeway keeps to the tops of the Chilterns for its eastern stretch, descending to cross the Thames at Goring Gap, where it meets the Thames Path. A recent creation, this trail follows England's most famous river from its source in Gloucestershire to the Thames Barrier at Woolwich, availing itself of 126 footbridges en route. The region has other longer paths that seek out the remoter corners of the countryside. Hampshire has the Hangers Way (17 miles (27km) through beechwoods between Alton and Petersfield) and the Solent Way (60 miles (96km) from Milford-on-Sea to Emsworth), and others besides. The Isle of Wight Coast Path circles the island in 69 glorious miles (110km).

How the other half lived

Those who enjoy that most compelling of pastimes – having a good look round somebody else's house – can indulge themselves to their heart's

Sandham Memorial Chapel

This chapel, at Burghclere in Berkshire, was built to house an extraordinary series of wall-paintings by the artist Stanley Spencer. He served in the army medical corps during World War I, and the murals record the everyday humdrum soldiers' duties: floor-cleaning, bed-making, laundry-sorting and a whole variety of other chores, but painted with exaggerated proportions and stylised perspective so that the scenes take on an aura of significance and horror. The chapel is dominated by a great Resurrection on the wall behind the altar.
www.nationaltrust.org.uk

Selborne's Natural History

Selborne, in a Hampshire back-water south of Alton, is largely synonymous with the work of late 18th-century clergyman-turned-naturalist, Gilbert White. Through a deep love of nature – and profound coach-sickness – White spent much of his time in the village of his birth. He eventually recorded his minute observation of natural phenomena in his masterpiece, The Natural History of Selborne, which has never been out of print since publication in 1789. His attractive home, The Wakes, is now a museum dedicated to his memory. http://selborne. parish.hants.gov.uk/house.html

Mad Jack Fuller

Nineteenth-century patron of the arts, bon viveur and local squire, 'Mad' Jack Fuller lives on thanks to his abiding passion for follies. His grave in the churchyard at Brightling, East Sussex, is a 25ft (7.5m)-high stone pyramid. Despite his wish to be interred at table, dressed for dinner and resplendent in top hat, he rests – in conventional repose – in the ground below. Nearby edifices include the 'Tower', a gothic-looking building with a battlemented top, and the Sugar Loaf, reputedly built in a night to enable Fuller to 'win' a bet that the spire of Dallington church was visible from his windows.

Folly Hill

When Gerald Tyrwhitt-Wilson, 14th Baron Berners, opened his 140ft (43m) folly to his friends in 1935 he displayed the following notice above the entrance: 'Members of the public committing suicide from this tower do so at their own risk'. Berners was an aristocratic eccentric, an accomplished painter, writer and composer, who entertained lavishly. Those who climb his folly (just outside Faringdon) are rewarded by a panoramic view of several counties stretching to the Berkshire Downs and the White Horse of Uffington.

content and without conscience. The choice is so wide that it can be a matter of choosing your scale, which starts at the very, very grand, such as Windsor Castle, Blenheim Palace, Osborne House, Waddesdon Manor and Goodwood House, and includes some comparatively modest houses. Closer to this end of the spectrum is the 14th-century Alfriston Clergy House, the very first property purchased by the National Trust, for just £10, in 1896. Lamb House, in the near-perfect town of Rye, was the home of the novelist Henry James; the 18th-century building is surrounded by an attractive garden. Other less celebrated historic homes include: Rousham House, a 17th-century Oxfordshire mansion now full of portraits but once used as a Royalist garrison in the Civil War; Haseley Manor, a rambling house of several periods happily rescued from dereliction in the 1970s; Dorney Court, Windsor, a 15th-century brick-and-timber house in the same ownership for almost 500 years; Chettle House, near Blandford Forum, an appealingly idiosyncratic, small Baroque country-house that feels – and is – very much a family home.

The coast is clear

England's southern coast has long been a playground for London, ensuring that most resorts offer a bewildering array of amenities. Margate, Eastbourne, Brighton, Bournemouth and Shanklin, amongst others, have long welcomed large numbers of visitors. Escaping the hurly-burly can be more of a challenge on this stretch of coastline, but try Minnis Bay, on Kent's north-facing shore, west of Margate; Pevensey Bay, between Bexhill and Eastbourne; the sand dunes west of Littlehampton; Bracklesham Bay, near Selsey Bill; Lepe, a small stretch of sand and shingle facing the Isle of Wight; Luccombe Bay, ten minutes' walk from Shanklin; and Shipstal Point, giving on to a quiet stretch of Poole Harbour.

The artistic year

The cultural capital for livelier, broad-minded souls is Brighton, with its avant-garde galleries, arthouse cinemas and never-ending supply of clubs. The Brighton Festival – held each May, and one of England's largest celebrations of the arts – includes events such as conducted walks through Victorian cemeteries, dance, theatre, jazz and classical music. Not far away, Arundel puts out the bunting in August and invites you to open-air theatre in the castle grounds, jazz, fireworks and classical concerts. The centrepiece of the Canterbury Festival is the cathedral – used for operatic performances – while other venues host drama, dance and much more, each October. Similarly, Chichester Festival's focal point is its Norman cathedral, though the refurbished ballroom of Goodwood House has also been called into service in the past; the July festivities add exhibitions of contemporary sculpture and lectures to the round of concerts and plays. Guildford holds two festivals each year: music in March and books in October. Henley makes the most of its superb Thames-side setting when theatre takes to the streets and bridges of the town each July. At the end of September and in early October, it is the turn of Windsor to stage musical and literary events, some held in the Castle itself. And for four weeks in February and March, the dance world turns its attention to north western Surrey, the home of the Woking Dance Festival.

A break with history

Most of the festival towns and cities are ideal for short breaks. There are a hundred other attractive bases suitable for a weekend away, of which these form an eclectic sample. Winchester, the nation's capital until the reign of Canute, claims the longest cathedral in Europe, and an impressive collection of Georgian townhouses too. Midhurst, a busy market town beneath the South Downs, seems only to have glorious 16th-, 17th- and 18th-century buildings, some of the best in the appealingly named Knockhundred Row. Tunbridge Wells' prosperity arrived with the discovery of chalybeate springs in 1606, and it has barely looked back since. Modern-day visitors can approach the springs along The Pantiles, a shopping area of sublime beauty. Arrive in early June and a cricket festival at one of the country's most picturesque grounds is in full swing. Hungerford, on the banks of the Kennet and close to more superb walking country, is a paradise for antique hunters. Thame, on the river of the same name, is equally popular with those happy to spend an evening in a fine old coaching inn; the town boasts four that date from the 15th century.

Some useful web addresses

Basingstoke Canal	www.basingstoke-canal.co.uk
The South Downs Way	www.nationaltrails.gov.uk/southdownsframeset.htm
The North Downs Way	www.nationaltrails.gov.uk/northdownsframeset.htm
The Ridgeway National Trail	www.nationaltrails.gov.uk/ridgewayframeset.htm
The Thames Path National Trail	www.nationaltrails.gov.uk/thamespathframeset.htm
Hangers Way	www.hants.gov.uk/countryside/row/ldr/hangway.html
Solent Way	www.hants.gov.uk/countryside/row/ldr/solentway.html
Isle of Wight Coast Path	www.walkthewight.org.uk/walkingroutes.htm
Windsor Castle	www.royal.gov.uk
Blenheim Palace, Woodstock	www.blenheimpalace.com
Osborne House, Isle of Wight	www.english-heritage.org.uk
Waddesdon Manor, Aylesbury	www.waddesdon.org.uk
Goodwood House, Chichester	www.goodwood.co.uk
Alfriston Clergy House	www.nationaltrust.org.uk
Lamb House, Rye	www.nationaltrust.org.uk
Rousham House, Bicester	www.oxfordshirecotswolds.org
Dorney Court, Windsor	www.dorneycourt.co.uk
Brighton Festival	www.brighton-festival.org.uk
Arundel Festival	www.arundelfestival.co.uk
Canterbury Festival	www.canterburyfestival.co.uk
Chichester Festivities	www.chifest.org.uk
Guildford International Music Festival	www.surrey.ac.uk/arts_office/festival
Guildford Book Festival	www.guildfordbookfestival.co.uk
Henley Festival	www.henley-festival.co.uk
Woking Dance Festival	www.wokingdancefestival.co.uk

Pallant House

Built in 1712, Chichester's Pallant House (tel: 01243 774557) is an interesting setting for a modern-art collection. Each room, lovingly restored, reflects a period in the house's history and contains furniture, porcelain, textiles, even pictures from the period. But amongst all this grace and refinement, the raw colour and abstract form of the modern paintings on its walls strike an exciting note of contrast. Picasso, Sutherland, Nash, Piper, Moore and others are represented, most donated by Walter Hussey, Dean of Chichester Cathedral from 1955 to 1977.
www.pallant.org.uk

The Gardens of Stowe

Perhaps the finest statement of the art of the 18th-century garden lives on at Stowe, near Buckingham. John Vanbrugh, William Kent, James Gibbs and 'Capability' Brown – the most talented gardeners and architects of their day – went to great lengths to create a landscape remodelled and replanted to look as natural as possible, in order to match the aesthetic blueprint of ancient Rome. To this end, grottoes were built, lakes dug, columns erected and monuments – thirty, all told – sited with consummate care. The National Trust is now restoring these majestic gardens.
www.nationaltrust.org.uk

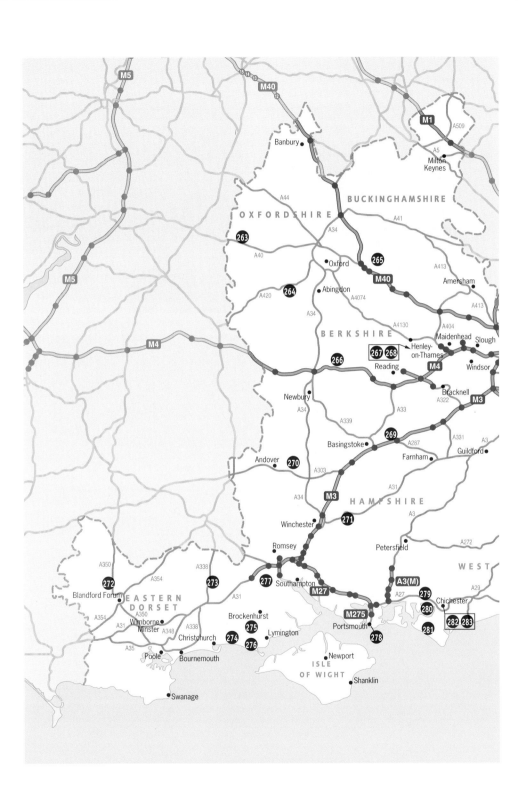

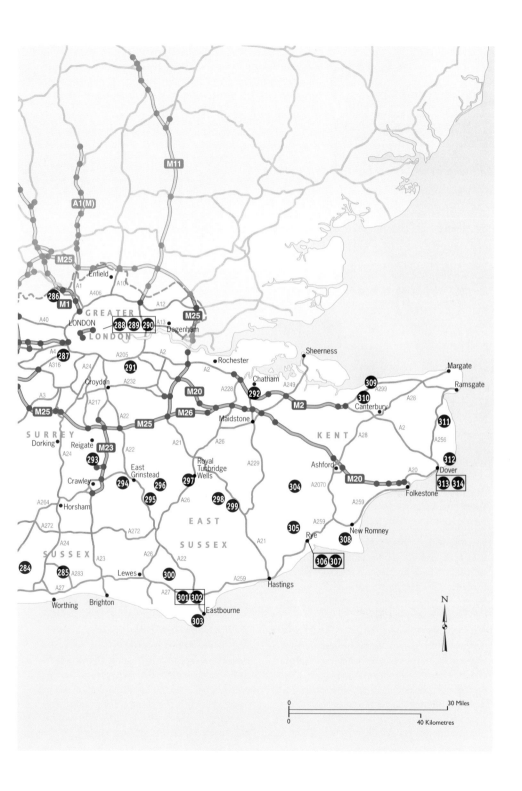

263 Burford House Hotel

◆ ◆ ◆ ◆ Gold Award

99 High Street, Burford, Oxford, Oxfordshire OX18 4QA **Tel:** (01993) 823151 **Fax:** (01993) 823240
Web: www.burfordhouse.co.uk **E-mail:** stay@burfordhouse.co.uk

Situated in one of the Cotswold's most historic towns, Burford House is perfectly placed for exploring this lovely area. Run with care by owners Jane and Simon Henty, importance is placed on comfort, a relaxed atmosphere and attention to detail, and the house is cosy and intimate with a wealth of personal touches. Wonderful breakfasts are served and guests can return to traditional afternoon tea in the sitting rooms or delightful courtyard garden. A warm welcome awaits.

Bed & Breakfast per night: single occupancy from £80.00–£125.00; double room from £105.00– £155.00
Lunch available: 1200–1400

Bedrooms: 2 four-poster, 3 double, 2 twin, 1 family
Bathrooms: 8 en-suite
Cards accepted: Mastercard, Visa, Switch/Delta, Amex

The Eastern Cotswolds

Mirroring the geography of the whole country, the Cotswolds slope gently down from west to east. Oxfordshire and the Eastern Cotswolds may not have great blustery tops and panoramic vistas, but the towns and villages – the true beauty of the area – continue to be of the highest level. The rivers – the Evenlode and Windrush (shown here) – are older and wiser here, flowing serenely through broader valleys and under stone bridges. Both are headed for the Thames and for Oxford, outside the Cotswolds proper, but an ideal basecamp for tackling the eastern fringes.

Southernmost of these Cotswold valleys is the Thames (known here as the Isis). The river is navigable as far as Lechlade on the Gloucestershire border, and is a popular attraction in its own right. Those who prefer dry land can follow almost the same route on the Thames Path. Buscot, west of the attractive market town of Faringdon, is perhaps the highlight of the upper Thames. An unspoilt estate village, it has a riverside church and two 18th-century properties belonging to the National Trust: the Old Parsonage (open by appointment only) and the larger Buscot Park, containing an important collection of paintings and set within fine parkland. Five miles downstream are Pusey House Gardens.

The evocatively named river Windrush flows over grey stone which has been used for St Paul's Cathedral,

many Oxford colleges and – on a more modest scale – the houses of Burford, a real Cotswold gem. Just south is the Cotswold Wildlife Park. Between Burford and Witney, an appealing town whose prosperity derived from blanket-making, is Minster Lovell, a charming, tucked-away village that conceals a gruesome legend. Desperate to escape capture after involvement in a failed insurrection, a 15th-century Lord Lovell had himself walled up by a servant, who suddenly died. The lord's remains were supposedly discovered in 1718. The ruined hall is open to the public.

The Evenlode makes its meandering way through remnants of the ancient Wychwood Forest towards Charlbury, where the quaint museum presents the history of this peaceful, former weaving town. The valley is good walking country – the Oxfordshire Way long-distance path follows the riverbank for some miles, as does the Oxford–Worcester railway line, which makes a good, leisurely vantage point. The Glyme, a tributary of the Evenlode, feeds the lakes of the sumptuous Blenheim Palace, given to the Duke of Marlborough by a grateful nation in the early 18th century after he had proved victorious in the War of the Spanish Succession. Nearby Woodstock is another magnificent village to dawdle in.

The greater part of the Cotswolds lie to the west – see feature on pages 78 & 79.

264 Fallowfields Country House Hotel

★★★ Silver Award

Kingston Bagpuize with Southmoor, Oxford, Oxfordshire OX13 5BH **Tel:** (01865) 820416 **Fax:** (01865) 821275
Web: www.fallowfields.com **E-mail:** stay@fallowfields.com

The Fallowfields' recipe – take near-organic garden produce, add meticulously chosen meat and fish, mix in a three-hundred-year-old (in parts) manor farmhouse, add interesting company, personal care of the owners, and serve in a candle-lit dining room, preferably by a log fire – leave with your bank manager still talking to you and you have the perfect recipe for a stay on business or pleasure. 'The next step is heaven' said one guest. AA Rosette.

Bed & Breakfast per night: single room from £95.00–£140.00; double room from £135.00–£170.00
Dinner, Bed & Breakfast per person, per night: £100.00–£152.50 (min 2 sharing)
Lunch available: 1200–1430

Evening meal: 1900 (last orders 2100)
Bedrooms: 8 double/twin, 2 family
Bathrooms: 10 en-suite
Parking: 73 spaces
Cards accepted: Mastercard, Visa, Switch/Delta, Amex, Barclaycard

265 The Dairy

◆◆◆◆◆ Gold Award

Moreton, Thame, Oxfordshire OX9 2HX **Tel:** (01844) 214075 **Fax:** (01844) 214075
Web: www.thedairy.freeuk.com **E-mail:** thedairy@freeuk.com

This former milking parlour, set in over four acres, provides a beautiful, peaceful and comfortable stay. All bedrooms are bright and airy and include hairdryers, writing tables, fresh flowers, biscuits and comfortable sofas and chairs. There is a large open plan lounge with views of the Chilterns. The property is very convenient for London, either by train (50 minutes from local station), coach or car. Oxford is 20 minutes by car.

Bed & Breakfast per night: single occupancy from £65.00; double room from £89.00

Bedrooms: 3 single/double
Bathrooms: 3 en-suite
Parking: 8 spaces
Cards accepted: Mastercard, Visa, Amex

266 Manor Farm House

◆◆◆◆ Silver Award

Church Street, Hampstead Norreys, Thatcham, Berkshire RG18 0TD **Tel:** (01635) 201276 **Fax:** (01635) 201035
Web: www.bettsbedandbreakfast.co.uk **E-mail:** bettsbedandbreakfast@hotmail.com

We enjoy welcoming guests to our 17th-century Grade II listed farmhouse with 21st-century comforts, including a splendid double en-suite with jacuzzi bath and a luxurious annexe apartment, also suitable for the disabled. Our arable/beef farm is in the centre of the village, two minutes to the pub. Lovely local walks - we can provide dogs! 10 minutes from M4/A34 juntion 13, 50 minutes from Heathrow. Convenient for Newbury Races, Basildon Park (NT), Highclere Castle, the Living Rainforest, one mile. Gateway to the West Country.

Bed & Breakfast per night: single occupancy from £35.00–£40.00; double room from £55.00–£60.00

Bedrooms: 1 double, 1 twin, 1 annexe suite
Bathrooms: 3 en-suite
Parking: 8 spaces

267 Holmwood

◆◆◆◆

Shiplake Row, Binfield Heath, Henley-on-Thames, Oxfordshire RG9 4DP **Tel:** (0118) 947 8747 **Fax:** (0118) 947 8637
E-mail: wendy.cook@freenet.co.uk

Holmwood is an elegant Georgian country house with a galleried hall, mahogany doors and marble fireplaces. The house is set in three acres of beautiful gardens with extensive views over the Thames Valley. The large bedrooms are furnished with antique and period furniture – all have bathrooms en-suite, colour television and tea/coffee making facilities. Holmwood is convenient for Windsor, Oxford, London and Heathrow. Nearby are several pubs offering excellent evening meals.

Bed & Breakfast per night: single room £45.00; double room £65.00

Bedrooms: 1 single, 2 double, 2 twin
Bathrooms: 5 en-suite
Parking: 10 spaces
Cards accepted: Mastercard, Visa, Switch/Delta

268 The Knoll

 ◆◆◆◆ Silver Award

Crowsley Road, Shiplake, Henley-on-Thames, Oxfordshire RG9 3JT **Tel:** (01189) 402705 **Fax:** (01189) 402705
Web: www.theknollhenley.co.uk **E-mail:** theknollhenley@aol.com

The Knoll, with extensive landscaped gardens, offers quiet luxury bed and breakfast accommodation. One of the loveliest homes, with riverside access in the village of Shiplake, it is situated just two miles from Henley-on-Thames. Winner of the 'Bed & Breakfast of the Year' Excellence Award for Southern England, The Knoll has also been nominated for the 'Best British Breakfast' Award. There is a regular train service from the village station to London, and you are also within easy driving distance of Windsor and Oxford. Minimum 2-night booking.

Bed & Breakfast per night: single occupancy £49.00; double room from £60.00

Bedrooms: 1 double, 1 twin, 1 family
Bathrooms: 3 en-suite
Parking: 5 spaces
Open: November–March and June–August

269 Tylney Hall Hotel

★★★★ Gold Award

Rotherwick, Hook, Hampshire RG27 9AZ **Tel:** (01256) 764881 **Fax:** (01256) 768141
Web: www.tylneyhall.com **E-mail:** sales@tylneyhall.com

Amidst sixty six acres of Hampshire countryside lies Tylney Hall, an independently-owned, Grade II listed country house hotel. The 112 bedrooms are beautifully decorated and fitted with all modern amenities. The award-winning Oak Room Restaurant offers innovative menus for those dining for business or pleasure, complemented by an extensive wine cellar and attentive, yet discreet, service. Twelve individually designed function suites cater for up to 120 people, whilst extensive and exclusive leisure facilities allow guests to relax in the luxurious surroundings.

Bed & Breakfast per night: single room from £135.00–£400.00; double room from £165.00–£430.00
Dinner, Bed & Breakfast per person, per night: £112.50–£200.00 (min 2 nights, 2 sharing)
Lunch available: 1230–1400

Evening meal: 1930 (last orders 2130)
Bedrooms: 1 single, 58 double, 23 twin, 1 family, 29 suites **Bathrooms:** 112 en-suite
Parking: 120 spaces
Cards accepted: Mastercard, Visa, Switch/Delta, Amex, Diners, JCB

270 Forest Edge

♦♦♦♦ Silver Award

Andover Down, Andover, Hampshire SP11 6LJ **Tel:** (01264) 364526
Web: www.forest-edge.co.uk **E-mail:** david@forest-edge.co.uk

Forest Edge abuts ancient oak woodland with its three species of deer, badgers, bluebell carpet and good network of footpaths. The RHS and other magazines have featured the one-acre, eco-friendly garden. The bedrooms have top-of-the-range beds and there is a spacious Garden Room, with cane furniture and library, for relaxation and breakfast. Forest Edge is five minutes from the A303, yet in a quiet location. Ideal for Stonehenge, Salisbury, Winchester and even Oxford. Many local gardens (Mottisfont, Longstock, Hillier's) open to the public.

Bed & Breakfast per night: single occupancy from £40.00–£45.00; double room from £55.00– £60.00
Dinner, Bed & Breakfast per person, per night: £45.00–£55.00 (min 2 nights)
Evening meal: 1900 (last orders 2000)

Bedrooms: 2 double, 2 twin, 1 family
Bathrooms: all en-suite
Parking: 4 spaces

271 Tichborne Grange B&B

♦♦♦♦

Grange Farm, Tichborne, Alresford, Hampshire SO24 ONE **Tel:** (01962) 732120 **Fax:** (01962) 732365
Web: www.tichbornegrange.co.uk **E-mail:** gussie@tichbornegrange.co.uk

A charming 17th-century farmhouse situated on a working farm in a picturesque village, just 2 miles from Alresford and 6 miles from Winchester. Large comfortable bedrooms and a cosy guest sitting room with open log fire. Breakfast is served in the conservatory overlooking the garden and paddocks. Excellent walking with a direct link to the South Downs Way. Good pubs and restaurants nearby and many local attractions including the Watercress Line, Northington Grange and Jane Austen's House.

Bed & Breakfast per night: single occupancy from £35.00–£50.00; double room from £50.00–£60.00

Bedrooms: 1 double, 1 twin
Bathrooms: 1 en-suite, 1 private
Parking: plenty

272 The Cricketers

♦♦♦♦♦ Silver Award

Main Street, Shroton, Blandford Forum, Dorset DT11 8QD **Tel:** (01258) 860421 **Fax:** (01258) 861800
E-mail: the_cricketers@hotmail.com

The Cricketers, the quintessential English country inn, set betwixt village green and cricket pitch at the foot of Hambledon Hill in a peaceful and pretty Dorset village. Superb pub renowned locally for fabulous food, fine ales and good wines and run enthusiastically by George and Carol Cowie. It offers a friendly welcoming atmosphere for that perfect 'get away break'. 'The Pavillion' accommodation is a separate garden room with a bay window overlooking the cleamtis-covered arbour. It features a super-king bed, a very high standard of soft furnishing and a separate shower room.

Bed & Breakfast per night: single room from £50.00; double room from £70.00
Lunch available: 1200–1400
Evening meal: 1830 (last orders 2100)

Bedrooms: 1 single/double/twin
Bathrooms: 1 en-suite
Parking: 20 spaces
Cards accepted: Mastercard, Visa, Switch/ Delta

At-a-glance symbols are explained on the flap inside the back cover

273 The Three Lions

◆◆◆◆◆ Gold Award

Stuckton, Fordingbridge, Hampshire SP6 2HF **Tel:** (01425) 652489 **Fax:** (01425) 656144
Web: www.thethreelionsrestaurant.co.uk **E-mail:** the3lions@btinternet.com

Built in 1863, The Three Lions nestles on the edge of the New Forest and is personally owned and run by Mike and Jayne Womersley. The rooms are all en-suite, airy and very peaceful, overlooking well-manicured gardens and the forest behind. There is also an open-air whirlpool therapy spa and sauna for residents' use. The restaurant is highly rated in all major UK food guides (Highly Commended Restaurant of the Year, 2001 Good Food Guide and Best Newcomer 2002 Good Hotel Guide) with 3 AA Rosettes and a 150-bin wine list.

Bed & Breakfast per night: single occupancy from £65.00–£75.00; double room from £75.00–£95.00
Dinner, Bed & Breakfast per person, per night: £55.00–£67.50 (min 2 nights)
Evening meal: 1900 (last orders 2100)

Bedrooms: 3 double/twin, 1 family
Bathrooms: 4 en-suite
Parking: 40 spaces
Cards accepted: Mastercard, Visa, Switch/ Delta, Amex, Barclaycard

The New Forest

The New Forest is the largest tract of uncultivated land in lowland Britain, escaping, by various accidents of history, the agricultural changes that have transformed most of southern England into fertile farmland. It was first granted special status in 1079 when William the Conqueror made it a Royal hunting preserve, imposing fierce and unpopular laws to protect his royal playground. His son, William Rufus, met his death here, killed by an arrow in the heart, but whether by accident or design remains a mystery. The Rufus Stone (actually made of cast iron – shown below) was erected in 1865 by Earl de la Warr at a lonely place in the Forest near Upper Canterton to commemorate the event, though there is scant evidence that this was actually the spot where Rufus died.

There is no record of any sovereign hunting here after James II, but by this time the status of the Forest had changed, from royal hunting ground to valuable timber resource. The Forest's trees, many planted by William I as coverts for his deer, were felled to supply timber for houses and for ships, and today large areas are devoted to the commercial cultivation of fast-growing conifers. But ancient broad-leaved woodland still clothes many parts of the New Forest, some of the finest undisturbed deciduous forest in Western Europe. At Mark Ash Wood, near Boldrewood, and Denny Wood, near Lyndhurst, for example, the mighty oaks and beeches have stood for hundreds of years, their leaves creating a vast canopy of dappled light and shade, their decayed trunks a rich habitat for fungi, insects and woodland-dwelling birds. These magnificent woodlands, however, are just one part of the New Forest's natural picture. Drive along the B3078 near Godshill, and a vista opens up of endless undulating heather-covered wilderness.

Explore on foot, and the diversity of flora and fauna becomes apparent. Rain collects in the ill-drained hollows of the heath to create acidic peat bogs, where the eagle-eyed may spot sundews, march gentian and bog orchid, rare types of dragonfly and damselfly, or all three of Britain's species of newt. The air is specked with butterflies, and loud with the call of the heathland and marshland birds – evening may even bring the churr of the shy and very rare nightjar. To learn more about aspects of the Forest's wildlife, visit the Holiday Hills Reptiliary, near Lyndhurst, or the New Forest Nature Quest, near Longdown.

274 Chewton Glen Hotel, Health & Country Club ★★★★★ Gold Award

Christchurch Road, New Milton, Hampshire BH25 6QS **Tel:** (01425) 275341 **Fax:** (01425) 272310
Web: www.chewtonglen.com **E-mail:** reservations@chewtonglen.com

A warm welcome awaits you at Chewton Glen where emphasis is placed on personal service. Local produce is well represented in the celebrated restaurant. Bedrooms are individually designed, most having a balcony or terrace. An amazing new spa, including a large gym and pool, ten treatment rooms, relaxation room, hydrotherapy spa, bar and lounge. Other facilities include a 9-hole, par 3 golf course and in/outdoor tennis within the grounds.

Bed & Breakfast per night: single occupancy from £195.00–£425.00; double room from £195.00–£745.00
Dinner, Bed & Breakfast per person, per night: £172.50–£447.50
Lunch available: 1230–1345

Evening meal: 1930 (last orders 2130)
Bedrooms: 37 double, 22 suites
Bathrooms: 59 en-suite
Parking: 125 spaces
Cards accepted: Mastercard, Visa, Switch/Delta, Amex, Diners, Eurocard

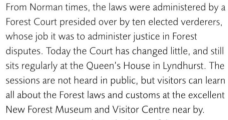

The whole New Forest is criss-crossed by footpaths and bridleways, and well provided with car parks and signposts, making this a paradise for walkers of all staminas, as well as horse-riders and mountain-bikers. At Rhinefield and Boldrewood ornamental trees and shrubs have been planted along the roadside, creating a spectacular splash of autumn colour; for more natural surroundings follow on foot the well-marked paths along the lovely Ober Water, near Brockenhurst, one of the Forest's finest beauty spots.

The New Forest also has a unique cultural heritage rooted in old custom and law. When William the Conquerer made the forest his own, he granted the commoners special rights, such as cutting turf, collecting fallen wood, and, in particular, grazing animals. Today, cows, sheep and ponies are permanent residents, their voracious nibbling continually re-shaping the landscape. The wild

ponies are a breed found nowhere else – it is said they are descended from animals who swam ashore from the Spanish Armada. In autumn you may chance upon a pony 'drift', a frenetic round-up at which ponies' tails are cut in a special pattern to record payment for grazing rights, and new foals are branded with their owner's number. For 60 days in autumn pigs, too, are allowed to forage in the woodlands for green acorns, poisonous to deer and cattle, an ancient privilege known as 'pannage'.

From Norman times, the laws were administered by a Forest Court presided over by ten elected verderers, whose job it was to administer justice in Forest disputes. Today the Court has changed little, and still sits regularly at the Queen's House in Lyndhurst. The sessions are not heard in public, but visitors can learn all about the Forest laws and customs at the excellent New Forest Museum and Visitor Centre near by.

Right in the heart of the Forest, Lyndhurst is considered its capital, a busy, important little town, with many picturesque old buildings, and a fine church noted for its pre-Raphaelite stained-glass. Not far away, Brockenhurst's medieval church is one of the oldest in the area. Its churchyard is dominated by the famous Brockenhurst yew, said to be over 1000 years old, but don't miss the fascinating Victorian monument to a disreputable local character, the snakecatcher Henry 'Brusher' Mills.

To the east is Beaulieu; its famous stately home, Beaulieu Abbey, was built upon the remains of a Cistercian monastery, and is still the ancestral home of the Montagu family, who created its fascinating motor museum. 5 miles (8km) downstream Buckler's Hard, once an important shipbuilding settlement, lies tranquilly beside the water. Amongst its mellow brick houses are a Maritime Museum and a house furnished with late 18th century interiors, interesting reminders of this once-great Forest industry.

275 The Nurse's Cottage ♦♦♦♦♦ Gold Award

Station Road, Sway, Lymington, Hampshire SO41 6BA **Tel:** (01590) 683402 **Fax:** (01590) 683402
Web: www.nursescottage.co.uk **E-mail:** nurses.cottage@lineone.net

Nothing equals a visit to this cosy New Forest cottage, for over 70 years home to Sway's successive District Nurses. Lovingly refurbished in recent years, the award-winning guest accommodation offers every possible creature comfort, while chef/proprietor Tony Barnfield's enterprising dinner menu and extensive wine list make this the perfect escape for that very special occasion. Invariably fully booked months ahead, advance reservations are essential. The popular, newly-extended restaurant is open to non-residents for breakfast, dinner and Sunday luncheon. 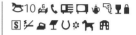 Accessible Mobility 1 Hearing 1

Dinner, Bed & Breakfast per night: single room £75.00; double/twin room £150.00 (reduced rates for short breaks)
Lunch available: Sunday 1230–1400
Evening meal: 1830 (last orders 2000)

Bedrooms: 1 single, 1 double, 1 twin
Bathrooms: 3 en-suite
Parking: 5 spaces
Open: all year except part March & November
Cards accepted: Mastercard, Visa, Switch/Delta, Amex, Eurocard, JCB

276 Alma Mater ♦♦♦♦

4 Knowland Drive, Milford-on-Sea, Lymington, Hampshire SO41 0RH
Web: www.almamater.org.uk **E-mail:** bandbalmamater@aol.com

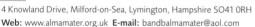

Eileen and John Haywood welcome guests to their beautiful chalet bungalow overlooking landscaped gardens in a quiet residential area. Close to the New Forest and the yachting centre of Lymington and Keyhaven. Ample on-site parking with the village and beach a short walk away. Four-course full English, Continental or vegetarian breakfasts served in the dining room. Comfortable ensuite bedrooms centrally heated with television, radio and courtesy beverages available.

Bed & Breakfast per night: single occupancy from £35.00–£40.00; double room from £54.00–£70.00

Bedrooms: 2 double, 1 twin
Bathrooms: 2 en-suite, 1 private
Parking: 4 spaces

277 Bartley Farmhouse ♦♦♦♦

Ringwood Road, Bartley, Southampton, Hampshire SO40 7LD **Tel:** (023) 8081 4194 **Fax:** (023) 8081 4117

When visiting the New Forest the old farmhouse is a lovely place to stay – warm, comfortable and welcoming. You will be invited to share our house and made to feel special. We can offer a paddock or stable if you bring a horse, a mountain bike or a map – alternatively a chair in the garden should you just want to relax. As a special treat, our hosted dinner party will give you an evening to remember (by arrangement).

Bed & Breakfast per night: single occupancy from £40.00; double room from £60.00
Dinner, Bed & Breakfast per person, per night: from £65.00

Bedrooms: 2 double
Bathrooms: 2 en-suite
Parking: 6 spaces
Cards accepted: Mastercard, Visa, Switch/Delta

278 131 High Street

◆◆◆◆

Portsmouth PO1 2HW **Tel: (**02392) 730903

Whether on business or pleasure, relax and enjoy yourself in this 18th-century Georgian House in the historic part of Old Portsmouth. Open all year round and just 5 minutes from the sea. '131' is also within walking distance of the town centre, harbour station, Gunwharf Quays leisure/shopping outlet, ferries, historic dockyard, museums and over 70 restaurants! Let Barbara and Lou spoil you with breakfast in bed at '131', as with everything so near this is the perfect place for that special break.

Bed & Breakfast per night: single occupancy £48.00; double room from £58.00–£60.00

Bedrooms: 1 double, 1 twin
Bathrooms: 1 en-suite, 1 private

279 Horse & Groom

◆◆◆◆

East Ashling, Chichester, West Sussex PO18 9AX   **Tel:** (01243) 575339   **Fax:** (01243) 575560
Web: www.horseandgroom.sageweb.co.uk and www.horseandgroomchichester.com   **E-mail:** horseandgroomea@aol.com

Charming 17th-century freehouse inn, conveniently situated near the South Downs, Chichester and Goodwood. Five of the eleven en-suite twin/double rooms are in a converted flint barn attached to the pub. All rooms have colour television, tea and coffee-making facitlities etc. At lunchtime and in the evenings (except Sunday) the restaurant provides bar snacks and our blackboard menu with freshly prepared local food. The bar itself has all the charm of a traditional English country pub with flagstones and an old-fashioned range. Parking available.

Bed & Breakfast per night: single occupancy from £40.00–£50.00; double room from £60.00–£100.00
Lunch available: 1200–1415
Evening meal: 1830 (last orders 2115)

Bedrooms: 6 double, 5 twin
Bathrooms: 11 en-suite
Parking: 30 spaces
Cards accepted: Mastercard, Visa, Switch/Delta, Amex

280 Millstream Hotel and Restaurant

★★★ Gold Award

Bosham Lane, Bosham, Chichester, West Sussex PO18 8HL   **Tel:** (01243) 573234 **Fax:** (01243) 573459
Web: www.millstream-hotel.co.uk   **E-mail:** info@millstream-hotel.co.uk

A beautifully appointed country house dating from 1701, set in a picturesque quayside village, only four miles west of Chichester. The friendly staff will make you feel very welcome. Bedrooms are all individually furnished, with every modern facility. The Millstream Restaurant is renowned for its superb food and extensive wine list and has been awarded an AA Rosette for culinary excellence. Enjoy walking on the beautiful shoreline or the rolling South Downs. Fishbourne Roman Villa, Goodwood House and Chichester Festival Theatre are all within easy reach.

Bed & Breakfast per night: single room from £79.00–£99.00; double room from £129.00–£149.00
Dinner, Bed & Breakfast per person, per night: £69.00–£92.00
Lunch available: 1230–1400

Evening meal: 1900 (last orders 2130)
Bedrooms: 5 single, 14 double, 10 twin, 2 family, 3 suites **Bathrooms:** 35 en-suite
Parking: 44 spaces
Cards accepted: Mastercard, Visa, Switch/Delta, Amex, Diners, Eurocard

At-a-glance symbols are explained on the flap inside the back cover

281 Millstone

◆◆◆◆ Gold Award

Clappers Lane, Earnley, Chichester, West Sussex PO20 7JJ **Tel:** (01243) 670116 or 07958 409724
E-mail: michaelharrington@btinternet.com

A friendly welcome awaits you in our elegant and spacious family home with a large double en-suite bedroom. Breakfast is served in the conservatory overlooking the secluded country garden. Pretty rural setting on quiet lane, close to sandy beaches and Chichester Harbour. Within easy reach of Chichester, Goodwood and the South Downs.

Bed & Breakfast per night: double room from £60.00–£65.00

Bedrooms: 1 double
Bathrooms: 1 en-suite
Parking: 4 spaces

282 The Royal Oak Inn

◆◆◆◆◆ Silver Award

Pook Lane, East Lavant, Chichester, West Sussex PO18 0AX **Tel:** (01243) 527434 **Fax:** (01243) 775062
Web: www.sussexlive.co.uk/royaloakinn **E-mail:** nickroyaloak@aol.com

Just two miles north of Chichester and set amongst rolling countryside, the Royal Oak Inn is in the picturesque village of East Lavant close to a whole host of attractions including 'Glorious Goodwood' race course and the renowned Festival Theatre. All bedrooms are individually styled with every modern facility including Plasma audio system, CD, direct dialling and internet access. If you want to dine in the evening the restaurant has a widespread reputation with a connoisseur's wine list to match. Stay at the Royal Oak and sleep in style.

Bed & Breakfast per night: single occupancy from £50.00–£70.00; double room from £70.00–£120.00
Dinner, Bed & Breakfast per person, per night: £70.00–£90.00
Lunch available: 1200–1430

Evening meal: 1800 (last orders 2130)
Bedrooms: 3 double, 2 double/twin, 1 cottage
Bathrooms: 6 en-suite
Parking: 25 spaces
Cards accepted: Mastercard, Visa, Switch/ Delta, Amex, Eurocard

283 Friary Close

◆◆◆◆ Silver Award

Friary Lane, Chichester, West Sussex PO19 1UF **Tel:** (01243) 527294 **Fax:** (01243) 533876
E-mail: friaryclose@btinternet.com

Friary Close is a Grade II listed Georgian house built astride the ancient city wall in central Chichester. The house stands in its own grounds and has a large walled garden. It is convenient for all city centre amenities, cathedral, theatre and Roman palace. Within a short drive it is possible to visit Chichester harbour (sailing and walking), Pagham harbour nature reserve and Goodwood (horse racing, motor events, golf and walking). Bus and mainline train station nearby.

Bed & Breakfast per night: double room from £56.00–£70.00

Bedrooms: 3 twin
Bathrooms: 3 en-suite
Parking: 3 spaces
Cards accepted: Mastercard, Visa

284 Amberley House

♦♦♦♦ Silver Award

Church Street, Amberley, Arundel, West Sussex BN18 9NF **Tel:** (01798) 839507 **Fax:** (01798) 839520
Web: www.amberleyhouse.co.uk **E-mail:** relax@amberleyhouse.co.uk

We offer that special touch of luxury with home comforts and charm – our emphasis is on harmony and relaxation. Our house has inglenook fireplaces and beams and the large tranquil garden with mature trees and lake overlooks water meadows and beautiful countryside. We offer a range of relaxing therapies. Breakfasts are mainly organic. We are in an enchanting village, at the foot of the South Downs, known as the 'Pearl of Sussex'. There are pubs and restaurants within walking distance and many outstanding attractions nearby.

Bed & Breakfast per night: single occupancy from £50.00; double room from £95.00– £140.00

Bedrooms: 2 double, 1 twin, 1 suite
Bathrooms: 2 en-suite, 1 shared
Parking: 1 space, unlimited on quiet road

285 The Old Tollgate Restaurant & Hotel

★★★ Silver Award

The Street, Bramber, Steyning, West Sussex BN44 3WE **Tel:** (01903) 879494 **Fax:** (01903) 813399
Web: www.oldtollgatehotel.com **E-mail:** info@oldtollgatehotel.com

In a lovely old Sussex village nestling at the foot of the South Downs, standing on the original Tollhouse site, a perfect blending of the old with the new. Award-winning, carvery-style restaurant – a well-known and popular eating spot – offers a magnificent hors d'oeuvres display followed by a vast selection of roasts, pies and casseroles, with delicious sweets and cheeses to add the final touch. Luxuriously-appointed bedrooms, including two four-posters with jacuzzi baths, and two suites.

Bed & Breakfast per night: single occupancy from £83.95–£135.45; double room from £91.90–£143.40
Dinner, Bed & Breakfast per person, per night: £69.90–£95.65 (min 2 sharing)
Lunch available: 1200–1345

Evening meal: 1900 (last orders 2130)
Bedrooms: 21 double, 10 twin, 3 family, 2 suites **Bathrooms:** 31 en-suite
Parking: 60 spaces
Cards accepted: Mastercard, Visa, Switch/Delta, Amex, Diners, Eurocard, JCB

286 Grim's Dyke Hotel

★★★ Silver Award

Old Redding, Harrow Weald, Harrow, Middlesex HA3 6SH **Tel:** 020 8385 3100 **Fax:** 020 8954 4560
Web: www.grimsdyke.com **E-mail:** reservations@grimsdyke.com

Restored in 1996 and once home to W S Gilbert of Gilbert and Sullivan fame. You can enjoy excellent food, fine wines, cream teas, guided tours, murder mystery dinners and Gilbert and Sullivan operettas with dinner. Set in 40 acres of woodland and landscaped gardens, it is ideal for a relaxing weekend break.

Bed & Breakfast per night: single occupancy from £85.00–£125.00; double room from £95.00–£152.00
Dinner, Bed & Breakfast per person, per night: £100.00–£150.00
Lunch available: 1230–1430

Evening meal: 1900 (last orders 2130)
Bedrooms: 44 double/twin
Bathrooms: 44 en-suite
Parking: 110 spaces
Cards accepted: Mastercard, Visa, Switch/Delta, Amex, Diners

287 Chalon House

◆◆◆◆◆ Gold Award

8 Spring Terrace, Paradise Road, Richmond, Surrey TW9 1LW **Tel:** 020 8332 1121 **Fax:** 020 8332 1131
E-mail: virgilioz@aol.com

London Tourism Award 2003 'Highly Commended' B&B of the Year. Elegant listed Georgian townhouse with garden. Quality en-suite bedrooms with big comfortable beds and breakfast tailored to your taste. Five minutes walk to Richmond station and seven miles to central London. Picnic in Kew Gardens or relax at one of the many traditional pubs along the Thames.

Bed & Breakfast per night: double room from £75.00–£80.00

Bedrooms: 1 double, 2 twin
Bathrooms: 3 en-suite
Parking: 4 spaces
Open: all year except Christmas/New Year

Epsom Derby

The Derby, the most famous horse-race in the world, was first run in 1780, and has attracted huge audiences of ordinary people ever since. 'On Derby Day,' wrote Charles Dickens, 'a population rills and surges and scrambles through the place, that may be counted in millions.' Dickens was surely exaggerating, but so great was the race's popularity in the second half of the 19th century that Parliament was suspended for the day. Currently crowds of some 100,000 or so attend the race, held on the first Saturday in June.

The Derby is named after the 12th Earl of Derby, Edward Smith Stanley, who, together with his colourful uncle, General John Burgoyne, organised the first contest for three-year old fillies in 1779. The race over Epsom Downs was named 'The Oaks' after Burgoyne's rambling house, once a pub, near Epsom, and was won by Derby's filly, Bridget. At the celebration dinnner which followed, Derby planned a second race for three-year-old colts and fillies, to be named after himself. On 4 May 1780 the first Derby took place – and a great English tradition was born. Both races continue to run, with The Oaks taking place the day before the Derby.

During its long history the race has had more than its fair share of dramatic occurrences. In 1913 the suffragette, Emily Davison, was killed when she threw herself in front of the King's horse, a deliberate act of martyrdom designed to generate maximum publicity. More recently, in 1981, the crowds thrilled to the most dramatic Derby win ever, when the legendary colt Shergar, ridden by Walter Swinburn, won effortlessly by a clear 10 lengths. Two years later Shergar was kidnapped from the Aga Khan's stud in Ireland, and to this day his fate remains a mystery.

From a racing point of view, the course over the Epsom Downs is supremely challenging. Run early in the season when the going can be heavy, the undulating and twisting 1½mile (2.4km) course requires great stamina. Rising 150ft (46m) in the first four furlongs, it then falls 100ft (30.5m) in varying gradients to the famous Tattenham Corner, before rising again towards the finishing post. The difficulties of winning such an event make the Derby a true test of equine greatness.

288 Windermere Hotel

◆◆◆◆ Silver Award

142-144 Warwick Way, Victoria, London SW1V 4JE **Tel:** (020) 7834 5163 or (020) 7834 5480 **Fax:** (020) 7630 8831
Web: www.windermere-hotel.co.uk **E-mail:** reservations@windermere-hotel.co.uk

Bed and Breakfast of the year - London Tourism Awards 2003. "The Windermere Hotel gives guests all the intimacy of a family run operation with all the professionalism of a large hotel." An ideal location, within minutes' walk of Buckingham Palace, Westminster Abbey and Tate Britain. All rooms are individually designed and include king, queen, double, twin and family rooms. A scrumptious English breakfast and gourmet dinner is served in the relaxed atmosphere of our licensed restaurant, the 'Pimlico Room'. Parking available.

Bed & Breakfast per night: single room from £69.00–£96.00; double room from £89.00–£139.00
Evening meal: 1730 (last orders 2230)

Bedrooms: 4 single, 10 double, 5 twin, 1 triple, 2 family
Bathrooms: 20 en-suite, 2 shared
Cards accepted: Mastercard, Visa, Switch/ Delta, Amex, Eurocard, JCB

289 Dolphin Square Hotel

★★★★ Silver Award

Dolphin Square, Chichester Street, London, SW1V 3LX **Tel:** (020) 7834 3800 **Fax:** (020) 7798 8735
Web: www.dolphinsquarehotel.co.uk **E-mail:** reservations@dolphinsquarehotel.co.uk

Dolphin Square Hotel is an all suite hotel set in three and a half acres of glorious private gardens, bordered by the River Thames and surrounded by the busy streets of Westminster. The hotel is home to Zest! Health and Fitness Spa that includes an 18 metre indoor swimming pool, air conditioned gym and treatment rooms. Allium, the Hotel's fine dining restaurant, is an exciting new venue under the direction of internationally renowned chef patron Anton Edelmann offering the best of French and British cuisine in a relaxed but sophisticated atmosphere.

Bed & Breakfast per night: single room from £95.00–£185.00; double room from £120.00–£475.00
Dinner, Bed & Breakfast per person, per night: £75.00–£265.00
Evening meal: 1800 (last orders 2230)

Bedrooms: 148 suites
Bathrooms: 148 en-suite
Parking: 18 spaces
Cards accepted: Mastercard, Visa, Switch/ Delta, Amex, Diners, JCB

290 Five Sumner Place Hotel

◆◆◆◆

South Kensington, London SW7 3EE **Tel:** (020) 7584 7586 **Fax:** (020) 7823 9962
Web: www.sumnerplace.com **E-mail:** reservations@sumnerplace.com

This delightful award-winning hotel (awarded best small hotel) is situated in South Kensington, one of the most fashionable areas of London. The hotel itself has been sympathetically restored to recreate the ambience and style of a bygone era. Family-owned and run, it offers excellent service and personal attention. All rooms are luxuriously appointed and come with private en-suite facilities, telephone, colour television, trouser press and full buffet breakfast.

Bed & Breakfast per night: single room from £70.00–£100.00; double room from £110.00–£152.00

Bedrooms: 3 single, 5 double, 5 twin
Bathrooms: 13 en-suite
Cards accepted: Mastercard, Visa, Switch/ Delta, Amex, Diners, Eurocard, JCB

291 Melrose House   ◆◆◆◆

89 Lennard Road, London SE20 7LY **Tel:** (0208) 776 8884 **Fax:** (0208) 325 7636
Web: www.uk-bedandbreakfast.com **E-mail:** melrose.hotel@virgin.net

We are a family-run guest house in a beautifully refurbished, traditionally built Victorian town house with parking,, situated in a quiet and pretty suberb only 15 minutes from the centre of London by public transport. The house has been carefully preserved with its 120 year old cornices and fireplaces still in place. The rooms are all charmingly furnished with private bathrooms. One room has a private marble bathroom with antique fittings and another has a king size, four-poster bed. We also have accommodation for disabled people.

Bed & Breakfast per night: single occupancy from £35.00–£50.00; double room from £55.00–£65.00

Bedrooms: 4 double, 1 twin, 1 suite
Bathrooms: 5 en-suite, 1 private
Parking: 4 spaces
Cards accepted: Mastercard, Visa, Switch/Delta

292 Bridgewood Manor Hotel   ★★★★ Silver Award

Bridgewood Roundabout, Walderslade Woods, Chatham, Kent ME5 9AX **Tel:** (01634) 201333 **Fax:** (01634) 201330
Web: www.marstonhotels.com **E-mail:** bridgewoodmanor@marstonhotels.com

Modern hotel built around a classical courtyard, with Gothic influences reflected in beautiful woodwork. Interconnecting rooms and suites available. Leisure facilities include a heated indoor pool, gym, tennis and beauty treatments. 2 AA Rosettes restaurant. Friendly and professional staff. Ideally located for exploring Kent's many interesting attractions, historic houses and gardens.

Bed & Breakfast per night: single occupancy from £89.00–£174.00; double room from £114.00–£208.00
Dinner, Bed & Breakfast per person, per night: £60.00–£100.00
Lunch available: 1230–1430 Monday–Friday

Evening meal: 1900 (last orders 2200)
Bedrooms: 70 double, 26 twin, 4 suites
Bathrooms: 100 en-suite
Parking: 100 spaces
Cards accepted: Mastercard, Visa, Switch/Delta, Amex, Diners

293 Rosemead Guest House   ◆◆◆◆

19 Church Road, Horley, Surrey RH6 7EY **Tel:** (01293) 784965 **Fax:** (01293) 430547
Web: www.rosemeadguesthouse.co.uk **E-mail:** info@rosemeadguesthouse.co.uk

A warm welcome awaits you at this TOTALLY NON-SMOKING guest house. Conveniently located for Gatwick Airport and within walking distance of shops, pubs and restaurants. The comforable rooms have been individually decorated with lots of extras to make your stay comfortable including teletext colour television, private bathrooms, a selection of hot drinks and complimentary biscuit tin. Full English breakfast is served from 0730–0830, with continental breakfast available anytime before 0730 for early morning departures. Long-term holiday parking is available by arrangement.

Bed & Breakfast per night: single room from £36.00–£40.00; double room from £52.00–£55.00

Bedrooms: 2 single, 1 double, 1 twin, 2 family
Bathrooms: 5 en-suite, 1 private
Cards accepted: Mastercard, Visa, Switch/Delta, Amex (surcharge of 7.5%)

294 Tiltwood House

♦♦♦♦♦ Silver Award

Hophurst Lane, Crawley Down, Crawley, West Sussex RH10 4LL   **Tel:** (01342) 712942
Web: www.tiltwood-bedandbreakfast.co.uk   **E-mail:** vjohnstiltwood@aol.com

The centre part of an elegant Victorian country house set in tranquil, large semi-landscaped gardens. Luxurious, spacious en-suite bedrooms, high ceilings with beautiful mouldings and cornices, king-size beds, television/videos, tea/coffee and light refreshment facilities. Full English breakfast, fresh fruits, cold meats and more, offering hearty sustenance for visiting National Trust gardens, Hickstead, South of England Showground, South Downs, Glynbourne, Lingfield Racecourse, Brighton, London. Ideally suited for honeymooners, being just 7 miles from Gatwick (Heathrow 35 miles).

Bed & Breakfast per night: single occupancy from £45.00–£55.00; double room from £65.00–£87.00

Bedrooms: 2 double
Bathrooms: 2 en-suite
Parking: 4 spaces

295 Ashdown Park Hotel

★★★★ Gold Award

Wych Cross, Forest Row, East Sussex RH18 5JR   **Tel:** (01342) 824988   **Fax:** (01342) 826206
Web: www.ashdownpark.com   **E-mail:** reservations@ashdownpark.com

Ashdown Park Hotel is an impressive Victorian mansion set in the heart of Ashdown Forest – home to 'Pooh Bear' yet within easy reach of London, Gatwick Airport and the South coast. Each of the bedrooms and suites are beautifully decorated, many with breathtaking views of the surrounding gardens and parklands. The award-winning Anderida Restaurant offers an unforgettable dining experience which can be enjoyed following an energetic or relaxing visit to our extensive country club.

Bed & Breakfast per night: single room from £135.00–£325.00; double room from £165.00–£355.00
Dinner, Bed & Breakfast per person, per night: £112.50–£200.00 (min 2 nights, 2 sharing)
Lunch available: 1230–1400

Evening meal: 1900 (lo 2130, Fri & Sat 2200)
Bedrooms: 6 single, 34 double, 31 twin, 36 suites   **Bathrooms:** 107 en-suite
Parking: 120 spaces
Cards accepted: Mastercard, Visa, Switch/Delta, Amex, Diners, Eurocard, Solo

296 Bolebroke Castle

♦♦♦♦

Edenbridge Road, Hartfield, East Sussex TN7 4JJ   **Tel:** (01892) 770061   **Fax:** (01892) 771041
Web: www.bolebrokecastle.co.uk   **E-mail:** bolebroke@btclick.com

Henry VIII's hunting lodge, Bolebroke Castle is set on a beautiful 30 acre estate with lakes, woodlands and views to Ashdown Forest where you will find 'Pooh Bridge' made famous by the 'Winnie the Pooh' stories. Antiques and beamed ceilings add to the atmosphere. Four-poster suite available. Audio tours of the castle can be made where you will see recreated the year 1528 with costumed servants and Henry VIII. It was from here he courted Anne Boleyn who lived at nearby Hever.

Bed & Breakfast per night: single occupancy from £35.00–£49.00; double room from £55.00–£150.00
Lunch available: 1100–1500

Bedrooms: 6 double, 2 family, 1 suite
Bathrooms: 6 en-suite, 1 private, 1 shared
Parking: 40 spaces
Cards accepted: Mastercard, Visa, Switch/Delta, Amex

297 The Spa Hotel

★★★ Silver Award

Mount Ephraim, Royal Tunbridge Wells, Kent TN4 8XJ   **Tel:** (01892) 520331 **Fax:** (01892) 510575
Web: www.spahotel.co.uk **E-mail:** reservations@spahotel.co.uk

Set in 14 acres of beautiful grounds, paddocks and stables with 69 en-suite bedrooms. The award-winning Chandelier Restaurant offers French cuisine with an English influence complemented by an international wine list. Seven conference and banqueting suites are available for meetings or private dining. The Sparkling Health Club has extensive leisure facilities including a beauty salon, swimming pool, steam room, gymnasium and saunas. The Spa is easily accessible from the M25, Gatwick and Heathrow airports and Tunbridge Wells railway station.

Bed & Breakfast per night: single room from £94.00–£104.00; double room from £119.00–£180.00
Dinner, Bed & Breakfast per person, per night: £91.00–£111.00
Lunch available: 1230–1400

Evening meal: 1900 (last orders 2130)
Bedrooms: 6 single, 45 double, 10 twin, 3 family, 5 suites
Bathrooms: 69 en-suite
Cards accepted: Mastercard, Visa, Switch/Delta, Amex, Diners

298 Bryants House

◆◆◆◆

Wards Lane, Wadhurst, East Sussex TN5 6HP   **Tel:** (01892) 784898 **Fax:** (01892) 784898
Web: www.bryants-house.co.uk **E-mail:** b-b@bryants-house.co.uk

Overlooking Bewl Water, the South East's largest lake, Bryants House offers comfortable, convenient accommodation with beautiful views and peaceful surroundings, with direct access to the 13-mile round Bewl Water walk. Guest accommodation comprises one double room and one twin-bedded room with private bathroom, each with colour television and tea/coffee making facilities. Leading off the dining room is a lounge for exclusive use of guests. The Bewl Water Visitor Centre offers cycle hire, fly fishing, windsurfing and sailing. The eastern side of the lake is a designated nature reserve which has a hide for bird watchers.

Bed & Breakfast per night: single occupancy £30.00; double room £54.00

Bedrooms: 1 double, 1 twin
Bathrooms: 1 shared
Parking: 6 spaces
Open: all year except Christmas/New Year

299 Dale Hill Hotel & Golf

★★★★ Gold Award

Ticehurst, Wadhurst, East Sussex TN5 7DQ   **Tel:** (01580) 200112 **Fax:** (01580) 201249
Web: www.dalehill.co.uk **E-mail:** info@dalehill.co.uk

The newly refurbished 4 Star Dale Hill Hotel is situated in an area of outstanding natural beauty, high on the Kentish Weald. All of our newly refurbished 35 en-suite bedrooms offer comfort and luxury, many have magnificent views overlooking our two 18-hole golf courses, one of which was designed to USGA specification by former US Masters Champion Ian Woosnam. Our award-winning Fairway restaurant and leisure facilities, which include an indoor swimming pool, sauna and gymnasium, complements the hotel.

Bed & Breakfast per night: single room from £90.00–£110.00; double room from £150.00–£210.00
Lunch available: 1100–1500
Evening meal: 1830 (last orders 2130)

Bedrooms: 6 single, 11 double, 11 twin, 4 family, 2 suites
Bathrooms: 35 en-suite
Parking: 220 spaces
Cards accepted: Mastercard, Visa, Switch/Delta, Amex, JCB

300 Eckington House

Ripe Lane, Ripe, Lewes, East Sussex BN8 6AR **Tel:** (01323) 811274 or 07720 601347
Web: www.eckingtonhouse.co.uk **E-mail:** sue@eckingtonhouse.co.uk

Beautiful 16th-century house with peaceful, mature garden in a rural village close to the South Downs and South coast. Facilities include oak-panelled guest sitting room with inglenook fireplace, croquet lawn and four-poster suite. Breakfast is served on the terrace during warm weather, with vegetarians catered for. Historic Lewes, famous Glyndebourne Opera House, and the coastal towns of Brighton and Eastbourne are nearby. London is one hour by rail from Lewes. Excellent for cycling, walking and sightseeing. Pub/restaurant within walking distance.

Bed & Breakfast per night: single room from £35.00–£40.00; double room from £50.00–£70.00

Bedrooms: 1 single, 3 double, 2 twin, 1 family, 1 suite
Bathrooms: 3 en-suite, 1 shared
Parking: 4 spaces

Rudyard Kipling and Bateman's

As soon as Rudyard Kipling set eyes upon Bateman's he knew he wanted it as his home: 'That's her! The only she!' he exclaimed, 'Make an honest woman of her – quick!' He then explored every room, finding 'no shadow of ancient regrets, stifled miseries, nor any menace'.

The beautiful manor house near Burwash in Sussex indeed has an atmosphere of venerable serenity. Built from warm local sandstone, its rooms all dark panelling and polished old wood, it is a perfect example of the English Jacobean manor house, almost unaltered since its completion in 1634. Of its early history little is known save that it may have been built by a prosperous Wealden ironmaster (17th-century Burwash was at the heart of a thriving iron industry). A large, rambling place with an oddly asymmetrical frontage, it is surrounded by large trees and the beautiful gardens the Kiplings created there.

Kipling was a successful author when he came to Bateman's. Literary acclaim had come early and by his late twenties he was already well known in London's intellectual circles. In 1892 he married Caroline Balestier and spent the next four years at her family's estates in America, where he wrote his famous *Jungle Book*. Kipling then returned to England and settled at Rottingdean, a village not far from Burwash, where a beautiful public garden has been created in his memory, adjacent to his former home, The Elms. The years there, however, were clouded by the death of his six-year-old daughter from pneumonia, and after only a year or so

the hunt began for a new house. After years of searching, Bateman's became his next, and final, home.

The Bateman's years were productive: here he wrote, amongst other works, *Traffics and Discoveries, Puck of Pooks Hill, Rewards and Fairies,* and the poems *If* and *The Glory of the Garden.* After his death in 1936, Caroline Kipling lived on at Bateman's for a further three years, finally bequeathing the house to the National Trust as a memorial to her husband. Many of the furnishings now on display belonged to the Kiplings, and particularly evocative is the author's study, barely touched since the day of his death. The table where he wrote, in front of the window, still bears his writing implements and paraphernalia, and the view is of a little grassy knoll, immortalised in his writings as Pooks Hill.

301 The Grand Hotel

★★★★★ Gold Award

King Edwards Parade, Eastbourne, East Sussex BN21 4EQ **Tel:** (01323) 412345 **Fax:** (01323) 412233
Web: www.grandeastbourne.com **E-mail:** sales@grandeastbourne.com

Benefiting from a complete restoration and spectacular improvement, the Grand takes pride of place as one of England's premier resort hotels. The atmosphere is restfully opulent but certainly not stuffy, with a wonderful location overlooking the sea in the elegant coastal town of Eastbourne. Boasting fine bedrooms and suites, two award-winning restaurants and comprehensive health and beauty facilities, including two pools, the Grand offers genuine service to match its elegant surroundings.

Bed & Breakfast per night: single occupancy from £135.00–£400.00; double room from £165.00–£430.00
Dinner, Bed & Breakfast per person, per night: £112.50–£230.00 (min 2 nights, 2 sharing)
Lunch available: 1230–1400

Evening meal: 1900 (last orders 2200)
Bedrooms: 68 double, 60 twin, 24 suites
Bathrooms: 152 en-suite
Parking: 60 spaces
Cards accepted: Mastercard, Visa, Switch/ Delta, Amex, Diners, Eurocard, JCB

302 Brayscroft Hotel

◆◆◆◆ Silver Award

13 South Cliff Avenue, Eastbourne, East Sussex BN20 7AH **Tel:** (01323) 647005
Web: www.brayscrofthotel.co.uk **E-mail:** brayscroft@hotmail.com

Brayscroft is an elegant, small award-winning hotel in an attractive, tree-lined avenue of red brick Edwardian houses. It is one minute from the seafront and a few minutes' walk from the bandstand, western lawns, theatres and Devonshire Park in the fashionable Meads district. Thoughtfully equipped guest rooms have stylish en-suite facilities, colour televisions and well-stocked hospitality trays. The hotel enjoys an excellent reputation for the quality of its food. For the comfort of guests, smoking is not allowed in guest or public rooms.

Bed & Breakfast per night: single room from £30.00–£32.00; double room from £60.00–£64.00
Dinner, Bed & Breakfast per person, per night: £43.00–£45.00
Evening meal: 1800

Bedrooms: 1 single, 2 double, 2 twin
Bathrooms: 5 en-suite
Parking: unrestricted road parking
Cards accepted: Mastercard, Visa, Switch/ Delta, Amex, Eurocard, JCB, Maestro, Solo

303 Pinnacle Point

◆◆◆◆◆ Gold Award

Foyle Way, Eastbourne, East Sussex BN20 7XL **Tel:** (01323) 726666 or 0796 7209958 **Fax:** (01323) 643946
Web: www.pinnaclepoint.co.uk **E-mail:** info@pinnaclepoint.co.uk

The house with the WOW factor! Pinnacle Point is reminiscent of a Mediterranean villa, with unrivalled views overlooking the English Channel. It has recently been featured in 'Real Homes' magazine and on the BBC 1 'South Today' programme. Peter and Elspeth Pyemont aim to give their guests a special and memorable time with award-winning breakfasts. "One feels like an honoured guest rather than a paying visitor." A tree house has recently been added for the use of guests.

Bed & Breakfast per night: single occupancy from £80.00; double room from £120.00

Bedrooms: 2 double, 1 twin
Bathrooms: 3 en-suite
Parking: 6 spaces

304 Little Silver Country Hotel

★★★ Silver Award

Ashford Road, St Michaels, Tenterden, Kent TN30 6SP **Tel:** (01233) 850321 **Fax:** (01233) 850647
Web: www.little-silver.co.uk **E-mail:** enquiries@little-silver.co.uk

Little Silver Country Hotel is set in its own landscaped gardens. The restaurant provides an intimate, tranquil atmosphere where local produce is enjoyed, pre-dinner drinks and after dinner coffee are offered in the beamed sitting room with its log fire. Breakfast is served in a Victorian conservatory overlooking the waterfall rockery. Luxury bedrooms, tastefully and individually designed, some with four-posters and jacuzzi baths, others with brass beds. Facilities for disabled. Personal attention, care for detail, warmth and friendliness create a truly memorable experience. Accessible Mobility 1

Bed & Breakfast per night: single room from £60.00–£85.00; double room from £90.00–£150.00
Dinner, Bed & Breakfast per person, per night: £62.00–£80.00
Lunch available: 1200–1400

Evening meal: 1900 (last orders 2100)
Bedrooms: 10 double/twin, 1 family
Bathrooms: 11 en-suite
Parking: 50 spaces
Cards accepted: Mastercard, Visa, Switch/Delta, Amex

305 Flackley Ash Hotel & Restaurant

★★★ Silver Award

London Road, Peasmarsh, Rye, East Sussex TN31 6YH **Tel:** (01797) 230651 **Fax:** (01797) 230510
Web: www.flackleyashhotel.co.uk **E-mail:** enquiries@flackleyashhotel.co.uk

A Georgian country house hotel, set in beautiful gardens with croquet and putting lawns. Indoor swimming pool and leisure centre with gym, saunas, whirlpool spa and steam room. Beauty salon offering aromatherapy massage. Warm, friendly atmosphere, fine wines and good food. Well situated for visiting the castles and gardens of East Sussex and Kent and the ancient Cinque port of Rye. Golf, bird-watching, country or seaside walks, potteries and steam trains are some of the attractions in the area.

Bed & Breakfast per night: single occupancy from £89.00–£99.00; double room from £132.00–£162.00
Dinner, Bed & Breakfast per person, per night: £69.00–£84.00 (min 2 nights)
Lunch available: 1230–1345

Evening meal: 1900 (last orders 2130)
Bedrooms: 27 double, 13 twin, 1 family, 4 suites **Bathrooms:** 45 en-suite
Parking: 70 spaces
Cards accepted: Mastercard, Visa, Switch/Delta, Amex, Diners, Eurocard, JCB

306 Rye Lodge Hotel

★★★ Silver Award

Hilders Cliff, Rye, East Sussex TN31 7LD **Tel:** (01797) 223838 or (01797) 226688 **Fax:** (01797) 223585
Web: www.ryelodge.co.uk **E-mail:** info@ryelodge.co.uk

Premier position on East Cliff, close to the historic 14th-century Landgate, High Street teashops, antique and art galleries, in this charming medieval Cinque Port with its cobbled streets and picturesque period buildings. Rye Lodge offers elegance and charm in a relaxed atmosphere. The luxurious de luxe bedrooms are all en-suite. Room service – breakfast in bed as late as you like! Candlelit dinners in the elegant marble-floored Terrace Room, delicious food and fine wines, attentive caring service, and an indoor swimming pool, sauna and aromatherapy steam cabinet! Private car park.

Bed & Breakfast per night: single occupancy from £65.00–£105.00; double room from £95.00–£180.00
Dinner, Bed & Breakfast per person, per night: £65.00–£100.00 (min 2 nights)
Evening meal: 1900 (last orders 2100)

Bedrooms: 12 double, 6 twin, 6 family
Bathrooms: 18 en-suite
Parking: 25 spaces
Cards accepted: Mastercard, Visa, Switch/Delta, Amex, Diners, Eurocard, JCB

307 Little Orchard House

◆◆◆◆◆ Silver Award

West Street, Rye, East Sussex TN31 7ES **Tel:** (01797) 223831 **Fax:** (01797) 223831
Web: www.littleorchardhouse.com

Elegant Georgian townhouse in a quiet cobbled street at the heart of ancient Rye. Perfectly situated for many excellent restaurants, shops, art/antique galleries as well as country/seaside walks, birdwatching or touring nearby National Trust properties like Sissinghurst. Antique furniture throughout, open fires, fine art, books and bears create a relaxed house-party atmosphere. Large, secluded walled garden for guests' use. Generous country breakfasts feature local organic and free range products. Parking available.

Bed & Breakfast per night: double room from £70.00–£100.00

Bedrooms: 2 double
Bathrooms: 2 en-suite
Cards accepted: Mastercard, Visa, Switch/ Delta, Eurocard, JCB

Flemings and Huguenots

The distinctive Flemish flavour of the streets of Sandwich, one of Southern England's most pleasant small towns, is difficult to miss. The clearest sign is the prevalence of Dutch gables – there are some on the corner of the church of St Peter (now the Tourist Information Centre during summer months) and others on Manwood Court, built in 1564 as a grammar school. Another indication is part of the local vocabulary; 'polder' – taken straight from the Dutch – is the word used by the townsfolk to describe the low-lying marshes between Sandwich and Canterbury.

In fact, the Flemings (as the immigrants from the Low Countries were known) were first invited by Edward III in the 14th century, since they were especially skilled in the art of weaving. The economy of this part of Kent had for some time been dependent upon trade through the port of Sandwich and upon cloth-making. The silting up of the harbour over many years (Sandwich is now some two miles from the sea) and the inefficiency of the old cloth-manufacturing techniques meant that the new arrivals were particularly welcome. Business boomed, and Sandwich's density of substantial timbered houses (Strand Street boasts some of the finest) bears witness to the fact that the town prospered greatly. The immigrants also brought other trades to this fertile corner of the land, such as hop-growing for the production of beer, and commercial market gardening; trades which have since become synonymous with Kent.

By the 16th century, many were fleeing the Low Countries to escape persecution for their Calvinist beliefs. Some French Protestants, too, had left their native land, but the Edict of Nantes in 1598 afforded them a measure of religious freedom. When in 1685 this was revoked, nearly half a million Protestants abandoned their homeland, many to cross the Channel to the South Coast. These new exiles, known as Huguenots, tended to stay on the eastern side of England, a significant number never leaving Kent. Echoing the achievements of their earlier Flemish counterparts, the Huguenots established in England the silk-weaving industry. At the peak of the trade, as many as 2,000 people were employed in the silk business in Canterbury alone. Indeed the contribution of the Huguenot community to the city was such that they were granted their own chapel within the cathedral.

308 Coxell House   ◆◆◆◆

9 Manor Road, Lydd, Romney Marsh, Kent TN29 9HR **Tel:** (01797) 322037 or 07762 627664
Web: www.coxellhouse.co.uk **E-mail:** coxellhouse@btopenworld.com

Located in a quiet corner of Lydd on Romney Marsh, Coxell House is a delightful 17th-century Grade II listed building recently tastefully renovated and converted to guest accommodation. Maggie and Robin assure you of a warm welcome and will suggest places of interest to visit for guests new to the area. Just 25 minutes from Ashford International station, 40 minutes from EuroTunnel and under an hour from the Dover ferries, we are ideally positioned for access to Europe or for sightseeing in Kent and East Sussex. Please phone for special three day break rates between 10th October - 21st December and 2nd January - 31st March.

Bed & Breakfast per night: single occupancy £36.00; double room £52.00

Bedrooms: 1 double, 1 twin
Bathrooms: 2 en-suite
Parking: 2 spaces

---

309 Victoria Villa   ◆◆◆◆ Gold Award

1 Victoria Street, Whitstable, Kent CT5 1JB **Tel:** (01227) 779191 **or (07950) 072680**
Web: www.victoria-villa.i12dotcom **E-mail:** victoria-villa@i12.com

Unrivalled Four Diamond accommodation with a coveted Gold Award. Victoria Villa is pleasantly situated in the heart of the conservation area just a stone's throw from the old town's maritime waterfront, harbour and beach. The tastefully furnished period villa comprises of just two guest rooms with large private or en-suite toilet and shower rooms. A newspaper of your choice will be delivered to your room before breakfast. Breakfast is served in the courtyard garden or the elegant dining room. Ideal for a romantic break, or a short escape from the children.

Bed & Breakfast per night: double room from £85.00–£110.00

Bedrooms: 1 double, 1 twin
Bathrooms: 1 en-suite, 1 private

---

310 Twin Mays   ◆◆◆◆ Gold Award

Plumpudding Lane, Dargate, Faversham, Kent ME13 9EX **Tel:** (01227) 751346
Web: www.twinmays.co.uk **E-mail:** jh@twinmays.co.uk

Sunday Times Top Ten bed and breakfasts. Ideal for Canterbury, Faversham and Whitstable. Thirty minutes from Dover, Ramsgate and the Channel Tunnel. In the countryside surrounded by apple orchards, built from a reclaimed French barn with huge oak beams and lovely views, virtually self-contained. Breakfasts include local fresh fruit, award-winning sausages, fish from Whitstable, homemade bread and preserves, served in the garden whenever possible. Excellent local gastropub close to Kent Archaeological Centre. Reduced rates for stays of more than one night.

Bed & Breakfast per night: single occupancy £50.00; double room £80.00
Dinner, Bed & Breakfast per person, per night: £54.00–£60.00

Bedrooms: 1 single/double/twin
Bathrooms: 1 en-suite
Parking: 4 spaces

311 Ilex Cottage

Temple Way, Worth, Deal, Kent CT14 0DA **Tel:** (01304) 617026
Web: www.ilexcottage.com **E-mail:** info@ilexcottage.com

This carefully modernised home dating from 1736 retains many character features. Our well-appointed, spacious en-suite guest rooms have co-ordinated furnishings and rural views. The Georgian conservatory provides a delightful reception area for relaxing and enjoying refreshments. Non-smoking throughout. Children and pets welcomed. Secluded, peaceful location, yet conveniently near picturesque conservation village centre. Sandwich and Deal are five minutes away, and Canterbury, Dover and Ramsgate are 20 minutes away. Numerous local tourist attractions and leisure facilities. An idyllic holiday base.

Bed & Breakfast per night: single occupancy from £35.00–£40.00; double room from £55.00–£60.00

Bedrooms: 1 double, 1 twin, 1 family
Bathrooms: 3 en-suite
Parking: 6 spaces
Cards accepted: Mastercard, Visa, Switch/Delta

Dickens' Kent

For eight days in late June, Broadstairs, on Kent's eastern coast, is thronged with characters in Victorian dress, parading the streets and participating in period cricket matches, bathing parties and other amusements. They are here for the Dickens festival, a literary event first staged in 1937 to mark the centenary of Dickens' first visit, and held annually ever since.

When Dickens came to Broadstairs he was 25 years old and on the point of achieving nationwide fame with the publication of *The Pickwick Papers*. He had spent part of his childhood in the Kent town of Chatham and had become well-acquainted with the county from accompanying his father on long country walks. For 14 years he frequently spent summer and autumn months in Broadstairs, eventually leasing Fort House, a fine residence overlooking Viking Bay. Now called Bleak House and open to the public as a museum, it is thought to have inspired its namesake in Dickens' famous novel, for it stands, tall and solitary, on the cliffs far above Broadstairs. Visitors may see rooms inhabited by the author, including the study where he completed *David Copperfield* and planned *Bleak House*. Also in Broadstairs is the Dickens House Museum once the home of Miss Mary Strong, an eccentric woman who was probably the inspiration for one of Dickens's most colourful creations, Miss Betsey Trotwood, David Copperfield's aunt.

In 1856, Dickens purchased Gad's Hill Place, near Rochester, which he had admired as a boy, and

always dreamed of owning. This substantial house, now a private school, is occasionally open to the public (details from Rochester's Tourist Information Centre, tel: 01634 843666). The town also provided inspiration for many places in Dickens' works. Eastgate House was both Nun's House School in *The Mystery of Edwin Drood* and Westgate House in *The Pickwick Papers*. Now the Rochester Dickens Centre, it recreates scenes and characters from the author's best-known works. In its gardens an elaborately carved Swiss chalet was a gift to Dickens from an actor friend who sent it to Higham station in 58 packing cases. It once stood in the shrubbery at Gad's Hill and in it Dickens wrote his last words before his death in 1870. Further Dickensian associations may be followed up using The Dickens Trail, available from local tourist information centres.

312 Lenox House ◆◆◆◆

Granville Road, St Margarets Bay, Dover, Kent CT15 6DS

Lenox House is a large unusual house of character in the heart of St. Margaret's Bay set on the hillside above the famous White Cliffs of Dover. The attractive bedrooms are spacious and well equipped and have stunning sea views across the bay, channel headland and cliffs. Ideally situated for cross channel ferries, being only three miles from Dover. Relax in the large drawing room or there are superb walks over National Trust land on the doorstep. A sloping garden path makes this home unsuitable for the disabled. One double with private facilities. One en-suite family suite.

Bed & Breakfast per night: single room from £30.00–£35.00; double room from £60.00–£65.00

Bedrooms: 1 double, 1 family suite
Bathrooms: 1 en-suite, 1 private

313 The Park Inn ◆◆◆◆ Silver Award

1-2 Park Place, Ladywell, Dover, Kent CT16 1DQ **Tel:** (01304) 203300 **Fax:** (01304) 203324
Web: www.theparkinnatdover.co.uk **E-mail:** theparkinn@aol.com

An extremely high standard of Victorian style decoration, furnishings and facilities prevails in our five en-suite rooms which complement our successful inn and restaurant. All rooms are cosy and comfortable and include satellite television and direct dial telephone with fax/modem points. Doubles, twins and superb four-poster rooms are available. All rooms are strictly non-smoking. The Park Inn offers an extensive à la carte and snack menu with a wide choice of ales and wines.

Bed & Breakfast per night: single room from £35.00–£45.00; double room from £54.00–£74.00
Evening meal: 1130 (last orders 2200)

Bedrooms: 1 single, 1 double, 2 twin, 1 family
Parking: secure parking by arrangement
Cards accepted: Mastercard, Visa, Switch/Delta, Amex, Diners, Eurocard, JCB, Electron, Solo

314 Loddington House Hotel ◆◆◆◆

14 East Cliff, (Seafront - Marine Parade), Dover, Kent CT16 1LX **Tel:** (01304) 201947 **Fax:** (01304) 201947
E-mail: sscupper@aol.com

Loddington House is a Regency Grade II listed building on the seafront, with panoramic views over the harbour and English Channel. The famous Dover Castle and White Cliffs form a spectacular backdrop to the property. Canterbury, Sandwich and Deal are all a short distance away, making it an excellent holiday choice for exploring Kent, or for a trip to France. Freshly prepared quality food, table d'hôte or à la carte, with a good selection of wines, by arrangement.

Bed & Breakfast per night: single room from £45.00–£50.00; double room from £54.00–£70.00
Evening meal: 1900 (last orders 2000)

Bedrooms: 1 single, 3 double, 2 twin, 1 family
Bathrooms: 4 en-suite, 2 private
Parking: 3 spaces
Cards accepted: Mastercard, Visa, Switch/Delta, Amex, Eurocard, JCB, Solo, Maestro

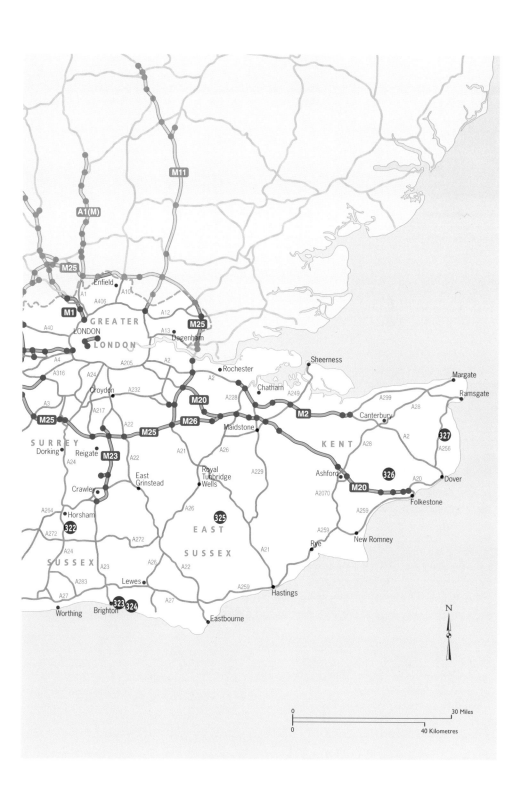

315 Heath Farm Holiday Cottages

★ ★ ★ ★ – ★ ★ ★ ★ ★

Heath Farm, Swerford, Chipping Norton, Oxfordshire **Web:** www.heathfarm.com

Contact: Mr & Mrs D Barbour, Heath Farm, Swerford, Chipping Norton, Oxfordshire OX7 4BN

Tel: (01608) 683270 or (01608) 683204 **Fax:** (01608) 683222 **E-mail:** barbours@heathfarm.com

Award-winning stone cottages set in 70 acres of woodland and flower meadows. Glorious views over unspoilt Cotswold countryside. Extensive use of local hardwoods in hand-crafted furniture and fittings. Stunning paved courtyard with water garden. Oxford, Stratford and all Cotwold attractions within easy reach. Exclusive, unusual, luxurious. Spoil yourself.

Low season per week: £255.00–£446.00
High season per week: £350.00–£586.00
Short breaks: from £180.00–£386.00

5 cottages: sleeping 2–4 people
Cards accepted: Mastercard, Visa, Switch/Delta

The Landmarks of White Horse Hill

The Lambourn Downs of South Oxfordshire, rising up bare and smooth from the Vale of the White Horse, are steeped in ancient history. Around 5,000 years ago our ancestors settled here, built their forts, buried their dead and walked their pathways; today the Downs are liberally sprinkled with the relics of their existence. Some sites have been excavated, but alongside the scant archaeological evidence, a vein of myth and legend has come down over the centuries to provide explanations for the mysterious landmarks.

Dominating the valley which is named after it, the strange elongated shape of a galloping horse is cut into the chalk near Uffington. The Iron Age tribes who lived in the nearby hillfort are believed to have carved it in about 50BC as a representation of the horse goddess, Epona. Possibly the oldest chalk carving in the country, it is, intriguingly, the only one which faces right. In more recent centuries the white horse became the focus of a seven-yearly tradition: people would climb the hill to 'scour' the accumulated weeds and debris from the horse to the accompaniment of fairground revels.

Just below the horse is a mound known as Dragon's Hill. Whether natural or man-made is unknown, but local legend asserts that this is where St George killed the dragon. The patches of bare chalk on its top and sides, the story goes, were formed by hot streams of dragon's blood, over which the grass can never grow.

Running along the ridge of the Downs, just south of the White Horse, is the Ridgeway. This track – used by people of the New Stone Age, the builders of Stonehenge – is one of the oldest roads in Britain. It leads south west past Wayland's Smithy, a neolithic burial chamber dating from around 2800BC. This remote spot is one of many places throughout Europe (usually either caves or burial mounds) imagined as the home of Wayland, the fearsome Saxon blacksmith-god.

The figure of the smith is also associated, somewhat menacingly, with another curiosity: a strangely-shaped stone beside the road leading south from Kingston Lisle, just east of the White Horse. The 'Blowing Stone', as it is called, was supposedly brought here by a blacksmith living in the nearby cottage who could blow into its many holes to create a gruesome, moaning roar. Another legend grew up that King Alfred summoned his troops to battle by blowing through the stone.

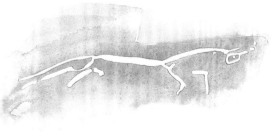

316 Beech House ★ ★ ★ ★ ★

Chalford Park, Old Chalford, Chipping Norton, Oxfordshire
Contact: Mrs D S Canty, Oak House, Chalford Park, Old Chalford, Chipping Norton, Oxfordshire OX7 5QR
Tel: (01608) 641435 **Fax:** (01608) 641345 **E-mail:** stuart.canty5@virgin.net

Magnificent 19th-century stone farmhouse with beautifully renovated interior, including marble floors and period fireplaces. Three fine reception rooms and large, modern, fully equipped kitchen-dining room with utility. Lovely enclosed private garden. Parking for nine cars. Situated in an Area of Outstanding Natural Beauty with wonderful country walks on bridleway directly from the property. Chipping Norton has a good range of shops, restaurant and pubs, a new leisure centre and the charming theatre. Blenheim Palace, Woodstock, Oxford, Stratford-upon-Avon, Warwick and Cheltenham within easy reach. Only 90 minutes from London by rail or car.

Low season per week: £1800.00–£2000.00
High season per week: £2000.00–£2600.00
Short breaks: from £1300.00–£2000.00

1 house: sleeping 20 people

317 Views Farm Barns ★ ★ ★ ★

Views Farm, Great Milton, Oxford   **Web:** www.viewsfarmbarns.co.uk
Contact: Mr & Mrs Peers, Views Farm, Great Milton, Oxford, Oxfordshire OX44 7NW
Tel: (01844) 279352 **Fax:** (01844) 279362 **E-mail:** info@viewsfarmbarns.co.uk

A stone farm building sensitively converted to six self-catering apartments which offer the holidaymaker luxury, comfort and easy access to places of interest and the motorway network. Situated between the Cotswolds and the Chilterns, seven miles from Oxford, 2–3 miles from junctions 7 and 8 of the M40 motorway. London and the centre of England are within easy reach, as is the Thames Valley and riverside attractions of towns such as Henley and Marlow. These luxury apartments have all the comforts of modern-day living and fully-equipped kitchens, added to the old world ambiance of stone walls and exposed beams.

Low season per week: £220.00–£265.00
High season per week: £370.00–£440.00

6 apartments: sleeping 2–5 people
Cards accepted: Mastercard, Visa, Switch/Delta, JCB

318 Purbeck Cliffs ★ ★ ★ ★

Swanage, Dorset   **Web:** www.purbeckcliffs.co.uk
Contact: Mrs McWilliams, Purbeck Cliffs, 3 Boundary Close, Swanage, Dorset BH19 2JY
Tel: (01929) 424352

A spacious ground floor apartment set in a two-acre, quiet, secluded garden next to the famous Heritage Coast and 300-acre Durlston Country Park. The accommodation is for a maximum of six people with exclusive use of a 40-foot indoor heated swimming pool with slide and diving board, sauna, snooker room, tennis court. Purbeck Cliffs is one mile from Swanage town/beach with its many local shops and restaurants. For more photographs and details visit our website: www.purbeckcliffs.co.uk or telephone: 01929 424352.

Low season per week: £495.00–£750.00
High season per week: £795.00–£975.00
Short breaks: from £250.00–£300.00

1 apartment: sleeping 6 people

319 Burgate Manor Farm Holidays ★ ★ ★ ★

Burgate Manor Farm, Fordingbridge, Hampshire **Web:** www.newforestcottages.com
Contact: Burgate Manor Farm Holidays, Burgate Manor Farm, Fordingbridge, Hampshire SP6 1LX
Tel: (01425) 653908 **Fax:** (01425) 653908 **E-mail:** holidays@newforestcottages.com

New Forest/Avon Valley. Fully equipped, single storey cottages and large, newly converted galleried, beamed granary with grand hall, log burner and facilities for disabled people. Situated alongside the Avon, with a pub/restaurant a short walk away. Cross the bridge by the farmyard and walk through unspoilt water meadows, rich in wildlife, into the New Forest. Picnic, bird watch or ramble on the owner's private land which is criss-crossed by streams and woodland. Large games barn with soft/table tennis, pool table, table football, darts and Wendy House. Beach 30 minutes. Fishing, stables, grazing.

6 single-storey cottages (sleeping 2–8)	1 converted granary (sleeping 12–16/18)	
Low season per week: £246.00–£468.00	**Low season per week:** £1092.00–£1404.00	
High season per week: £358.00–£798.00	**High season per week:** £1508.00–£2704.00	
Short breaks: from £148.00–£338.00	**Short breaks:** from £1040.00–£1768.00	

320 Gorse Cottage ★ ★ ★ ★

Balmer Lawn Road, Brockenhurst, Hampshire **Web:** www.gorsecottage.co.uk
Contact: Mr J Gilbert, Suite E, Chiltern House, 180 High Street North, Dunstable, Bedfordshire LU6 1AT
Tel: (08703) 210020 **Fax:** (08702) 330151 **E-mail:** info@gorsecottage.co.uk

Beautifully appointed cottage/bungalow, set in secluded garden opposite open forest, close to the village of Brockenhurst in the New Forest. Spacious yet cosy accommodation, lounge, dining hall with wood-burning stove and attractive conservatory. Small luxurious bathroom with whirlpool bath. Two well designed bedrooms, well equipped kitchen with microwave, Miele washer/dryer, dishwasher etc. Baxi clean air system. Ideal location for lovers of the countryside. Many fine amenities and attractions close by.

Low season per week: max £410.00	1 cottage: sleeping 4 people	
High season per week: max £780.00		

321 Mares Tails Cottage ★ ★ ★ ★

Beaulieu, Brockenhurst, Hampshire
Contact: Mrs A Barber, Mares Tails, Furzey Lane, Beaulieu, Brockenhurst, Hampshire SO42 7WB
Tel: (01590) 612160 **E-mail:** marestails@ukonline.co.uk

Well appointed modern cottage with own secluded garden in the grounds of architect's house. One mile from the lovely village of Beaulieu with direct access to the open forest and backing onto farmland. The cottage is fully carpeted and comprises of lounge, bedroom with en-suite bathroom and unusual sit-in bath with hand-held shower, galley kitchen, 30ft conservatory. Gas central heating or curl up beside a lovely log fire. Ideal for walking, birdwatching. Two miles from the Solent shore. Peace and quiet.

Low season per week: £320.00–£330.00	1 cottage: sleeping 2 people	
High season per week: £330.00–£360.00	**Open:** May–October	

322 Walnut Barn & Walnut Cottage ★ ★ ★ ★ – ★ ★ ★ ★ ★

Kerves Lane, Horsham, West Sussex **Web:** www.sussexholidaycottages.com
Contact: Mrs Cole, Hard's Farm Cottage, Kerves Lane, Horsham, West Sussex RH13 6RJ
Tel: (01403) 249159 **E-mail:** jpcole@lineone.net

Magnificent timber-framed barn and farm buildings set in unspoilt Sussex countryside, in the grounds of the owners' home. Guests have access to the owners' extensive grounds and heated outdoor swimming pool. The accommodation is very flexible so parties of 1 to 11 are welcome. Children and pets are welcome. Cot and high chair can be provided on request.

Low season per week: £280.00–£1080.00
High season per week: £525.00–£2080.00
Short breaks: from £196.00–£756.00 (low season only)

1 house: sleeping 8 people
1 cottage: sleeping 3 people

Isle of Wight Geology

No part of the Isle of Wight's complex geology is unaffected by the action of the waves. The sea has periodically inundated the land and then retreated, laying down sediments and battering away at them, carving out dramatic cliffs and steep-sided valleys and creating some of the most spectacular coastal scenery in southern England.

The island is bisected by a high chalk ridge running east–west and rising to a height of some 650ft (198m). At its western end this chalk band forms a narrow headland pointing out to sea, shaped by the waves into the spectacular snow-white cliffs of Freshwater Bay and, at its furthest extremity, eroded into a series of jagged, white teeth poking from the sea: the famous Needles (shown below).

The character of the landscape north and south of the band of chalk differs markedly. The soils of the northern half of the island were laid down about 60 million years ago, in sedimentary layers of sand (crushed quartz) and clay. At Alum Bay, just north of the Needles, some of these layers have been exposed by the sea to create an extraordinary phenomenon. Mineral impurities have changed the colour of the usually white quartz, creating an amazing variety of coloured sands: white, black, green, red and yellow.

On the southern side of the island, ancient earth movements have exposed sedimentary layers laid down between 120 and 65 million years ago. Of these, the Wealden group, Wight's oldest rocks, meet the sea in just two places, one north of Sandown, the other along the south-west coast. They were deposited when dinosaurs roamed the area and now yield some of the richest sources of dinosaur bones in Europe. On the beach at Hanover Point is Pine Raft, the fossilised remains of tree-trunks, some beautifully preserved, with annular growth rings still visible.

The southernmost region of the island is a complex arrangement of soft gault clay sandwiched between harder layers of sandstone. The gault, known as 'blue slipper', creates a highly unstable lubricant layer, causing the hard strata above to collapse periodically in giant landslips. Between Shanklin and Chale, each of the distinctive terraces falling down to the sea represents a different landslip. Known as the Undercliff, this picturesque terrain is the largest area of coastal landslip in north-western Europe.

The Museum of Isle of Wight Geology at Sandown records the island's geological history and displays some spectacular fossil remains.

323 Brighton Marina Holiday Apartments ★★★★

Mariners Quay, Brighton Marina Village, Brighton, East Sussex **Web:** www.brightonmarinaholidayapartments.co.uk
Contact: Mrs A M Wills, 5 Mariners Quay, Brighton Marina Village, Brighton, East Sussex BN2 5UZ
Tel: (0208) 940 6945 **Fax:** (0208) 940 8907 **E-mail:** info@brightonholidaymarinaholidayapartments.co.uk

Luxury 2-bedroom apartments overlooking the inner harbour, with private balconies or terrace. Each individually furnished apartment has a separate living room, modern kitchen, bathroom, en-suite shower room and private parking. Situated a mile east of Brighton, the Marina boasts an extensive range of leisure, shoping and dining facilities.

Low season per week: £350.00–£450.00
High season per week: £450.00–£600.00
Short breaks: from £250.00–£300.00 (winter months only)

3 apartments: sleeping 4 people

324 Kilcolgan Bungalow ★★★★★

Rottingdean Village, Brighton, East Sussex
Contact: Mr J St George, 22 Baches Street, London N1 6DL
Tel: (0207) 250 3678 **Fax:** (0207) 250 1955 **E-mail:** jc.stgeorge@virgin.net

Welcome to excellence in self-catering accommodation. An exceptional Five Star quality detached 3-bedroomed bungalow which sleeps 2–5 people. Comprehensively equipped with an emphasis on comfort and with secluded, landscaped gardens overlooking farmland. Garage and parking for two vehicles. Rottingdean, which is only four kilometres from Brighton City, is a delightful seaside village with seafront promenade. The village has retained much of its 'olde worlde' charm, offering quaint tea houses, traditional inns and cottages. An ideal retreat for discerning people who dislike large tourist resorts.

Low season per week: £530.00–£650.00
High season per week: £700.00–£800.00
Short breaks: from £420.00–£450.00 (low season only)

2 bungalows: sleeping 2–5 people

325 Coopers Farm Cottage ★★★★★

Coopers Farm, Stonegate, Wadhurst, East Sussex **Web:** www.coopersfarmstonegate.co.uk
Contact: Jane Howard, Coopers Farm, Stonegate, East Sussex TN5 7EH
Tel: (01580) 200386 **E-mail:** jane@coopersfarmstonegate.co.uk

Off the beaten track, recently restored 18th-century Coopers Cottage combines the charm of an ancient listed building with the comforts of 21st-century Five Star accommodation. Inside there is an interesting mix of antique furniture, huge comfy sofas, log fires and oak beams while outside there is a very secluded southwest facing terrace garden with panoramic views across unspoilt countryside. Situated on a traditional family-run farm, Coopers is a truly peaceful retreat yet only an hour on the train from London. Horses welcome.

Low season per week: from £375.00
High season per week: max £650.00
Short breaks: from £200.00

1 cottage: sleeping 4 people

326 Lower Court Cottage ★★★★

Shuttlesfield Lane, Ottinge, Canterbury, Kent
Contact: Mr & Mrs Caunce, Lower Court, Shuttlesfield Lane, Ottinge, Canterbury, Kent CT4 6XJ
Tel: (01303) 862124 **Fax:** (01303) 864231 **E-mail:** caunce@ottinge.fsnet.co.uk

Recently refurbished, light and airy country cottage near the beautiful village of Elham. Easy access to Canterbury, Hythe and the Channel Tunnel. Peaceful courtyard setting off a delightful country lane. Two bathrooms, one en-suite, sitting and dining rooms, modern kitchen, garden, tennis court and secluded patio.

Low season per week: £265.00–£320.00
High season per week: £300.00–£520.00
Short breaks: from £225.00

1 cottage: sleeping 4 people

327 Updown Park Farm ★★★★

Nr Sandwich, Kent **Web:** www.montgomery-cottages.co.uk
Contact: Mrs J R Montgomery, Little Brooksend Farm, Birchington, Kent CT7 0JW
Tel: (01843) 841656 **Fax:** (01843) 841656 **E-mail:** info@montgomery-cottages.co.uk

Set in 30 acres of beautiful parkland, approached by a long private roadway, these two cottages, converted from the former dairy, retain original beams and features and yet have all modern facilities. Extremely peaceful and yet within easy reach of Canterbury, Dover (ferry ten minutes), Deal and Sandwich (three golf links in six miles) and Thanet's coastal towns and sandy beaches. Both have three bedrooms on the ground floor with bath/shower rooms, plus twin beds on upper floor. Suitable for disabled people.
Accessible Mobility 1   Accessible Mobility 2

Low season per week: £300.00–£375.00
High season per week: £375.00–£600.00
Short breaks: from £240.00–£265.00

2 cottages: sleeping 6–7 people

Welcome *to* Excellence

The network of Regional Tourist Boards run a range of training recognition awards which demonstrate a commitment to improving customer service within all types of accommodation and other tourism organisations.

Wherever you find the Welcome to Excellence logo, you can be assured of a commitment to:

- achieving excellence in customer service
- exceeding guest needs and expectations
- providing an environment where courtesy, helpfulness and a warm welcome are standard
- a focus on developing individual skills.

Those displaying the logo have at least 50% of staff trained to the required standard.

Where to Stay 2004

The official and best selling guides,
offering the reassurance of quality assured accommodation

Hotels, Townhouses and
Travel Accommodation
in England 2004
£10.99

Guesthouses, Bed &
Breakfast, Farmhouses, Inns
and Campus Accommodation
in England 2004
£11.99

Self-Catering
Holiday Homes
in England 2004
£10.99

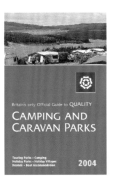

Camping & Caravan Parks, Hostels,
Holiday Villages and Boat
Accommodation in Britain 2004
£6.99

Somewhere Special
in England 2004
£8.99

Look out also for:
SOMEWHERE SPECIAL
IN ENGLAND 2004

Accommodation
achieving the highest
standards in facilities
and quality of service -

the perfect guide for the
discerning traveller.

**NOW ALSO FEATURING
SELF-CATERING
ACCOMMODATION**

The guides include

- **Accommodation entries packed with information • Full colour maps**
- **Places to visit • Tourist Information Centres**

INFORMATIVE • EASY TO USE • GREAT VALUE FOR MONEY

From all good bookshops or by mail order from the:
VisitBritain Fulfilment Centre, c/o Westex Ltd, 7 St Andrews Way, Devons Road, Bromley-by-Bow,
London E3 3PA Tel: 0870 606 7204 Fax: 020 8563 3279 Email: fulfilment@visitbritain.org

Useful Information

Booking checklist

When enquiring about accommodation make sure you check prices and other important details. You will also need to state your requirements clearly and precisely – for example:

- Your intended arrival and departure dates, with acceptable alternatives if appropriate.
- The type of accommodation you require.
- The number of people in your party and the ages of any children.
- Any particular requirements, such as a special diet or a ground-floor room.
- If you think you are likely to arrive late in the evening, mention this when you book. Similarly, if you are delayed on your journey a telephone call to inform the management may well help avoid any problems on your arrival.
- If you are asked for a deposit or the number of your credit card, find out what the proprietor's policy is if, for whatever reason, you can't turn up as planned – see 'cancellations' opposite.
- Exactly how the establishment's charges are levied – see opposite.

Misunderstandings can easily occur over the telephone, so it is advisable to confirm in writing all bookings, together with special requirements. Please mention that you learnt of the establishment through *Somewhere Special*. Remember to include your name and address, and please enclose a stamped, addressed envelope – or an international reply coupon if writing from outside Britain. Please note that VisitBritain does not make reservations; you should address your enquiry directly to the establishment.

Prices

The prices given throughout this publication will serve as a general guide, but you should always check them at the time of booking.

- Prices were supplied during the autumn of 2003 and changes may have occurred since publication.
- Prices include VAT where applicable.
- Prices are often much cheaper for off-peak holidays; check to see whether special off-season packages are available.

For hotels and guest accommodation the following information may also prove useful when determining how much a trip may cost:

- You should check whether or not a service charge is included in the published price.
- Prices for double rooms assume occupancy by two people; you will need to check whether there is a single person supplement if a single occupancy rate is not shown.
- A full English breakfast may not always be included in the quoted price; you may be given a continental breakfast unless you are prepared to pay more.
- Establishments with at least four bedrooms or eight beds are obliged to display overnight accommodation charges in the reception area or at the entrance.
- Reduced prices may apply for children; check exactly how these reductions are calculated, including the maximum age for the child.

Deposits and advance payments

When booking a hotel or guest accommodation, reservations made weeks or months ahead will usually require a deposit which will be deducted from the total bill at the end of your stay.

Some establishments, particularly the larger hotels in big towns, will require payment for the room upon arrival if a prior reservation has not been made. This is especially likely to happen if you arrive late and have little or no luggage. If you are asked to pay in advance, it is sensible to see your room before payment is made to ensure that it meets your requirements.

When booking self-catering accommodation, the proprietor will normally ask you to pay a deposit immediately and then to pay the full balance before your holiday date. This is to safeguard the proprietor in case you decide to cancel at a late stage, or simply do not turn up. He or she may have turned down other bookings on the strength of yours and may find it hard to re-let.

If you book by telephone and are asked for your credit card number, you should note that the proprietor may charge your credit card account even if you subsequently cancel the booking. Ask the owner what his or her usual practice is.

Credit/charge cards

Any credit/charge cards that are accepted by the establishment are indicated at the end of the written description. If you intend to pay by either credit or charge card you are advised to confirm this at the time of booking.

Please note that when paying by credit card, you may sometimes be charged a higher rate for your accommodation in order to cover the percentage paid by the proprietor to the credit card company. Again find this out in advance.

When making a booking, you may be asked for your credit card number as 'confirmation'. The proprietor may then charge your credit card account if you have to cancel the booking, but if this is the policy, it must be made clear to you at the time of booking – see opposite.

Cancellations

When you accept offered accommodation, including over the telephone, you are entering into a legally binding contract with the proprietor. This means that if you cancel a reservation or fail to take up all or part of the accommodation booked, the proprietor may be entitled to compensation if the accommodation cannot be re-let for all or a good part of the booked period. If you have paid a deposit, you will probably forfeit this, and further payment may well be asked for. You should be advised at the time of booking of what charges would be made in the event of cancelling the accommodation or leaving early. If this does not happen, you should ask, to avoid any future disputes.

No claim can be made by the proprietor until after the booked period, during which time every effort should be made to re-let the accommodation. It is therefore in your interests to advise the management immediately in writing if you have to cancel or curtail a booking. Travel or holiday insurance, available quite cheaply from travel agents and some hotels, will safeguard you if you have to cancel or curtail your stay.

And remember, if you book by telephone and are asked for your credit card number, you should check whether the proprietor intends charging your account should you later cancel your reservation. A proprietor should not be able to charge for a cancellation unless he or she has made this clear at the time of your booking and you have agreed. However, to avoid later disputes, we suggest you check whether he or she intends to make such a charge.

Hotels and guest accommodation

Service charges and tipping

Some establishments levy a service charge automatically, and, if so, must state this clearly in the offer of accommodation at the time of booking. If the offer is accepted by you, the service charge becomes part of the contract. If service is included in your bill, there is no need for you to give tips to the staff unless some particular or exceptional service has been rendered. In the case of meals, the usual tip is 10% of the total bill.

Telephone call charges

There is no restriction on the charges that can be made by hotels for telephone calls made from their premises. Unit charges are frequently considerably higher than telephone companies' standard charges in order to defray the costs of providing the service. It is a condition of the National Rating Standard that unit charges are displayed by the telephone or with the room information. But in practice it is not always easy to compare these charges with standard telephone rates. Before using a hotel telephone, particularly for long-distance calls, it is advisable to ask how the charges compare.

Security of valuables

It is advisable to deposit any valuables for safe-keeping with the management of the establishment in which you are staying. If the management accept custody of your property they become wholly liable for its loss or damage. They can however restrict their liability for items brought on to the premises and not placed in their special custody to the minimum amounts imposed by the Hotel Proprietors Act, 1956. These are the sum of £50 in respect of one article and a total of £100 in the case of one guest. In order to restrict their liability the management must display a notice in the form required by the Act in a prominent position in the reception area or main entrance of the premises. Without this notice, the proprietor is liable for the full value of the loss or damage to any property (other than a motor car or its contents) of a guest who has booked overnight accommodation.

Code of Conduct and Conditions of Participation

The operator/manager is required to observe the following Code of Conduct:

▶ To maintain standards of guest care, cleanliness, and service appropriate to the type of establishment;

▶ To describe accurately in any advertisement, brochure, or other printed or electronic media, the facilities and services provided;

▶ To make clear to visitors exactly what is included in all prices quoted for accommodation, including taxes, and any other surcharges. Details of Charges for additional services/ facilities should also be made clear;

▶ To give a clear statement of the policy on cancellations to guests at the time of booking i.e. by telephone, fax, email as well as information given in a printed format;

▶ To adhere to, and not to exceed prices quoted at the time of booking for accommodation and other services;

▶ To advise visitors at the time of booking, and subsequently of any change, if the accommodation offered is in an unconnected annexe or similar, and to indicate the location of such accommodation and any difference in comfort and/or amenities from accommodation in the establishment;

▶ To give each visitor, on request, details of payments due and a receipt, if required;

▶ To deal promptly and courteously with all enquiries, requests, bookings and correspondence from visitors;

▶ Ensure complaint handling procedures are in place and that complaints received are investigated promptly and courteously and that the outcome is communicated to the visitor;

▶ To give due consideration to the requirements of visitors with special needs, and to make suitable provision where applicable;

▶ To provide public liability insurance or comparable arrangement and to comply with applicable planning, safety and other statutory requirements;

▶ To allow a VisitBritain representative reasonable access to the establishment, on request, to confirm the Code of Conduct is being observed.

Feedback

Let us know about your break or holiday. We welcome suggestions about how the guide itself may be enhanced or improved and you will find our addresses on page 4 of the guide.

Details listed were believed correct at time of going to press (October 2003), but we advise telephoning in advance to check that details have not altered and to discuss any specific requirements.

Most establishments welcome feedback. Please let the proprietor know if you particularly enjoyed your stay. We sincerely hope that you have no cause for complaint, but should you be dissatisfied or have any problems, make your complaint to the management at the time of the incident so that immediate action may be taken.

In certain circumstances VisitBritain may look into complaints. However, we have no statutory control over establishments or their methods of operating. We cannot become involved in legal or contractual matters, nor can we get involved in seeking financial recompense.

If you do have problems that have not been resolved by the proprietor and which you would like to bring to our attention, please write to:
Quality Standards Department
VisitBritain
Thames Tower
Black's Road
Hammersmith
London W6 9EL

QUALITY ASSURED
VISITOR ATTRACTION

Visitor Attraction Quality Assurance

VisitBritain operates a Visitor Attraction Quality Assurance Standard. Participating attractions are visited annually by trained, impartial assessors who look at all aspects of the visit, from initial telephone enquiries to departure, customer service to catering, as well as all facilities and activities. Only those attractions which have been assessed by VisitBritain and meet the standard receive the quality marque, your sign of a 'Quality Assured Visitor Attraction'.

Look out for the quality marque and visit with confidence.

www.visitengland.com

What makes the perfect break? Big city buzz or peaceful country panoramas? Take a fresh look at England and you may be surprised that everything is here on your very own doorstep. Where will you go? Make up your own mind and enjoy England in all its diversity.

....remember paddling on sandy beaches, playing Poohsticks in the forest, picnics at open-air concerts, tea-rooms offering home-made cakes........

....make your own journey of discovery through England's cultural delights: surprising contrasts between old and new, traditional and trend-setting, time-honoured and contemporary........

....while you're reading this someone is drinking in lungfuls of fresh air on a hill-side with heart-stopping views or wandering through the maze that can be the garden of a stately home or tugging on the sails of a boat skimming across a lake....

....no rush to do anything or be anywhere, time to immerse yourself in your favourite book by a roaring log fire or glide from a soothing massage to a refreshing facial, ease away the tension......

To enjoy England, visitengland.com